STEFAN BOGNER • JAN KARL BAEDEKER

PORSCHE DRIVE – PASS PORTRAIT
GROSSGLOCKNER
HOCHALPENSTRASSE · ÖSTERREICH/AUSTRIA – 2504 M

DELIUS KLASING VERLAG

EDITORIAL

Warum baut man eine Straße über die Alpen? Warum sprengt man tonnenschwere Felsen, trägt Pflasterstein um Pflasterstein in eisige Höhen, baut Brücken über schwindelerregende Abgründe, lässt auf karstigen Steilhängen Serpentinen wachsen, schickt Armeen von Arbeitern für Jahre in die karge Welt jenseits der Baumgrenze, trotzt Wind und Wetter, Schneestürmen, Lawinen und Geröll? Die meisten Alpenstraßen, die im späten 18. und 19. Jahrhundert auf den Spuren alter Saumpfade entstanden, wurden aus strategischen Erwägungen gebaut – sie sollten kurze Verbindungen schaffen, das Reisen von einem Ort zum nächsten erleichtern, dem Militär neue Bewegungsräume eröffnen, den Handel zwischen Nord und Süd zum Blühen bringen.

Mit den ersten Alpinisten und schließlich dem Einzug des Fremdenverkehrs im Hochgebirge ab Mitte des 19. Jahrhunderts verloren die Berge jedoch ihre Schrecken. Die schneebedeckten Gipfel der Alpen waren nicht mehr bloß Hindernis für Schnellreisende, Händler und Armeen – sie waren mit einem Mal zum Ziel naturromantischer Sehnsüchte, sportlicher Ambitionen und schließlich, ab der Jahrhundertwende, erster automobiler Vergnügungsfahrten geworden. Auch die Passstraßen selbst wurden in diesem Zuge zu touristischen

Why does one build a road over the Alps? Why does one blast away tons upon tons of rock; carry tremendous quantities of cobblestones up to icy heights; build bridges over dizzying chasms; carve hairpin bends into steep rocky slopes; send veritable armies of workers into the austere world beyond the tree line, year after year, despite the wind and weather, blizzards, avalanches and boulders? Most of the Alpine roads constructed in the late 18th and 19th centuries along the routes of the old mule tracks were built for strategic reasons – their purpose being to establish short connections, simplify travel between one place and the next, open up access to new spaces for military operations, and foster trade between the north and south.

With the first mountaineers and eventually the advent of tourism in the high mountains starting in the mid-19th century, however, the mountains ultimately lost their frightening aura. The snow-capped summits of the Alps were no longer merely a hindrance for travelers, traders and armies – at once they also became the object of nature-romanticizing passions, athletic ambitions, and, from the turn of the century onwards, a playground for the first automotive pleasure drives. In the process, the pass roads

Erlebnisorten und erfahrbaren Sehenswürdigkeiten, auf denen man am Steuer seines Automobils komfortabel die höchsten Höhen erklimmen und dabei – immer mit einem Rad am Abgrund, wie man daheim stolz berichten würde – die wohligsten Schauer genießen konnte. Für die Alpenländer wurde der Fremdenverkehr schnell zum wichtigen Wirtschaftsfaktor. In einfachen Bauerndörfern erwuchsen auf Kuhwiesen glamouröse Grand Hotels. Neue Passstraßen wurden so geplant, dass sie die Landschaft besonders eindrücklich inszenierten und die Wahrnehmung der Automobilisten – fast wie im Kinofilm, dem neuen Massenmedium dieser Zeit – möglichst effektvoll steuerten.

Das bis heute eindrucksvollste Beispiel einer als ästhetischen und medialen Gesamtkomposition angelegten Alpenstraße ist die Großglockner Hochalpenstraße, die in den Zwanzigerjahren des letzten Jahrhunderts geplant und zwischen 1930 und 1935 unter Leitung des vielseitig begabten Ingenieurs Franz Wallack und mit politischer Unterstützung des Salzburger Landeshauptmanns Franz Rehrl errichtet wurde. Dabei war die 48 Kilometer lange Straße jedoch von Anfang an mehr als eine befahrbare Aussichtsplattform mit Blick auf den Großglockner, den höchsten Gipfel des Landes, und die majestätische Pasterze des größten Gletscher Österreichs.

Zum einen schuf die Großglockner Hochalpenstraße eine dringend benötigte Nord-Süd-Verbindung im verkehrstechnisch unerschlossenen Hochgebirge zwischen dem Brenner und dem Radstädter Tauern. Noch maßgeblicher für die Durchsetzung des Bauvorhabens war jedoch ihre politische Rolle: Nach dem Ersten Weltkrieg und dem Zusammenbruch der Donaumonarchie war das gewaltige Straßenbauprojekt in den Hohen Tauern eines der wichtigsten Symbole für die ungebrochene Schaffenskraft und Leistungsfähigkeit der jungen Republik Österreich sowie für die touristische Anziehungskraft der Länder Salzburg und Kärnten. Darüber hinaus und sicher ebenso wichtig war der Bau auch eine titelseitentaugliche Strukturmaßnahme mit Signalwirkung im Kampf gegen Arbeitslosigkeit und Rezession. Letztlich war es der ab 1933 in Österreich entstehende autoritäre Ständestaat, der die Vollendung der Großglockner Hochalpenstraße im Zuge seiner Automobilisierungspolitik gegen zahlreiche Widerstände finanzierte und ermöglichte, bevor die Nationalsozialisten sich die Strecke nach dem »Anschluss« Österreichs 1938 politisch und propagandistisch aneigneten. So ist der Blick in die Historie der Straße auch eine Reise in die wechselvolle Geschichte Österreichs in der Zwischenkriegszeit.

Und doch ist es im Rückblick vor allem die Vision und Zielstrebigkeit eines einzelnen Menschen, die der Glocknerstraße zu jener bis heute nachwirkenden zeitlosen Qualität verholfen hat: Für den Konstrukteur Franz Wallack endete das Projekt nämlich nicht bei der Wahl der Straßenbeläge und Streckenführungen – er engagierte sich in allen Bereichen der Planung und Umsetzung,

themselves became tourist destinations and sights to be experienced, where one could comfortably scale the highest of heights from the driver's seat of an automobile – always with one wheel practically dangling over the edge of the abyss, as one would boast later at home – while enjoying the most delightful exhilaration. For the countries of the Alps, tourism quickly became one of the most important economic drivers. In simple farming villages, grand hotels rose up in erstwhile cow pastures. New mountain passes were planned in such a way as to stage the landscape in the most striking way possible and steer the impressions of the automobile drivers as effectively as possible – almost cinematically, as it were, to borrow the language of the emerging mass medium of the time.

To this day, the most impressive example of an Alpine road as a holistic composition designed with a view to its aesthetic and media impact is the Grossglockner High Alpine Road. It was planned in the 1920s and built between 1930 and 1935 under the able leadership of the polymath and engineer Franz Wallack with the political support of Salzburg state governor Franz Rehrl. Yet the 48-kilometer road was from the very outset more than just a drivable viewing platform with stunning vistas of the Grossglockner, the highest peak in the country, and the majestic Pasterze, the biggest glacier of Austria.

On the one hand, the Grossglockner High Alpine Road established an urgently needed north-south connection in the high mountains between the Brenner Pass and the Radstadt Tauern, which until then lacked transportation infrastructure. Even more important to the success of the plan, however, was its political role: After World War II and the collapse of the Austro-Hungarian Empire, the massive road-building project in the High Tauern was one of the most important symbols of the unbroken productive force and capability of the young Republic of Austria, as well as the tourism appeal of the states of Salzburg and Carinthia. Moreover, and certainly just as importantly, the building of the road was also a headline-worthy structural measure significant in the fight against unemployment and recession. Ultimately, it was the authoritarian corporate state that began to emerge in Austria in 1933 that financed and pushed through the completion of the Grossglockner High Alpine Road against fierce resistance of its automotive policies, before the Nazis took political and propagandistic control of the roadway following the "Anschluss" – annexation – of Austria in 1938. A look back into the history of the road is therefore also a trip into the tumultuous history of Austria in the interwar period.

And yet for all that, it is above all the vision and perseverance of one person that gave the Glockner Road the timeless quality that has resounded through the ages: For designer Franz Wallack, the project was by no means finished after the selection of road surfaces

Das bis heute eindrucksvollste Beispiel einer als ästhetischen und medialen Gesamtkomposition angelegten Alpenstraße ist die Großglockner Hochalpenstraße, die in den Zwanzigerjahren des letzten Jahrhunderts geplant und zwischen 1930 und 1935 unter Leitung des vielseitig begabten Ingenieurs Franz Wallack und mit politischer Unterstützung des Salzburger Landeshauptmanns Franz Rehrl errichtet wurde.

To this day, the most impressive example of an Alpine road as a holistic composition designed with a view to its aesthetic and media impact is the Grossglockner High Alpine Road. It was planned in the 1920s and built between 1930 and 1935 under the able leadership of the polymath and engineer Franz Wallack with the political support of Salzburg state governor Franz Rehrl.

hielt Vorträge und betrieb Pressearbeit, buhlte um Investoren, ließ sich von den wichtigen Alpenpässen Europas vor Ort inspirieren, plante Hotels entlang der Straße, erdachte das Logo der Maut-Vignetten, entwickelte die Rotationspflüge zur jährlichen Schneeräumung, koordinierte Instandhaltung und Reparaturen und schrieb schließlich auch die erste Biografie der Straße selbst. Es ist dieser holistische Ansatz, diese bis ins kleinste Detail durchdachte Idee einer architektonischen und medialen Gesamtkomposition, welche die Großglockner Hochalpenstraße so einzigartig macht – und der sich auch in der Bewerbung um den Welterbetitel der UNESCO wiederfindet.

Mit ihrem Mautsystem, den zahlreichen Informations- und Ausstellungsorten und den strengen Naturschutzregeln hat die Glocknerstraße durchaus Modellcharakter für andere Passstraße in Europa, auf denen sich bis heute ungebremst die Blechkarawanen durch die Bergwelt schieben. Die Strecke von Bruck hinauf zum Fuscher Törl, hoch zur Edelweiß-Spitze, weiter zum Hochtor, zur Franz-Josefs-Höhe und wieder hinab bis nach Heiligenblut gehört darüber hinaus sicherlich zu den schönsten und eindrucksvollsten Fahrstrecken der Alpen. Wir haben in den vergangenen Jahren und während der Produktion dieses Buches unzählige Tage auf der Großglockner Hochalpenstraße verbracht – fad oder gar langweilig wurde uns jedoch nicht, ist doch hier oben

and the exact route. He was involved in all areas of the planning and implementation, gave speeches and did public relations work, wooed investors, sought inspiration by visiting the important Alpine passes in Europe, planned hotels along the route, designed the logo for the toll stickers, developed the rotating plows for the annual snow removal operation, coordinated maintenance and repair and, finally, wrote the first biography of the road itself. It is this holistic approach, this vision of a unified composition designed with a view to its aesthetic and media impact and meticulous attention to detail, that makes the Grossglockner High Alpine Road so unique – and which was highlighted in its application for the UNESCO World Heritage Site designation.

With its toll system, numerous information and exhibition sites, and its strong nature preservation rules, the Glockner Road took on an undeniable model character for other pass roads in Europe, on which the endless caravans of motorized vehicles continue to snake their way through the mountains even today. The stretch from Bruck up to Fuchser Törl, further up to Edelweiss-Spitze, continuing to Hochtor and Franz-Josefs-Höhe before heading back down to Heiligenblut is unquestionably among the most beautiful and impressive driving routes in the Alps. Over the past few years and throughout the production of this book, we have spent countless days on the Grossglockner High Alpine

kein Tag wie der andere. Mal fährt man im Tal bei schönstem Frühlingswetter durch blühende Wiesen, nur um eine halbe Stunde später zwischen meterhohen Schneewänden im Nebel kaum die nächste Kurve zu erkennen. Dann wieder blickt man bei Kaiserwetter und tiefblauem Himmel auf ein unbeschreibliches Gipfelpanorama und sieht mit dem Fernglas sogar die Bergsteiger am Großglockner oder die Segelboote als kleine weiße Dreiecke in Zell am See übers Wasser gleiten.

Und doch gibt es Fragen, denen man sich auch auf dieser Vorzeige-Passstraße nicht entziehen kann, wenn man sein Auto oder Motorrad als einer von rund einer Million jährlicher Besucher einmal quer durch den größten Nationalpark der Alpen und entlang eines rapide schmelzenden Gletschers steuert. Wie können wir die Bergwelt genießen, ohne sie gleichzeitig existenziell zu gefährden? Die reduzierten Mautpreise für Elektrofahrzeuge und die Stromtankstellen entlang der Strecke mögen ein erstes Signal für einen nachhaltigeren Alpentourismus sein. Letztlich ist es jedoch eine Frage der Haltung und des Respekts – gegenüber der Natur, gegenüber den Bewohnern, gegenüber den anderen Besuchern, den Wanderern, Radlern und Bergsteigern –, die den Unterschied macht. In diesem Sinne soll auch dieses Buch einen Beitrag leisten, die Großglockner Hochalpenstraße nicht als alpine Rennstrecke für Serpentinenjäger erscheinen zu lassen, sondern als komplexes Meisterwerk der Architekturgeschichte sowie als Zugang zu einer ebenso eindrucksvollen wie fragilen Bergwelt, der man trotz aller Freude am sportlichen Fahren stets mit Ehrfurcht und Hochachtung begegnen sollte.

Road, but it never got tedious or boring; up here, no day is like another. One time you set off through blooming meadows in the valley amid perfect spring weather only to encounter, not half an hour later, meters-high snow-drifts in fog so thick that you can't see around the next bend. Another time, with deep blue skies and glorious weather, you survey an indescribable panoramic view of the peaks, or, with a pair of binoculars, even track the mountain climbers on the Grossglockner or sailboats as little triangles as they glide across the water in Zell am See.

And yet there are questions that none of the million annual visitors who travel this exemplary pass road with their cars and motorcycles can avoid as they traverse the largest national park in the Alps, skirting a rapidly melting glacier. How can we enjoy the mountain landscape without, at the same time, endangering its very existence? The reduced tolls for electric vehicles and electric filling stations along the route may represent a first step along the way to a more sustainable form of Alpine tourism. Ultimately, however, it is a question of attitude and respect – for nature, for local residents, for other visitors, for hikers, cyclists and mountain climbers – that will make the difference. It is in this spirit that this book, too, intends to portray the Grossglockner High Alpine Road not as a mountain race track for switchback-junkies, but as a complex masterpiece of architectural history and a point of access to a mountainous region that is as fragile as it is impressive, and which should, for all the pleasure of driving it with vigorous exuberance, always be treated with respect and reverence.

STEFAN BOGNER ist Autor, Fotograf und Inhaber einer Designagentur – und ein leidenschaftlicher Porsche-Fahrer. Mit seinen eindrücklichen Fotografien von Kurven, Kehren und Serpentinen hat er die Schönheit der Alpenpässe sichtbar gemacht. Sein Magazin *Curves* und sein Bildband *Escapes* gelten unter sportlichen Automobilisten als perfekte Anleitungen zum Glücklichsein.

Stefan Bogner is a writer, photographer, founder of a Munich Design Agency – and a passionate Porsche driver. With his stunning photos of curves, hairpins and serpentines, he has captured the magnificence of the Alpine passes. Sporty drivers consider his magazine *Curves* and his coffee-table book *Escapes* as the ultimate guides to happiness.

JAN KARL BAEDEKER ist Reisender aus Leidenschaft – und zudem Autor, Fotograf sowie Chefredakteur des Magazins *Classic Driver*. Sozusagen genetisch vorbelastet ist er als Urenkel von Karl Baedeker, der ab 1828 das Reisen zu einer Kulturform erhob und mit seinen roten Reisehandbüchern viele Generationen von Fernwehgetriebenen auf die richtige Spur brachte. Jan Karl Baedeker hat Medienwissenschaften und Europäische Ethnologie in Hamburg studiert, lebt heute in Zürich – und ist immer auf dem Sprung zur nächsten Tour.

Jan Karl Baedeker is an avid traveller – as well as author, photographer and editor-in-chief of the magazine *Classic Driver*. One could say he is genetically predisposed: he is, after all, the great-grandson of Karl Baedeker, who from 1828 turned travelling into a form of culture and, with his red travel guides, opened the way for many generations of adventurers to whet their wanderlust. Jan Karl Baedeker learned Media Studies and European Ethnology in Hamburg, he now lives in Zurich – and is always set to take off on his next adventure.

DIE GROSSGLOCKNER HOCHALPENSTRASSE

THE GROSSGLOCKNER HIGH ALPINE ROAD

MIT FREUNDLICHER GENEHMIGUNG
COURTESY OF:
GROHAG ARCHIV

Die frühe Geschichte Die Großglockner Hochalpenstraße folgt – anders als die berühmten Passstraßen über den Großen Sankt Berhard oder den Brenner – keiner bedeutenden antiken Transitstrecke. Dennoch dienten das Hochtor und das Fuscher Törl den Bewohnern der Alpentäler seit Jahrtausenden als Übergang. Die frühesten Spuren in den Hohen Tauern hinterließen vor mehr als dreitausend Jahren kupfer- und bronzezeitliche Jäger, deren in der Neuzeit gefundenen Schwerter und Dolche von Streifzügen durch die alpine Bergwelt zeugen. Auch keltische Stämme passierten den 2.576 Meter hohen Pass auf ihren Pfaden und huldigten am Scheitelpunkt der gefährlichen Strecke ihren Göttern. Die Römer, die den Alpenraum mit einem Netz von Wegen und Straßen überzogen und den transalpinen Handel professionalisierten, reisten ebenfalls über das Hochtor – bei den Bauarbeiten der Straße wurde 1933 eine bronzene Herkulesstatue gefunden, die auf ein römisches Passheiligtum schließen ließ. Spätere Grabungen bestätigten diese Vermutung. Im Gegensatz zu den hochfrequentierten Römerstraßen über den Reschen- und den Brennerpass dürfte der Weg über die Hohen Tauern jedoch nur unregelmäßig begangen worden sein.

Mit dem Niedergang des Römischen Reiches und der einsetzenden Völkerwanderung versiegte der Transitverkehr über das Hochtor und das Fuscher Törl. Erst mit dem spätmittelalterlichen Bergbau und dem erneuten Aufblühen des Handels

Early history The Grossglockner High Alpine Road doesn't follow any significant ancient transit route, unlike other famous pass roads, such as the Great St. Bernard Pass or the Brenner Pass. Yet the Hochtor and the Fuscher Törl have served the inhabitants of the Alpine valleys as passageways for millennia. The earliest human traces in the High Tauern mountains were left by hunters from the Copper and Bronze Ages more than three thousand years ago. The swords and daggers discovered in modern times bear witness to their forays through the Alpine mountain landscape. Celtic tribes also crossed over the 2,576-meter-high pass on their travels and paid homage to their gods at the summit of the dangerous route. The Romans, who blanketed the Alps with a network of paths and roads and professionalized transalpine trade, also journeyed over the Hochtor – during road construction in 1933, a bronze Hercules statue was found, which suggested a Roman mountain pass shrine. Later excavations confirmed this assumption. In contrast to the highly frequented Roman roads across the Reschen and Brenner Passes, the route traversing the High Tauern was most likely used only intermittently.

With the decline of the Roman Empire and the onset of the Migration Period, the transit traffic over the Hochtor and Fuscher Törl petered out. It was only when mining in the late Middle Ages and the newly thriving trade between Northern and Southern Europe arrived did the old bridle paths of the Celts and Romans experience a renaissance. Kilometers-long

zwischen Nord- und Südeuropa erlebten die alten Saumpfade der Kelten und Römer ihre Renaissance. Bis weit hinauf in die Gipfelregionen wurden Stollen kilometerweit in den Stein gehauen und tonnenweise Gold, Silber und Erz gefördert. Doch das Einsetzen der »Kleinen Eiszeit« ab dem 15. Jahrhundert und die wachsenden Gletscher machten dem alpinen Bergbau den Garaus, die Werkstätten und Unterkünfte der Knappen verfielen. Heute gibt der zurückweichende Permafrost immer wieder Stollen, Halden und andere Relikte dieser Zeit frei.

Neben den mittelalterlichen Bergleuten und Saumhändlern, die beladen mit Salz und Eisen, Wein und Stoffen zwischen Fusch und Heiligenblut verkehrten, gab es noch andere Reisende, die auf der »Glocknerroute« ihre Spuren hinterließen: So erinnerte der Fund einer acht Meter langen Sträflingskette an die im 17. Jahrhundert durch den Erzbischof von Thun eingeführte Galeerenstrafe für Wilderer, die von Salzburg über das Hochtor nach Venedig ihrem schaurige Schicksal entgegenwandern mussten. Auch auf die Pinzgauer Wallfahrer, die alljährlich über den Pass nach Heiligenblut pilgerten, wartete am Ende ihrer Reise nicht immer die erhoffte Erlösung – Namen wie »Beindlkar« und »Elendbogen« entlang der Straße erinnern noch immer an jene neun Pilger, die im Hochsommer 1683 von einem Schneesturm überrascht ihr Leben ließen.

Alpinismus und Bergtourismus Doch mit der Zeit verloren die eisigen Höhen ihre Schrecken. Im ausgehenden 18. Jahrhundert begannen die ersten wagemutigen Bergsteiger, die vergletscherten Gipfel der Zentralalpen zu erstürmen und im Namen der noch jungen Naturwissen-

> Namen wie »Beindlkar« und »Elendbogen« entlang der Straße erinnern noch immer an jene neun Pilger, die im Hochsommer 1683 von einem Schneesturm überrascht ihr Leben ließen.
>
> Names like Beindlkar and Elendbogen ("misery bend") along the road are reminders of the nine pilgrims who lost their lives in an unexpected snowstorm at the height of summer in 1683.

mining tunnels were hewn into the rock far up into the summit areas to mine tons of gold, silver and ore. However, the onset of the "Little Ice Age" in the 15th century and the expanding glaciers put an end to the Alpine mining, and the miners' workshops and living quarters fell into ruin. Today the receding permafrost continues to reveal relics from this era, such as tunnels and slag heaps.

Besides the medieval miners and pack train tradesmen, who travelled between Fusch and Heiligenblut loaded with salt and iron, wine and textiles, there were other travelers who left their traces behind on the Glockner route: thus the unearthing of an 8-meter-long convict chain served as a reminder of the gruesome fate awaiting 17th century poachers as they were led from Salzburg across the Hochtor to Venice: the Archbishop of Thun had decreed that their punishment was to serve as galley slaves. The hoped-for salvation was also not always the expected result for the Pinzgau pilgrims, who undertook annual pilgrimages across the pass to Heiligenblut – names like Beindlkar and Elendbogen ("misery bend") along the road are reminders of the nine pilgrims who lost their lives in an unexpected snowstorm at the height of summer in 1683.

Alpine mountaineering and tourism
Nonetheless, the icy heights lost their ability to instill terror over time. In the final years of the 18th century, the first bold mountain climbers began taking

MIT FREUNDLICHER GENEHMIGUNG
COURTESY OF:
GROHAG ARCHIV

Der Grossglockner, von der Pasterze aus gesehen.

Glocknerhaus mit Pasterzengletscher

13. Aug. 1902.

schaften zu erforschen. Am 28. Juli des Jahres 1800 erreichten die Teilnehmer einer durch Fürstbischoff Franz II. Xaver von Salm-Reifferscheidt-Krautheim organisierten Expedition erstmals den 3.798 Meter hohen Gipfel des Großglockners – und hinterließen neben dem obligatorischen Gipfelkreuz auch ein Barometer. Die Vermessung der Bergwelt hatte begonnen.

Der im 19. Jahrhundert in ganz Europa Einzug haltende Geist der Romantik mit seiner Natursehnsucht und dem wehmütigen Wunsch, im Angesicht schöner wie erhabener Landschaften die eigene Existenz und Vergänglichkeit zu erspüren, trieb immer mehr Wanderer und Alpinisten in die Berge. Das Aufkommen neuer Verkehrsmittel für Schnellreisende wie die Eisenbahn und das Dampfschiff sowie der rasante Ausbau der Gleisverbindungen und Straßen in ganz Europa beschleunigte überdies die touristische Eroberung der Alpen. Dabei wurden nicht nur die Täler für den Verkehr erschlossen, sondern auch die Berge selbst: Einer der eindrucksvollsten Straßenbauten der Habsburgermonarchie war die von Carlo Donegani in nur fünf Jahren errichtete, 1825 eröffnete Straße über das 2.757 Meter hohe Stilfser Joch. Und ab 1854 bewies die Semmeringbahn, dass selbst tonnenschwere Eisenbahnzüge die Höhen der Alpen erklimmen konnten. Mit den Reisenden kehrte in den Bergdörfern neues Leben ein. Dabei waren es nicht nur Forscher und Gipfelstürmer, die in der abgeschiedenen Welt für Aufsehen sorgten: Im September 1856 besuchten Kaiser Franz Joseph und Kaiserin Elisabeth das am obersten Ende des Mölltals gelegene Heiligenblut und machten sich mitsamt einer Entourage von mehr als 100 Mann auf den Weg in Richtung Großglockner. Während »Sissi« picknickend im Tal verweilte, bestieg seine Majestät den Hohen Sattel – der seitdem den Namen Kaiser-Franz-Josefs-Höhe trägt.

Durch die ab Mitte des 19. Jahrhunderts in Österreich und Deutschland entstehenden Alpenvereine wurde der Fremdenverkehr im Hochgebirge erstmals umfassend organisiert. Alte Saumpfade und Wege wurden ausgebaut, Hütten errichtet, Bergführer ausgebildet, die Idee des Naturschutzes gefördert und selbst die entlegensten Höhenregionen erschlossen, kartografiert und durch Werbung den Naturfreunden im Flachland nahe gebracht. Neue alpine Verkehrsmittel wie die 1887 in Betrieb genommene Zahnradbahn auf den Gaisberg bei Salzburg rückten die Gipfel derweil immer näher an die Städte heran. Auch die erste, um 1908 fertiggestellte und 12 Kilometer lange Fahrstraße vom kärntnerischen Heiligenblut hinauf zum Glocknerhaus oberhalb des damals noch gewaltigen Pasterze-Gletschers geht auf die Initiative der Sektion Klagenfurt des Deutschen und Österreichischen Alpenvereins zurück. Erstmals konnten nun auch jene Automobilisten, die seit der Jahrhundertwende aus der ganzen Welt in die Alpen reisten, um ihre Fahrkünste sowie die Leistungsfähigkeit ihrer Maschinen unter Beweis zu stellen und nur noch ungern zu Fuß

the glacier-covered mountaintops of the Central Alps by storm and conducting research in the name of the still young natural sciences. On July 28 in the year 1800, the participants of an expedition organized by Prince-Bishop Franz II. Xaver von Salm-Reifferscheidt-Krautheim reached the 3,798-meter summit of the Grossglockner for the first time – and also left a barometer next to the obligatory summit cross. Measurement had begun in the mountains.

The advent of Romanticism and its sensibility, which spread throughout Europe in the 19th century along with its longing for nature and the wistful desire to gain a sense of one's own existence and mortality in the presence of beautiful and noble landscapes, drove ever more travelers and mountaineers into the mountains. The emergence of new modes of transportation for quick travel, such as the railroad and the steam ship, and the rapid expansion of rail connections and roads throughout Europe also accelerated the touristic conquest of the Alps. In the process, not only did the valleys become accessible to traffic, but the mountains themselves did, too: one of the most impressive road construction projects of the Habsburg monarchy was the road crossing the 2,757-meter Stilfser Joch, which opened in 1825. It was built by Carlo Donegani in only five years. Starting in 1854, the Semmering railway also proved that even trains weighing tons could scale the heights of the Alps.

The arrival of the travelers brought new life to the mountain villages. However, it wasn't only researchers and ambitious mountain-climbers who caused a sensation in this isolated world: in September 1856, Emperor Franz Joseph and Empress Elisabeth visited the village of Heiligenblut at the uppermost end of the Möll Valley and set off in the direction of the Grossglockner with an entourage of more than 100 people. While "Sissi" lingered in the valley to enjoy a picnic, His Majesty ascended to the Hoher Sattel – which has borne the name of Kaiser-Franz-Josefs-Höhe ever since.

Starting in the middle of the 19th century, Alpine clubs began forming in Austria and Germany, which led to tourism in the high mountains being organized comprehensively for the first time. Old pack train trails and paths were improved, huts were built, mountain guides trained, the idea of nature conservation was encouraged and even the most remote high-altitude areas accessed, mapped and brought closer to the nature lovers in the flatlands through advertising. Meanwhile, new means of Alpine transportation, like the rack railway on the Gaisberg that began operating in 1887, brought the peaks ever closer to the cities. The first paved road from Heiligenblut in Carinthia up to the Glockner House above the then still massive Pasterze Glacier was 12 kilometers long and built at the initiative of the Klagenfurt chapter of the German and Austrian Alpine Club. For the first time, those drivers who had traveled to the Alps from around the world since the turn of the century – and only went on foot grudgingly

MIT FREUNDLICHER GENEHMIGUNG
COURTESY OF:
GROHAG ARCHIV

gingen, den Anblick des Großglockners genießen. Auch auf Salzburger Seite wurden Anfang des 20. Jahrhunderts die Verkehrswege von Zell am See, Bruck und Ferleiten in Richtung der Hohen Tauern weiter ausgebaut. Dabei entstanden auch immer neue Aussichtspunkte, um den höchsten Gipfel des österreichisch-ungarischen Kaiserreichs zu bewundern und zu erwandern.

Die Idee einer Straße Während die befahrbaren Alpenübergänge in den West- und Zentralalpen mitunter nur zehn Kilometer Luftlinie voneinander entfernt waren, musste man seine transalpinen Reisen in den Ostalpen genauer planen – schließlich lagen zwischen dem Radstädter Tauernpass und dem Brennerpass fast 160 Kilometer für Automobile unpassierbaren Hochgebirges. Schon Ende des 19. Jahrhunderts hatte man erstmals über eine Nord-Süd-Verbindung am Glockner nachgedacht, um die Länder Salzburg und Kärnten sowie das nördliche Alpenvorland und die Adria miteinander zu verbinden. Die Lage auf halber Strecke zwischen Radstädter Tauern und Brenner sowie die einmalige landschaftliche Schönheit der umliegenden Glocknergruppe ließen den alten Saumweg über das Hochtor als geradezu prädestinierte Strecke erscheinen. Doch schon die Straße des Alpenvereins zum Glocknerhaus, an der Bergwetter- und Erosionskräfte zehrten, zeigten deutlich, dass ein Straßenbau im Hochgebirge keine leichte Angelegenheit sein würde.

Nach dem Ersten Weltkrieg wurde die Idee einer Zentralalpenquerstraße zwischen Bruck und Heiligenblut erneut aufgenommen – allerdings unter neuen politischen Vorzeichen: Nach dem Zerfall des Habsburgerreiches, der Ausrufung der Republik Österreich im Jahr 1918 und dem Friedensvertrag von Saint-Germain war das Land auf ein Siebtel seiner vormaligen Größe zusammengeschrumpft. Südtirol – und mit ihm nicht nur der höchste Alpenpass des Landes, das Stilfser Joch, sondern auch die prestigeträchtige Große Dolomitenstraße – waren nunmehr italienisch. Zu den identitären Phantomschmerzen der Bevölkerung kamen handfeste Machtkämpfe zwischen rechten und linken politischen Bewegungen, die in den kommenden zwei Dekaden weiter eskalieren sollten, sowie eine desolate Wirtschaftslage unter dem Druck der Sparauflagen der Siegermächte. In diesem fortwährenden Krisenzustand wurde der Straßenbau im Hochgebirge zu einem Symbolprojekt, das sich mit unterschiedlichsten politischen und gesellschaftlichen Botschaften aufladen ließ: Als Arbeitsbeschaffungsmaßnahme, Magnet für den volkswirtschaftlich dringend benötigten Fremdenverkehr und Zeichen fortwährender österreichischer Leistungsfähigkeit wurde die Straße auch jenseits aller architektonischen und verkehrstechnischen Überlegungen zu einem gewaltigen Bauvorhaben, das mit seinem universellen Anspruch ganz in den für Großprojekte aller Art so empfänglichen Geist der deutsch-österreichischen Zwischenkriegszeit passte. Dabei war nicht nur der Straßen-

to enjoy the view of the Grossglockner – could now show off their driving skills as well as their high-performance machines. On the Salzburg side, too, the transportation routes from Zell am See, Bruck and Ferleiten toward the High Tauern were upgraded further at the beginning of the 20th century. The process resulted in the emergence of ever more panoramic viewpoints that enabled travelers to marvel at and hike on the highest peak in the Austro-Hungarian Empire.

The idea of a road While the driveable Alpine crossings in the Western and Central Alps were sometimes a mere ten kilometers apart as the crow flies, it was obligatory to plan trips to the Eastern Alps more thoroughly – after all, the distance between the Radstädter Tauern Pass and the Brenner Pass was nearly 160 kilometers of high mountains impassable by car. Thoughts about a North-South connection at the Glockner had first begun at the end of the 19th century – a project that would link the states of Salzburg and Carinthia as well as the northern Alpine foothills and the Adriatic Sea to each other. Based on its location halfway between Radstädter Tauern and the Brenner as well as the unique natural beauty of the surrounding Glockner group, the old pack train track across the Hochtor seemed absolutely predestined as the perfect route. However, the Alpine Club's road to the Glocknerhaus, which was being worn down by mountain weather and the powers of erosion clearly showed that road construction in the high mountains would not be a simple matter.

After WWI, the idea of a central road to traverse the Alps between Bruck and Heiligenblut was taken up again – but under new political circumstances: following the collapse of the Habsburg Empire, the proclamation of the Austrian Republic in 1918 and the peace treaty of St. Germain, the country had shrunk to one-seventh of its former size. South Tirol – and with it not only the country's highest Alpine Pass, the Stilfser Joch, but also the prestigious Great Dolomites Road – were now Italian. In addition to the populace's phantom pain caused by identity loss, there were substantial power struggles between right and left-wing political movements, which were to escalate during the coming two decades, along with a desolate economic situation caused by pressure from the fiscal restraints imposed by the victors. During this continuing crisis, the construction of the road in the high mountains became a symbolic project, which could have the most varied political and social messages loaded onto it: as a job creation scheme, as a magnet for the desperately needed tourism and a representation of Austria's ongoing economic viability. The road was also made into a massive building project beyond all architectural and technological traffic-related considerations, which fit into the spirit of the German-Austrian interwar period – an era that was receptive to large-scale projects of all kinds – because of its universal aspirations. At the same time, not only was the construction itself controversial, but the routing from the start was as well. At the suggestion of the civil servant and

bau selbst, sondern auch die Streckenführung von Anfang an umstritten. Auf Anregung des Beamten und begeisterten Bergsteigers Adolf Jahn hatte sich das Bureau für Fremdenverkehr des österreichischen Bundesministeriums für Handel und Gewerbe, Industrie und Bauten im Hochsommer 1922 erstmals für die Schaffung einer Fahrverbindung von Bruck im Salzburger Land bis zur bereits bestehenden Glocknerhausstraße des Alpenvereins auf Kärntner Seite ausgesprochen – allerdings über den damals beliebten Kurort Bad Fusch und die Heiligenbluter Tauern. Die Vertreter des Landes Tirol favorisierten derweil eine westlichere Alpenquerung von Matrei über die Felber Tauern nach Mittersill. Nachdem eine Kommission beide Strecken in Augenschein genommen und begangen hatte, verwarfen die Experten zwar die Idee einer Straße über die Steilhänge bei Bad Fusch, gaben generell aber vom Standpunkt der technischen Linienführung aus einer Hochtorstraße gegenüber dem Felber-Tauern-Projekt den Vorzug. Auch die landschaftliche Schönheit der Strecke mit Blick auf den Großglockner wurde in den Gutachten erstmals explizit genannt.

Der richtige Mann Erst im Frühjahr 1924 wurde die Idee auf Initiative der Salzburger Landesregierung erneut aufgenommen, schließlich zusammen mit dem Land Kärnten ein Ausschuss zur Erbauung einer Großglockner-Hochalpenstraße gegründet und ein Fonds zur Finanzierung eingerichtet. Der Grundstein war gelegt – doch wer sollte die anspruchsvolle Aufgabe der Trassierung übernehmen? Von Kärntner Seite wurde der 36 Jahre alte Wiener Zivilingenieur, Straßenfachmann, Landesbaurat und Kenner der Bergwelt Franz Wallack ins Spiel gebracht. »Eines Tages im Frühsommer des Jahres 1924 wurde ich in Klagenfurt auf der Straße von zwei Herren mit der Frage überrumpelt, ob ich Lust hätte, eine Straße ins Glocknergebiet zu trassieren, die eine neue Verbindung von Salzburg mitten durch das Massiv der Hohen Tauern nach Kärnten und Osttirol schaffen soll«, erinnerte sich Franz Wallack gut ein Jahrzehnt später an die »Stunde Null« seines Glocknerstraßenprojekts. »Als guter Bergsteiger, als begeisterter Freund der herrlichen Hochgebirgsnatur, als Feind allzu umfangreicher Büroarbeit, die gerade zu jeder Zeit die Verfassung zahlreicher ›Projekte am Papier‹ zum Gegenstand hatte, deren Verwirklichung in nebelhafter Ferne lag, ließ meine Antwort auf die gestellte Frage nicht lange auf sich warten, und ich sagte sofort: Ja.«

Als Spezialist für Wasserkraftwerke kannte Franz Wallack das Kärntner Hochgebirge durch seine Terrainaufnahmen und Tiefenlotungen bereits wie kaum ein anderer Ingenieur. Doch innerhalb von nur zwei Monaten ein Projekt für die Trassierung einer Alpenstraße über die Hohen Tauern vorzulegen, war selbst für den erfahrenen Bergsteiger und Hochgebirgskenner eine sportliche Aufgabe. Den Sommer 1924 verbrachte Franz Wallack in den Bergen zwischen Ferleiten und Heiligenblut, schlief nachts im Zelt, begann seine Arbeit im Morgengrauen,

enthusiastic mountain climber Adolf Jahn, the Bureau for Tourism of the Austrian Federal Ministry for Trade and Commerce, Industry and Construction voiced approval for the creation of a road connecting Bruck in the state of Salzburg to the already existing Alpine Club's Glocknerhaus road on the Carinthian side for the first time – but via the then popular spa Bad Fusch and the Heiligenblut Tauern. Meanwhile, the representatives of Tirol state favored a more westerly Alpine crossing from Matrei to Mittersill via the Felber Tauern. After a commission had taken a close look at and walked both routes, the experts rejected the idea of a road across the steep slopes by Bad Fusch, but in general preferred the Hochtor road over the Felber-Tauern project based on a technical routing perspective. The scenic beauty of the route with its view of the Grossglockner was also explicitly named for the first time in the report.

The right man It was only in the spring of 1924 that the idea was taken up once again at the initiative of the Salzburg state government, which in the end set up a committee jointly with the state of Carinthia to build the Grossglockner High Alpine Road and established a fund to finance it. The cornerstone was laid, but who would undertake the demanding task of laying out the route? The 36-year-old Viennese civil engineer, road expert, Public Works Board member and authority on mountains, Franz Wallack, was brought into the discussion by the Carinthian side. "One day in the early summer of 1924, I was blindsided by two men on the street in Klagenfurt who asked me out of the blue if I felt inclined to route a road into the Grossglockner area, which was intended to create a new link between Salzburg and Carinthia and Eastern Tirol through the middle of the High Tauern Massif," Franz Wallack reminisced a good decade later about the "zero hour" of his Glockner Road project. "As a good mountain climber, enthusiastic friend of the magnificent nature in the high mountains, and as a foe of extensive office work, which always seemed to involve the writing of numerous 'paper projects', the implementation of which lay at some nebulous time in the future, my answer to the question posed was not long in coming, and I immediately said yes."

As a specialist in hydro power stations, Franz Wallack already knew the Carinthian high mountains like no other engineer due to the terrain documentation and depth soundings he had done there. Yet submitting a project for the laying of an Alpine road across the High Tauern within a span of only two months was a marathon task even for the experienced mountain climber and high mountain expert. Franz Wallack spent the summer of 1924 in the mountains between Ferleiten and Heiligenblut, slept in a tent at night, took up his work again at dawn, ended it at dusk and ultimately presented his plan for a road to the committee – on time. A call for tenders for the construction and financing of the road based on Wallack's project template was issued in the fall. The public was informed

beendete sie mit der Dämmerung und legte dem Ausschuss schließlich seinen Plan einer Straße vor – fristgerecht. Auf Basis von Wallacks Projektvorlage erfolgte im Herbst die Ausschreibung für Bau und Finanzierung. Zum Weihnachtsfest 1924 wurde die Öffentlichkeit über den geplanten Bau der Großglockner Hochalpenstraße informiert. Wie das ambitionierte Bauvorhaben in der notorisch klammen, vom Völkerbund mittels Krediten am Leben erhaltenen Republik finanziert werden soll, stand allerdings noch in den Sternen.

Dennoch lief die Planung weiterhin munter voran: Im Frühjahr 1925 wurde Franz Wallack eine Studienreise zu den wichtigsten Passstraßen Europas gewährt. Im Sommer besuchte er in fünf Wochen die 13 großen Alpenhauptübergänge sowie 30 weitere Alpenpässe. Wallack begutachtete Streckenführungen und Straßenbeläge, vermaß Kehren und Steigungen, Tunnels und Galerien, prüfte Randsteine, Geländer und Brüstungsmauern, inspizierte Brücken aus Stein, Eisen, Holz und Beton, zählte Automobile, Busse und Motorräder, fuhr ferner mit zahllosen Zahnrad- und Schwebebahnen, besichtigte Wasserkraftwerke, schlief in Berghotels – und verfasste dabei eine ebenso einzigartige wie umfassende Bestandsaufnahme des alpinen Straßenbaus und Gebirgstourismus der 1920er-Jahre.

»Ich muss gestehen«, so erinnerte sich Franz Wallack mehr als zwei Jahrzehnte später in seinen Glocknerstraßenbiografie, »daß ich mit einigem innerem Zagen und Bangen die Kraftwagen auf das Stilfser Joch, auf die Grimsel und Furka sowie auf den Col du Lauteret bestieg, immer darauf gefasst, Ähnliches und landschaftlich Schöneres – vielleicht sogar weitaus Schöneres – zu Gesicht zu bekommen, als es die Großglockner Hochalpenstraße je zu bieten vermochte. Doch je weiter ich kam und je mehr ich sah, um so vorteilhafter hob sich das Projekt der Großglockner Hochalpenstraße von den anderen Alpenstraßen ab, am deutlichsten, als ich im unmittelbaren Anschluß an diese Reise wieder ins Glocknergebiet fuhr.«

Franz Wallack war auf seiner Reise endgültig zu der Überzeugung gelangt, dass es neben der verkehrstechnischen Bedeutung vor allem die landschaftliche Schönheit war, die den Bau der Straße rechtfertigte – und die in der Trassierung einer wahrhaften Panoramastraße berücksichtigt werden musste. Vor allem die Abzweigung zur Kaiser-Franz-Josefs-Höhe mit ihrem einzigartigen Gletscherblick galt es im Sinne des Fremdenverkehrs zu inszenieren. Doch so sehr der Konstrukteur auch an seiner Vision festhielt, die Strecke erneut trassierte, die Straßenbreite von drei auf fünf Meter erhöhte, die Strecke von 27 Kilometer auf 38 Kilometer verlängerte und alle weiteren Erkenntnisse seiner Studienreise ergänzend in das Projekt einfließen ließ – auch im Winter 1925 war kein Investor für die benötigten fünf Million Goldschilling in Sicht. Mittlerweile regte sich auf Bundesebene

about the planned buiding of the Grossglockner High Alpine Road at Christmastime in 1924. How the ambitious construction project would be financed in the notoriously cash-strapped republic, which was barely clinging to life through loans from the League of Nations, remained to be seen.

Nevertheless, the planning continued to advance blithely: in spring 1925, Franz Wallack was given permission to take a study tour to Europe's most important mountain road passes. In the summer he visited the 13 most important Alpine crossings as well as an additional 30 Alpine passes in a five-week period. Wallack examined routing and road surfaces, measured hairpin turns and inclines, tunnels and galleries, checked curbstones, railings and retaining walls, inspected bridges made of stone, iron, wood and concrete, counted cars, busses and motorcycles, furthermore rode on countless cable and suspension railways, visited hydro power stations, slept in mountain hotels – all while writing a unique and comprehensive inventory of Alpine road engineering and mountain tourism in the 1920s. "I have to admit," Franz Wallack recalled more than two decades later in his Glockner Road biography, "that as I ascended the Stilfserjoch, the Grimsel and the Furka as well as the Col du Lauteret by car, I felt some inner apprehension and fear and was always prepared to come face to face with similar and even more scenically beautiful – perhaps even significantly more beautiful – landscapes than the Grossglockner High Alpine Road would ever have to offer. However, the farther I got and the more I saw, the more favorably the Grossglockner High Alpine Road project set itself apart from the other Alpine roads, and most clearly when I drove back to the Glockner area immediately after making this trip."

Franz Wallack ultimately became convinced during this trip that besides the traffic-related technological significance, it was primarily the scenic beauty that justified the construction of the road – and the aspect of a truly panoramic road had to be taken into account in its planning. In particular, it was important to showcase the branch road to the Kaiser-Franz-Josefs-Höhe and its unparalleled view of the glacier as a tourist highlight. But as tightly as the builder held onto his vision, reworked the routing, increased the road width from three to five meters, lengthened the route from 27 to 38 kilometers and brought in all additional insights he had gained from his study tour – even in the winter of 1925 there was still no investor for the required five million gold schillings. In the meantime, political opposition to the project was stirring at government level, the advocates for a Felber-Tauern variant were also piping up again, and a pass road over the Lower Tauern was brought into play from Badgastein. Meanwhile, Wallack's Grossglockner project, which had been prepared down to the composition of the dry masonry and could be implemented immediately, was still lying untouched in the committee's drawer in 1928, four years after the planning had been initiated.

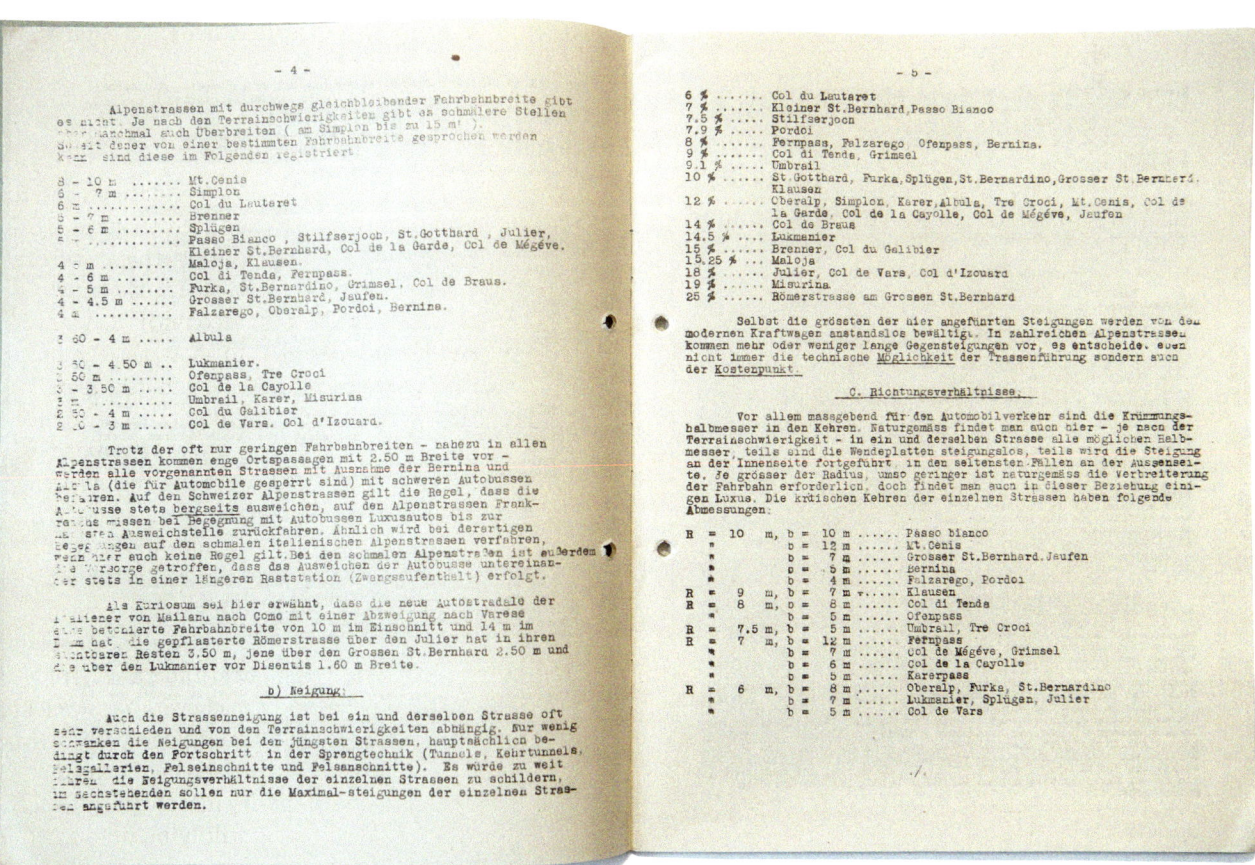

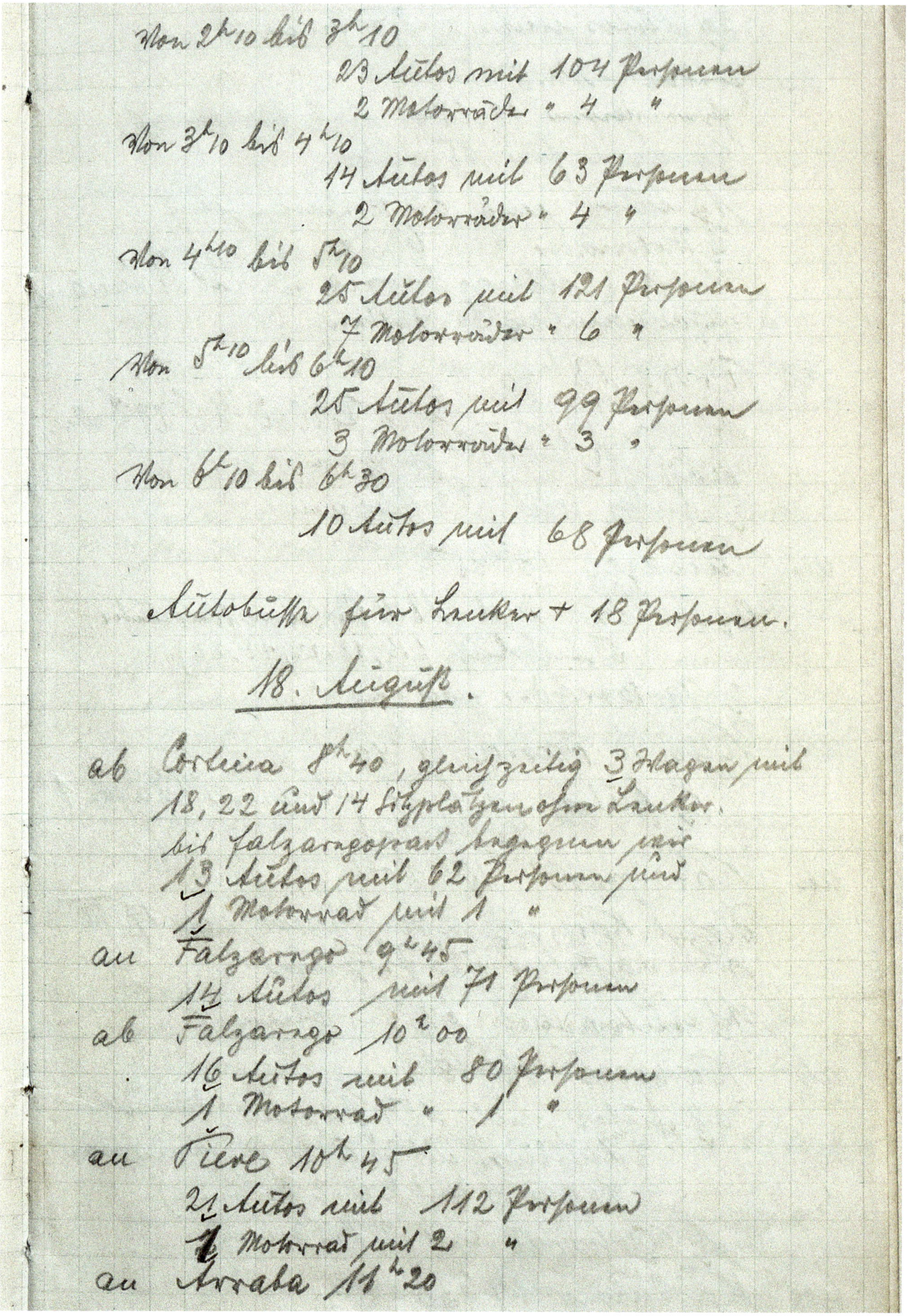

Von 2h10 bis 3h10
    23 Autos mit 104 Personen
    2 Motorräder „ 4 „

Von 3h10 bis 4h10
    14 Autos mit 63 Personen
    2 Motorräder „ 4 „

Von 4h10 bis 5h10
    25 Autos mit 121 Personen
    7 Motorräder „ 6 „

Von 5h10 bis 6h10
    25 Autos mit 99 Personen
    3 Motorräder „ 3 „

Von 6h10 bis 6h30
    10 Autos mit 68 Personen

Autobusse für Lenker + 18 Personen.

18. August.

ab Cortina 8h40, gleichzeitig 3 Wagen mit
18, 22 und 14 Sitzplätzen ohne Lenker.
bis Falzaregopass begegnen wir
13 Autos mit 62 Personen und
1 Motorrad mit 1 „

an Falzarego 9h45
    14 Autos mit 71 Personen

ab Falzarego 10h00
    16 Autos mit 80 Personen
    1 Motorrad „ 1 „

an Pieve 10h45
    21 Autos mit 112 Personen
    1 Motorrad mit 2 „

an Arabba 11h20

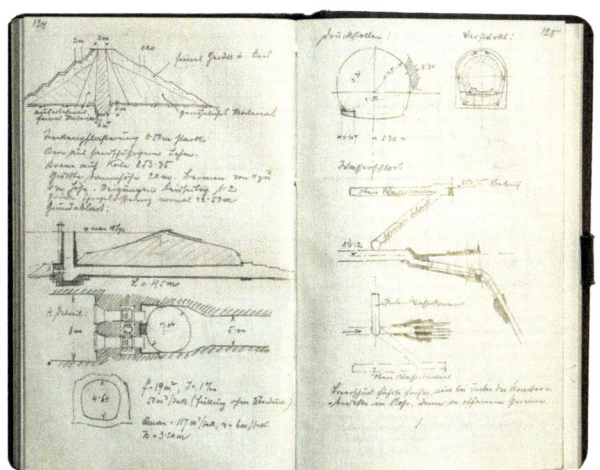
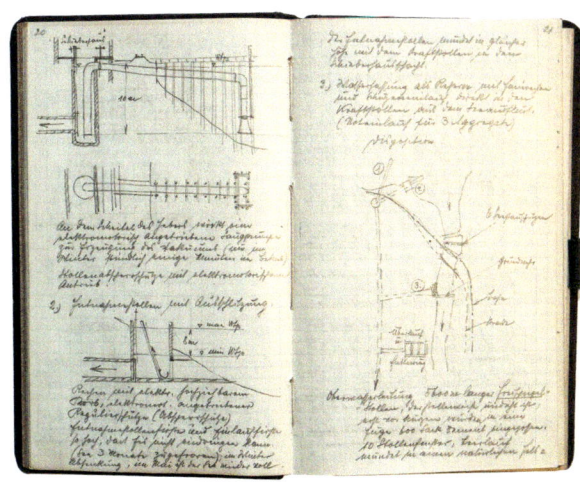
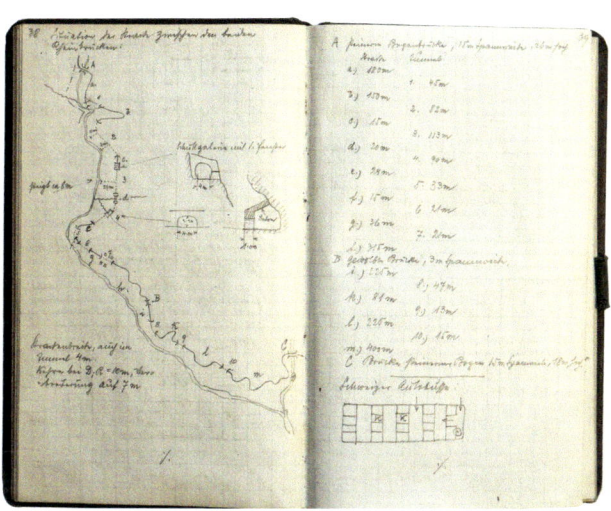
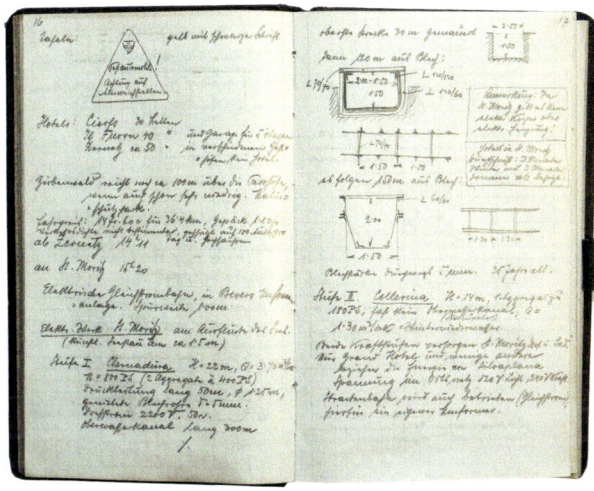
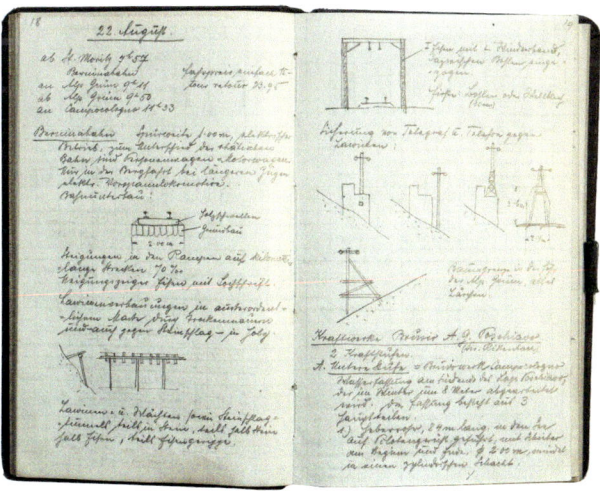
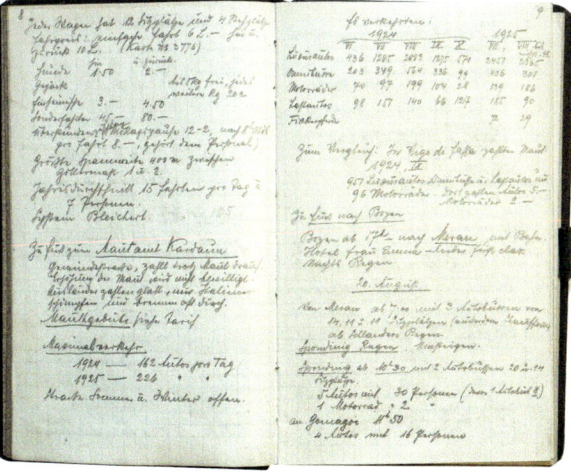

MIT FREUNDLICHER GENEHMIGUNG
COURTESY OF:
GROHAG ARCHIV

politischer Widerstand gegen das Projekt, auch die Fürsprecher einer Felber-Tauern-Variante meldeten sich erneut zu Wort, aus Badgastein wurde zudem eine Passstraße über die Niederen Tauern ins Spiel gebracht. Währenddessen lag Wallacks bis hin zur Beschaffenheit der Trockenmauern ausgearbeitetes und sofort realisierbares Großglockner-Projekt auch 1928, vier Jahre nach Planungsbeginn, unangetastet in der Schublade des Ausschusses.

Gegen alle Widerstände Franz Wallack war nicht der einzige, der bereit war, die Idee einer Großglockner Hochalpenstraße durchzusetzen. Bereits 1922 hatte Salzburg mit dem damals 31-jährigen Franz Rehrl einen neuen Landeshauptmann erhalten. Der impulsive Machtpolitiker, ökonomisch ambitionierte Großdenker und begeisterte Automobilist hatte die touristische Entwicklung des Salzburger Landes ganz oben auf die Agenda gesetzt und die Festspielhäuser ausbauen sowie die Gaisbergstraße und die Schmittenhöhen-Seilbahn in Zell am See errichten lassen. Nachdem er die Hochtorstrecke im Oktober 1926 zum ersten Mal begangen und bei schönstem Herbstwetter den Gletscher bewundert hatte, sollte Franz Rehrl auch zur treibenden Kraft hinter dem Glocknerstraßenbau und zum Sparringspartner für Franz Wallack werden. Für Rehrl war die Straße jedoch nicht nur eine willkommene touristische Ergänzung zu »seinen« Salzburger Festspielen und die Verbindung zu einem zukünftigen Skizentrum in der Glocknergruppe, sie war auch für sein anderes Mammutprojekt essenziell: die Tauernkraftwerke.

Das von der Allgemeinen Elektricitäts-Gesellschaft in Berlin getragene Vorhaben sah vor, alle Wasserkräfte der Hohen Tauern, die sich oberhalb von 2.000 Meter Seehöhe befanden, zu konzentrieren und in drei nördlich des Tauernhauptkammes gelegene Speicher zu leiten. Das gewaltige Tauernkraftwerk sollte jährlich mehr als sechs Milliarden Kilowattstunden Strom erzeugen, der bis in die nördlichsten Teile Europas geleitet werden würde. Franz Rehrl versprach sich von dem 250 Millionen Dollar teuren Kraftwerksprojekt nicht nur die wirtschaftliche Sanierung seines Landes, sondern auch en passant die Lösung der Glocknerstraßenfrage. In seiner Silvesteransprache des Jahres 1928 verkündete der Landeshauptmann, man könne statt der Strecke über das Fuscher Törl und den rund 255 Meter langen Hochtortunnel auf 2.506 Meter Höhe auch einfach einen künftigen Kraftwerkstollen auf etwa 2.080 Meter Höhe mitbenutzen.

Doch statt eines neuen Tauernkraftwerks brachte das neue Jahr 1929 die Weltwirtschaftskrise. Die Reichsmark befand sich im freien Fall, verschiedene Ministerien äußerten ihre Bedenken, die Kohleindustrie intrigierte erfolgreich, und eine Realisierung des Kraftwerks rückte in weite Ferne. Franz Rehrl mochte seine Pläne nicht vollends aufgeben und verfolgte nun die Idee,

In spite of all resistance Franz Wallack was not the only one who was prepared to push the idea of the Grossglockner High Alpine Road to fruition. The state of Salzburg had gotten a new governor in 1922, the then 31-year-old Franz Rehrl. The impulsive power politician, economically ambitious big thinker and enthusiastic car driver had put Salzburg's state tourist development at the top of his agenda along with upgrading the venues for festival events, and had had the Gaisbergstrasse and the Schmittenhöhen cable car built at Zell am See. After he inspected the Hochtor route for the first time and marveled at the glacier during the most glorious fall weather in October 1926, Franz Rehrl also became a driving force behind the Glockner Road construction and a sparring partner for Franz Wallack. For Rehrl the road was, however, not only a welcome touristic addition to "his" Salzburg Festival and the connection to a future skiing center in the Glockner group, it was also essential to his other mammoth project: the Tauern power plants.

The plan, which was to be financed by the Allgemeine Elektricitäts-Gesellschaft in Berlin stipulated that all the High Tauern's hydropower located above an altitude of 2,000 meters was to be concentrated and conducted to three storage facilities to the north of the main Tauern ridge. The massive Tauern power plant was to generate more than six billion kilowatts of electricity annually, which would be transmitted up to the northernmost reaches of Europe. Franz Rehrl not only expected the economic rehabilitation of his state from the 250-million dollar power plant project, but also the solution of the Glockner Road issue as a secondary benefit. In his 1928 New Year's Eve speech, the governor announced that instead of the route via the Fuscher Törl and the approximately 255-meter long Hochtor Tunnel at an altitude of 2,506 meters, one could simply share use of a future power station utility tunnel at approx. 2,080 meters above sea level.

Yet instead of a new Tauern power plant, the new year of 1929 brought a worldwide economic crisis. The Reichsmark was in free fall, various ministries were expressing their misgivings, the coal industry plotted successfully against it, and thus making the power plant a reality moved far into the future. Franz Rehrl didn't like giving up on his plans completely and began pursuing the idea of building the Grossglockner High Alpine Road at least as a preliminary step for a future power plant project – and demanding the construction costs back later from the respective power plant operator. With the backing of the Finance Minister Otto Juch and by pointing out the dramatic unemployment situation, Rehrl in fact succeeded in getting the Salzburg state government to approve the construction of the road under these highly speculative circumstances.

Shortly thereafter Franz Wallack received a telegram with the message that the Glockner Road was to become a reality. Wallack's initial joy, however, quickly turned into disillusionment as Franz Rehrl explained his idea of the

Großglockner Hochalpenstraße zumindest als Vorstufe für ein künftiges Kraftwerksprojekt zu errichten – und später die Baukosten vom jeweiligen Kraftwerksbetreiber zurückzufordern. Mit Rückendeckung des Finanzministers Otto Juch und Verweis auf die dramatische Arbeitslosigkeit gelang es Rehrl im März 1930 tatsächlich, den Salzburger Landtag dazu zu bewegen, dem Bau der Straße unter diesen reichlich spekulativen Vorzeichen zuzustimmen.

Kurz darauf erhielt Franz Wallack per Telegramm die Nachricht, dass die Glocknerstraße Realität werden sollte. Wallacks anfängliche Freude schlug jedoch in Ernüchterung um, als Franz Rehrl bei einer ersten Begehung des Geländes seine Idee der Straßenführung erklärte: Von Wallacks Projekt waren nur die Nordrampe von Ferleiten bis zum Oberen Naßfeld und die Südrampe von Heiligenblut bis zur Franz-Josefs-Höhe übrig geblieben – dazwischen erstreckte sich eine offensichtlich mit dem Lineal gezogene Scheitelstrecke inklusive eines 1.950 Meter langen Pfandlschartentunnels. Der Beschaffenheit des Geländes, der Eignung für einen Straßenbau und dem panoramatischen Fahrerlebnis war offensichtlich wenig Aufmerksamkeit geschenkt worden. Dafür hatte Rehrl den auf Kärntner Seite gelegenen Pasterze-Gletscher deutlich näher an Salzburg herangerückt. »Gegen diesen Linienzug«, so erinnerte sich Wallack später, »sträubte sich mein Inneres«.

Der Bau beginnt Während sich Wallack und Rehrl ihrem Variantenstreit hingaben, rutschte Österreich weiter in die Rezession. Für die Regierung wurde die Großglockner Hochalpenstraße immer mehr zum beschäftigungspolitischen Symbolprojekt. Sobald Bundeskanzler Johann Schober bei einer Wirtschaftskonferenz den Bau verkündet hatte, strömten Tausende Arbeiter aus dem ganzen Land nach Ferleiten und Heiligenblut, um als sogenannte »Baraber« auf den Baustellen der Nord- und Südrampen anzuheuern – doch nur wenige waren für die schwere und gefährliche Arbeit im Hochgebirge tatsächlich qualifiziert. Hinter den Kulissen wurde derweil weiter um die Finanzierung gekämpft: Nachdem Österreich im August 1930 neue Anleihen gewährt worden waren, gab der Ministerrat unter Beteiligung des Bundes den Weg für die Gründung einer Großglockner Hochalpenstraßen AG frei. Mithilfe eines alten Verordnung aus dem Kaiserreich ließ sich die Glocknerstraße zudem zum begünstigten Bau erklären, um Genehmigungen zu beschleunigen, Einspruchsrechte zu entkräften und Enteignungen zu ermöglichen. Kaum dass in Heiligenblut und Ferleiten die Lokalverhandlungen stattgefunden hatten und die Bewilligungen für den Bau der Nordrampe bis Hochmais und der Südrampe bis zur Franz-Josefs-Höhe ausgesprochen waren, begann die Einrichtung der Baustellen und Baracken, die mit Tragtieren, Trägerkolonnen und Traktoren auf den Berg geschafft wurden. Magazine, Kantinen, Verkaufsstände, Werkstätten, Büro-

routing during their initial inspection of the terrain: what remained of Wallack's project were only the north ramp from Ferleiten to the Oberes Nassfeld and the south ramp from Heiligenblut to Franz-Josefs-Höhe – between them was a summit route obviously drawn with a ruler which included a 1,950-meter-long Pfandlscharte tunnel. It was obvious that little attention had been paid to the make-up of the terrain, its suitability for building a road or to providing the best panoramic experience for visitors in cars. Instead, Rehrl had moved the Pasterze Glacier, which is on the Carinthian side, significantly closer to Salzburg. "My innermost being," as Wallack reminisced later, "rebelled against that line".

Construction begins While Wallack and Rehrl indulged in their disagreement about their preferred road versions, Austria slid deeper into recession. To the government, though, the Grossglockner High Alpine Road increasingly became a symbolic political project for employment. As soon as Chancellor Johann Schober announced the construction at an economic conference, thousands of workers from all over the country streamed to Ferleiten and Heiligenblut to sign up for the north and south ramp construction sites as so-called "Glockner laborers" – but few were actually qualified for the heavy and dangerous work in the high mountains. Meanwhile, the fight for the financing continued behind the scenes: after Austria was granted new bonds in August 1930, the Council of Ministers and the participating federal government gave the green light for founding the Grossglockner High Alpine Road AG. With the help of an old regulation from the time of the Empire, the Glockner Road was also declared a favored construction project in order to speed up permits, to invalidate objections and to enable expropriations. Hardly had the local negotiations taken place in Heiligenblut and Ferleiten and the permits for the construction of the north ramp to Hochmais and the south ramp to the Franz-Josefs-Höhe been issued when the work to set up the construction sites and barracks began, with materials being hauled up the mountain by pack animals, work crews and tractors. Storerooms, canteens, stalls selling goods, workshops and office buildings were built on both sides of the tree line, and the nearly one thousand laborers were equipped with hammer drills, gravel crushers, sand grinders and all other required tools. On the morning of August 30, 1930, Franz Rehrl's daughter finally initiated the first explosive blasts. While the governor spoke words of encouragement to the laborers, Franz Wallack and his wife clasped hands in silence – the building of the Grossglockner High Alpine Road had indeed begun.

And it progressed rapidly: by the end of the season in October 1930, the laborers in the north had worked up to the third construction section between Piffkar and Hochmais when the onset of winter stopped the work at that high altitude. In the meantime, the work on the road in the valley continued until shortly before Christmas. On the south side, the construction work on the four sections

häuser wurden diesseits wie jenseits der Baumgrenze errichtet, und die fast eintausend Arbeiter mit Bohrhämmern, Schotterquetschen, Sandmühlen und allen erforderlichen Werkzeugen ausgestattet. Am Morgen des 30. August 1930 löste Franz Rehrls Tochter in Ferleiten schließlich die ersten Sprengschüsse aus. Während der Landeshauptmann den Arbeitern Mut zusprach, drückten sich Franz Wallack und seine Frau stumm die Hand – der Bau der Großglockner Hochalpenstraße hatte tatsächlich begonnen.

Und es ging zügig voran: Bis zum Ende der Saison im Oktober 1930 hatten sich die Baraber im Norden bis zum dritten Baulos zwischen Piffkar und Hochmais emporgearbeitet, dann stoppte der Wintereinbruch die Arbeiten in der Höhe. Im Tal ging derweil die Arbeit an der Straße bis kurz vor Weihnachten weiter. Auf der Südseite konnten die Bauarbeiten an den vier Baulosen zwischen Heiligenblut und der Franz-Josefs-Höhe bis Mitte November fortgesetzt werden. Während der Bauarbeiten hatte sich gezeigt, dass viele der zu 80 Prozent zugewiesenen Arbeitslosen – darunter auch Kellner und Friseure – für die schwere Arbeit im Hochgebirge weder ausgebildet noch gekleidet waren. Manch ein Arbeiter, so schilderte es Franz Wallack, hatte offensichtlich noch nie eine Schaufel in der Hand gehabt. Auch festes Schuhwerk fehlte allerorts. Ein ständiger Wechsel in der Arbeiterschaft war die Folge.

Im Februar 1931 wurde die Großglockner Hochalpenstraßen AG gegründet – Hauptaktionär war mit 60 Prozent der Anleihen die Österreichische Republik, 33 Prozent der Aktien hielt fortan die Tauernwerke AG, hinter der noch immer die A.E.G. stand. Doch das optimistische Konstrukt hielt nur kurz, die Berliner zogen sich zurück, der Bund übernahm auch die restlichen Anteile. Das Tauernkraftwerksprojekt wurde erst 1938 – nach dem »Anschluss« Österreichs an das deutsche NS-Reich, auf Initiative Hermann Görings und mithilfe Hunderter Zwangsarbeiter – in Kaprun wieder aufgenommen und in der Nachkriegszeit als Sinnbild des Österreichischen Wiederaufbaus vollendet.

Der Bauplan für die Glocknerstraße sah derweil weiterhin vor, zunächst die Rampen zu errichten und die Straßen in Nord und Süd schließlich durch die Scheitelstrecke zu verbinden. Ob Wallacks Variante I von Hochmais über das Fuscher Törl und das Hochtor zum Kasereck oder die von Franz Rehrl präferierte Variante II von Hochmais durch einen Pfandlschartentunnel zur Franz-Josefs-Höhe gebaut werden sollte, war zu diesem Zeitpunkt noch immer nicht klar und wurde in vielen Varianten hitzig diskutiert und durchgerechnet. Im März 1931 wurden die Bauarbeiten wieder aufgenommen, im Juli die Straße von Fusch nach Ferleiten dem Verkehr übergeben. Am Schluss der Bausaison 1931 waren auf beiden Rampen 11 Straßenkilometer fertiggestellt, rund zwanzig Kilometer standen noch im Bau.

between Heiligenblut and the Franz-Josefs-Höhe was able to continue until mid-November. During the construction work it became clear that many of the up to 80 percent assigned unemployed people – who included waiters and hairdressers – were neither trained nor clothed for the hard work in the high mountains. Some of the laborers, as Franz Wallack described it, had obviously never even so much as held a shovel in their hands. In addition, sturdy footwear was lacking everywhere. The result was a constant turnover in the workforce.

In February 1931, the Grossglockner High Alpine Roads AG was founded – the main shareholder was the Austrian Republic with 60 percent of the shares, Tauernwerke AG, behind which AEG still stood, held 33 percent of the shares from then on. However, the optimistic arrangement only lasted a short time, the Berliners withdrew, and the federal government took over the remaining shares. The Tauern power plant project was only taken up again in Kaprun in 1938 – after the Austrian "reunification" with the German Nazi Reich, at the initiative of Hermann Göring and with the help of hundreds of forced laborers – and completed in the post-war period as a symbol of Austrian reconstruction.

Meanwhile, the blueprint for the Glockner Road continued to plan that the ramps would be built first and then ultimately the roads in the north and south would be linked via the crest route. At that point it still wasn't clear whether Wallack's version I from Hochmais via the Fuscher Törl and the Hochtor to Kasereck or Franz Rehrl's preferred version II from Hochmais through a Pfandlscharte tunnel to Franz-Josefs-Höhe was going to be built – several variations were subjects of heated discussions and calculations. In March 1931, the construction work was taken up again, and in July the road from Fusch to Ferleiten was opened to traffic. At the end of the construction season of 1931, eleven road kilometers had been completed on both ramps, and around twenty kilometers were still under construction.

The privy councilor and the "Glockner laborers" Privy Councilor Wallack was quite the character: gruff, determined, disciplined, tough on the laborers, but also on himself – and always had his mind on production value for the media. In the five-year construction period he was said to have traversed the Alpine crest on foot around 260 times, always marching while wearing his typical knickerbockers. The tour de force was when he covered the distance from Heiligenblut to Ferleiten in a brisk three hours and twenty minutes. He undertook nighttime Alpine hikes in order to be the first one at the construction site and surprise his laborers. No construction foreman was safe from his sudden inspections. In wind and weather, ice and snow, the chain-smoking engineer was not too self-important to give the "Glockner laborers" detailed instructions and to coordinate the road construction one stone at a time. The approximately 4,000 laborers who lived in

MIT FREUNDLICHER GENEHMIGUNG
COURTESY OF:
GROHAG ARCHIV

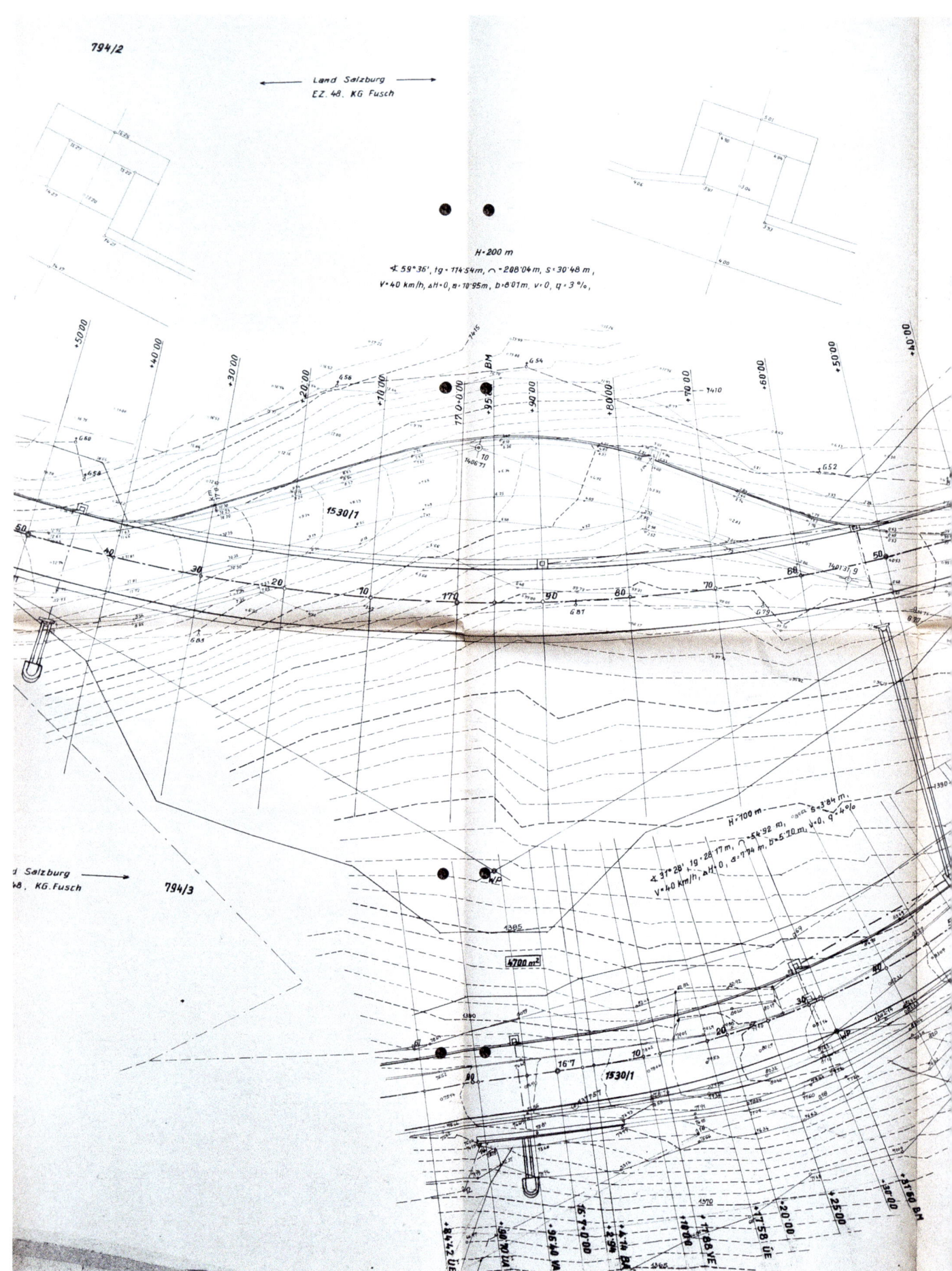

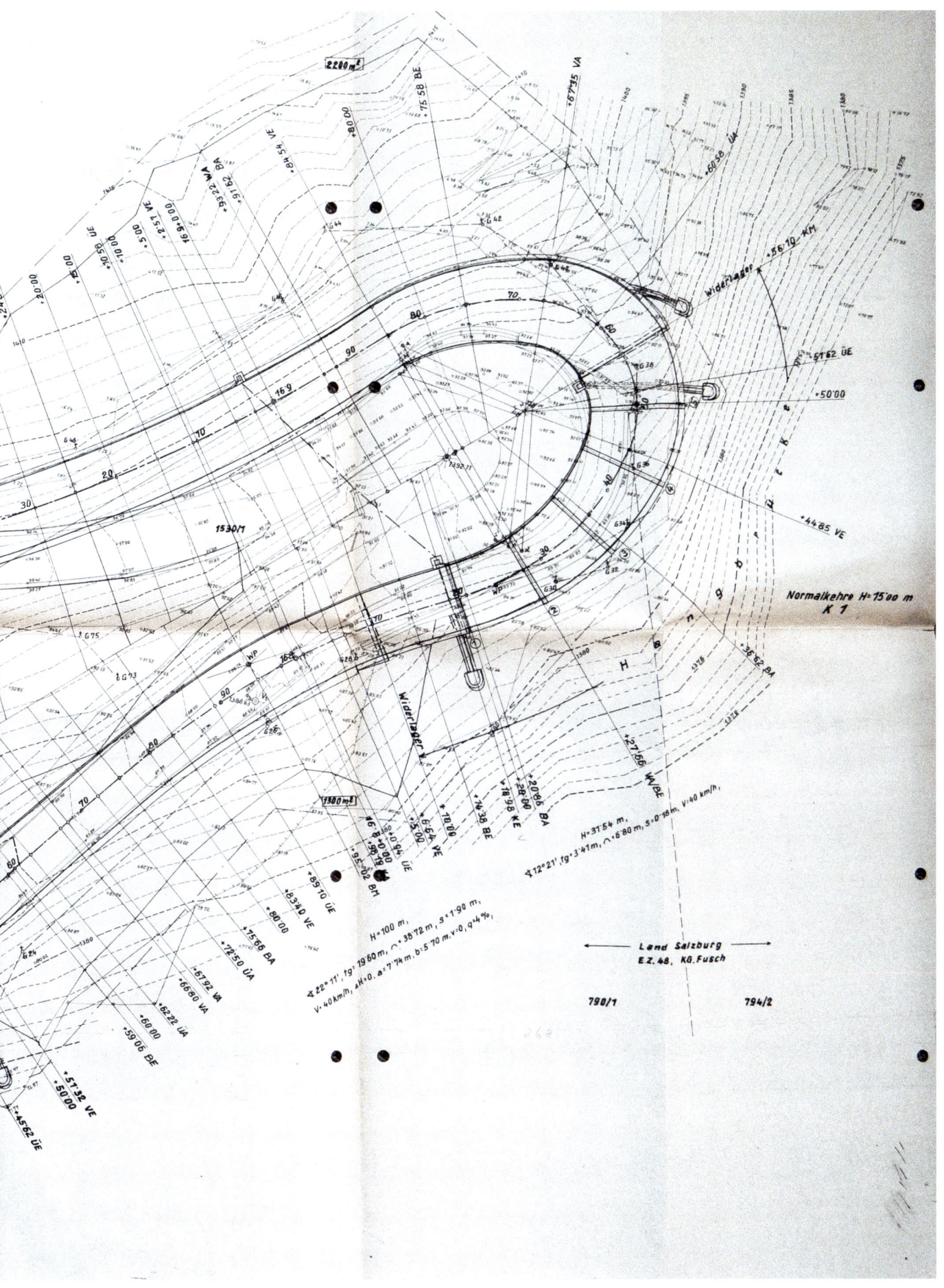

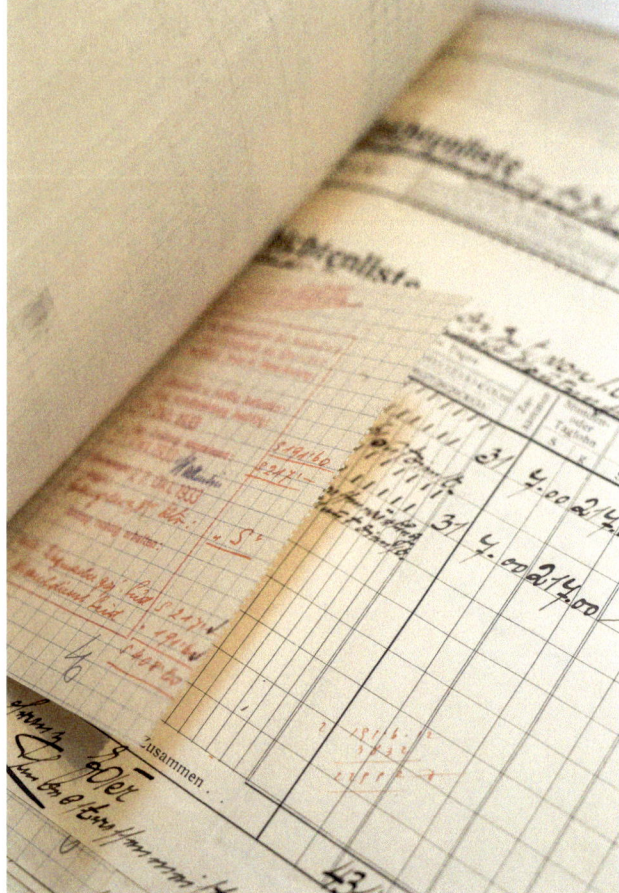

34 — GESCHICHTE / HISTORY

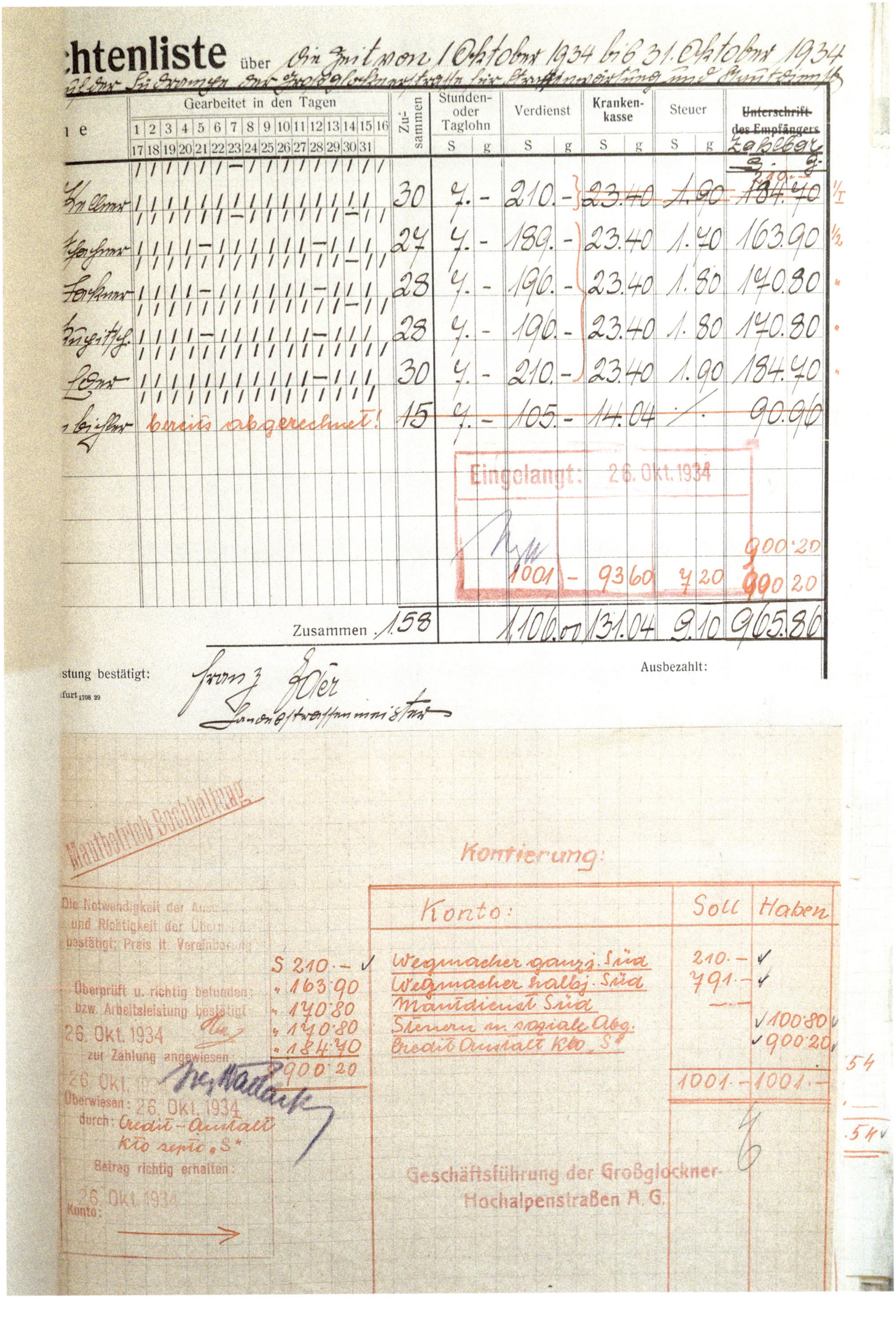

...chtenliste über die Zeit von 1. Oktober 1934 bis 31. Oktober 1934

e	Gearbeitet in den Tagen 1–31	Zusammen	Stunden- oder Taglohn S g	Verdienst S g	Krankenkasse S g	Steuer S g	Unterschrift des Empfängers
	/////////////-////////////////	30	7.–	210.–	23.40	1.90	184.70
	//////////////////////////////	27	7.–	189.–	23.40	1.40	163.90
	//////////////////////////////	28	7.–	196.–	23.40	1.80	170.80
	//////////////////////////////	28	7.–	196.–	23.40	1.80	170.80
	//////////////////////////////	30	7.–	210.–	23.40	1.90	184.70
bisher bereits abgerechnet!		15	7.–	105.–	14.04	/	90.96
				1001.–	93.60	7.20	900.20
Zusammen		158		1106.00	131.04	9.10	965.80

Eingelangt: 26. Okt. 1934

Leistung bestätigt: **Franz Eder** Landesstraßenmeister

Ausbezahlt:

Mautbetrieb Buchhaltung

Die Notwendigkeit der Aus... und Richtigkeit der Über... bestätigt; Preis lt. Vereinbar...

Überprüft u. richtig befunden: bzw. Arbeitsleistung bestätigt:

26. Okt. 1934 zur Zahlung angewiesen

26. Okt. 1934
Überwiesen: 26. Okt. 1934
durch: Credit-Anstalt
Kto septo "S"
Betrag richtig erhalten:
26. Okt. 1934
Konto:

S 210.–
„ 163.90
„ 170.80
„ 170.80
„ 184.70
„ 900.20

Kontierung:

Konto:	Soll	Haben
Wegmacher ganzj. Süd	210.–	
Wegmacher halbj. Süd	791.–	
Mautdienst Süd		
Steuern u. soziale Abg.		100.80
Credit Anstalt Kto "S"		900.20
	1001.–	1001.–

Geschäftsführung der Großglockner-Hochalpenstraßen A.G.

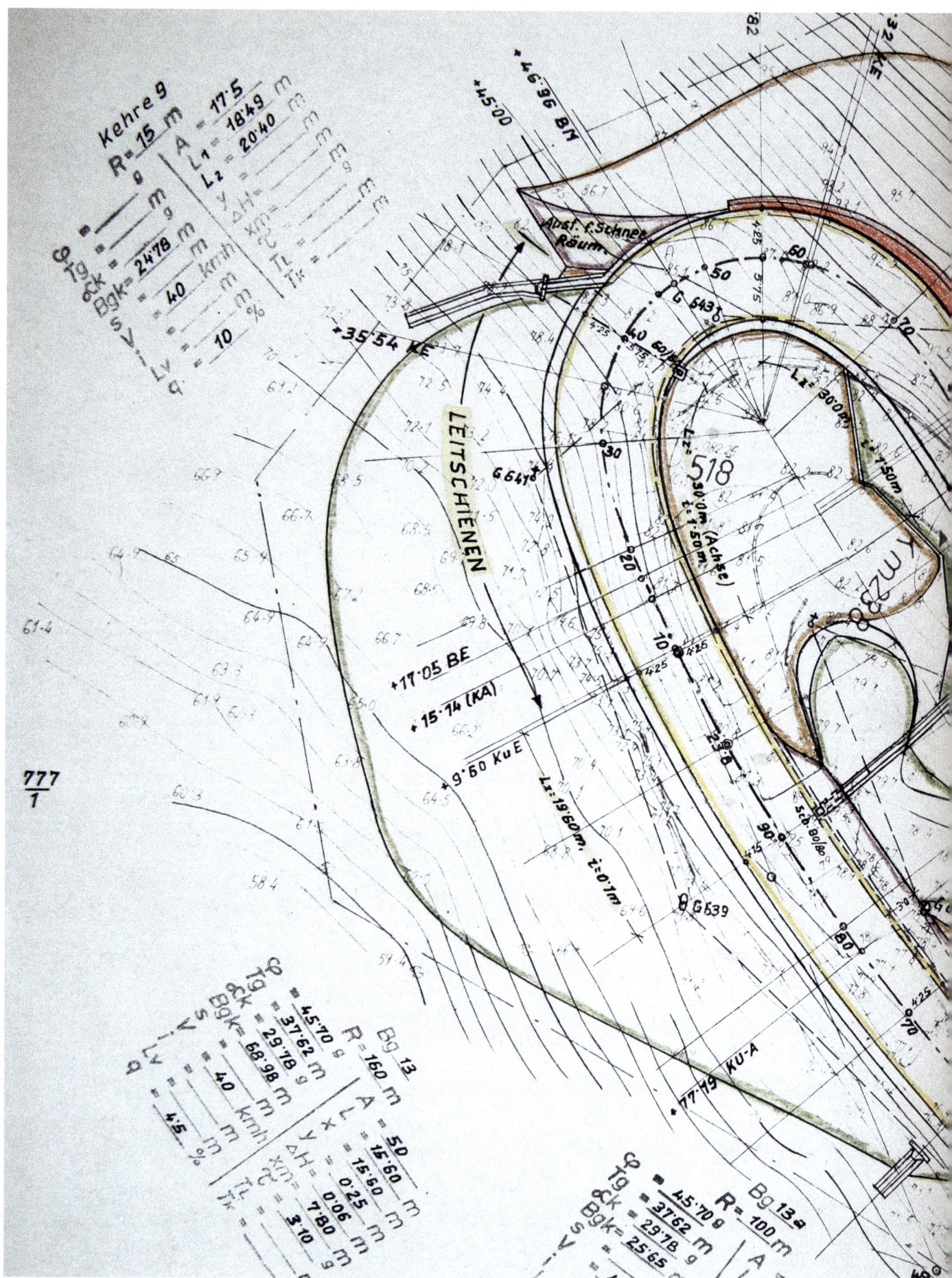

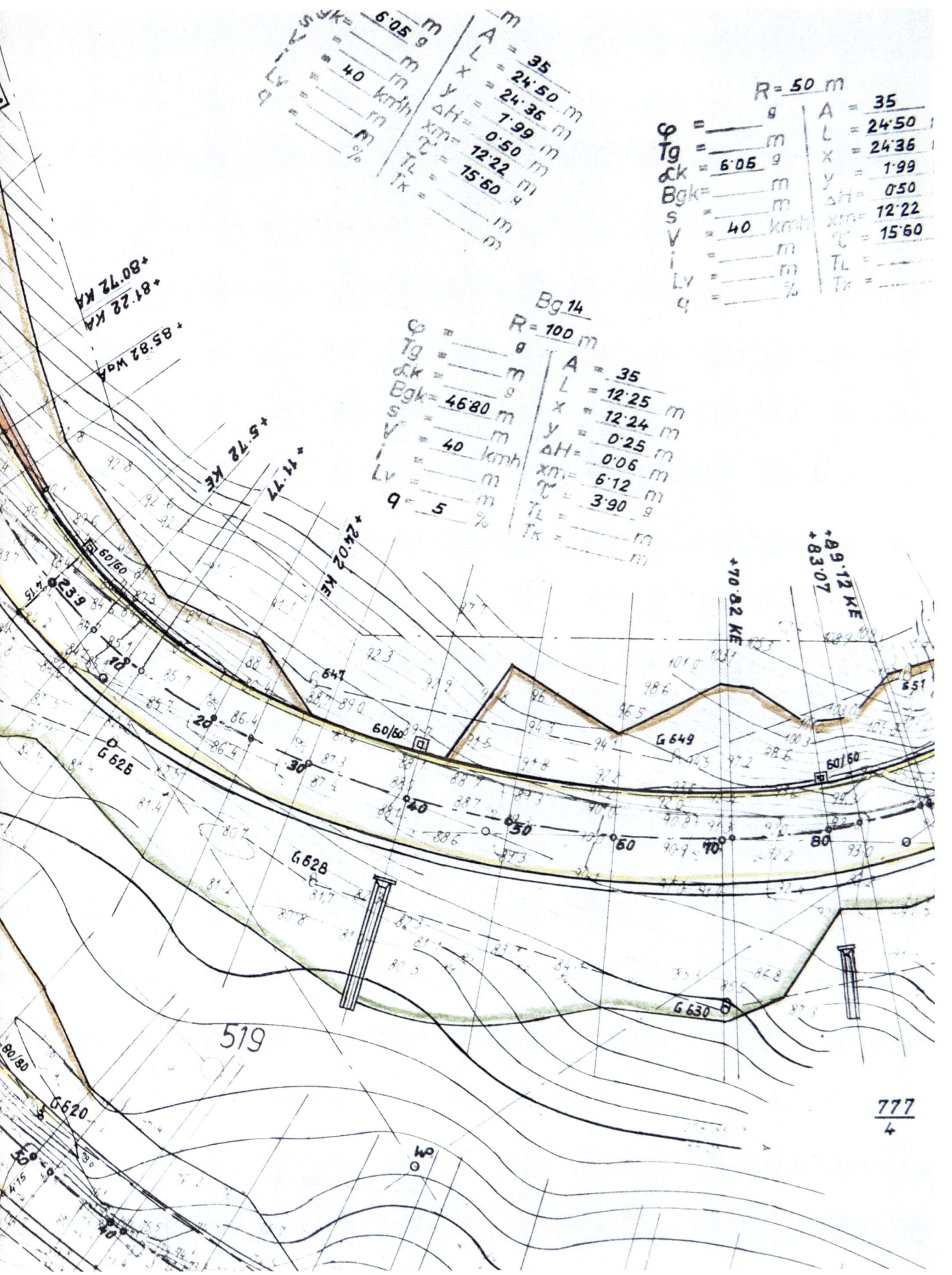

Der Hofrat und die »Glocknerbaraber« Hofrat Wallack war ein spezieller Charakter: barsch, zielstrebig, diszipliniert, hart zu den Arbeitern, aber auch zu sich selbst – und stets auf seine mediale Inszenierung bedacht. In fünf Jahren Bauzeit soll er den Alpenhauptkamm zu Fuß, im Stechschritt und in seinen charakteristischen Kniebundhosen, rund 260 Mal überquert haben. Die Tour de Force von Heiligenblut bis Ferleiten legte er nach eigenen Aussagen in drahtigen drei Stunden und zwanzig Minuten zurück. Um morgens als Erster an der Baustelle zu sein und seine Arbeiter zu überraschen, legte er alpine Nachtwanderungen ein. Kein Capo war vor seinen plötzlichen Inspektionen sicher. Bei Wind und Wetter, Eis und Schnee war sich der kettenrauchende Ingenieur nicht zu schade, den »Glocknerbarabern« detaillierte Anweisungen zu geben und den Straßenbau Stein für Stein zu koordinieren. Von den rund 4.000 Arbeitern, die während der gesamten Bauzeit in 30 Baulagern entlang der Straße lebten und bis zur Eröffnung etwa 1,8 Millionen Arbeitsstunden leisteten, wurde Wallack wohl durchaus geschätzt – hatte er doch erstmals eine Schlechtwetterregelung eingeführt, die eine Lohnfortzahlung garantierte, auch wenn ein Schneesturm im Sommer einmal wieder die Bauarbeiten unmöglich machte. Als leidenschaftlicher Schlittschuhläufer ließ Wallack für die Arbeiter zudem einen Eislaufplatz auf der Fuscher Lacke errichten – die harten Männer, die auf 2.262 Meter Höhe ihre Pirouetten drehten, müssen ein faszinierendes Bild abgegeben haben.

So unnachgiebig Wallack bei der Durchsetzung seiner Ziele war, so feinfühlig zeigte sich der begeisterte Alpinist gegenüber der Natur. Er wusste die Schönheit der Topographie zu schätzen und folgte mit der Straßenführung den Vorgaben des Geländes, statt die alpine Landschaft mit gewaltigen Kunstbauten dominieren zu wollen. »In dieser erhabenen Bergwelt«, so schrieb Wallack später, »wäre es eine Vermessenheit gewesen, hätte ich mit den Mitteln der Technik der Natur den Rang ablaufen wollen.« Wie bereits in seinem Bericht von 1924 formuliert, war es Franz Wallacks anspruchsvolles Ziel, zwei Sackgassen zu einer Durchzugsstraße von großartiger landschaftlicher Schönheit zu verbinden, die dazu berufen sein würde, einen der ersten Plätze unter den Hochalpenstraßen Europas und den Gebirgsstraßen der ganzen Welt einzunehmen. Dass es zum Zweck eines möglichst eindrücklichen Landschaftserlebnisses zu Mehrkosten kommen würde – wie etwa bei der später eingefügten »Panoramaschleife« um den Törlkopf südwestlich des Fuscher Törls – war für Wallacks Gesamtkunstwerk natürlich nur Makulatur.

Straßenbau mit Hindernissen So hoch der ästhetische Anspruch des Baumeisters auch sein mochte – die Finanzen mussten stimmen. Im Frühjahr 1932 fehlte es erneut nicht nur an Geldmitteln, sondern auch an politischer Rückendeckung zur Fortsetzung des Baus. Sollte die Glocknerstraße als Ruine unvollendet am Berg

30 construction camps along the road over the entire construction period and carried out around 1.8 million hours of work by the time of the opening seem to have thoroughly appreciated Wallack – after all, he had introduced a bad weather regulation that guaranteed continued payment of wages even when a snowstorm in summer made working impossible yet again. As a passionate ice skater, Wallack also had an ice skating area created for the laborers on the Fuscher Lacke – it must have been a fascinating sight to see hardened men pirouetting on the ice at an altitude of 2,262 meters.

As unrelenting as Wallack was when it came to pushing his goals through, the enthusiastic Alpinist proved to be very sensitive when it came to nature. He placed great value on the beauty of the topography and ensured that the routing followed the demands of the terrain instead of wanting to dominate the Alpine landscape with massive engineering structures. "In this sublime mountain landscape," Wallack wrote later, "it would have been presumptuous if I had wanted to outdo nature with technological means". As he had already formulated in his 1924 report, it was Franz Wallack's ambitious goal to link two dead end roads into a thoroughfare of spectacular beauty that would be destined to become one of Europe's top high Alpine roads as well as take a prominent position among the world's mountain roads. That it would incur additional expenses for the purpose of providing the most impressive scenic experience possible – such as, for example, the "panorama loop" around the Törlkopf southwest of the Fuscher Törl – was naturally only a minor defect in Wallack's complete work of art.

Road construction with obstacles As high as the master builder's aesthetic demands may have been – the finances had to add up. In spring 1932, not only was there a shortage of funds again, but there was a lack of political backing for continuing the construction. Was the Glockner Road to be left behind on the mountain as an unfinished ruin? Franz Rehrl advanced the road construction project in Salzburg and at the federal level, campaigned with the Glockner laborers, and in the end showed Austria's chancellor Engelbert Dollfuß around the construction site in the early summer of 1932 – and was able to convert him from an opponent to a supporter of the road on the spot. At the end of June, the National Assembly resolved to at least complete the partial routes that had been started. At the beginning of September 1932, the north ramp from Ferleiten to Hochmais was finally fit for traffic: "Hundreds of cars in a long line," as Franz Wallack recalled, "now drove up the road, which had an abundance of wonderful views". A month later, the south ramp from Heiligenblut to Franz-Josefs-Höhe via the Glocknerhaus was also opened. Before Federal President Wilhelm Miklas opened the road, Franz Wallack went to the small church cemetery in Heiligenblut, which afforded a view of the Grossglockner, and paid his respects to the laborers who had lost their lives building the road.

> Als leidenschaftlicher Schlittschuhläufer ließ Wallack für die Arbeiter zudem einen Eislaufplatz auf der Fuscher Lacke errichten – die harten Männer, die auf 2.262 Meter Höhe ihre Pirouetten drehten, müssen ein faszinierendes Bild abgegeben haben.

> As a passionate ice skater, Wallack also had an ice skating area created for the laborers on the Fuscher Lacke – it must have been a fascinating sight to see hardened men pirouetting on the ice at an altitude of 2,262 meters.

zurückbleiben? Franz Rehrl trug das Straßenbauprojekt in Salzburg und auf Bundesebene weiter voran, machte mit den Glocknerarbeitern Wahlkampf, führte im Frühsommer 1932 schließlich Österreichs Bundeskanzler Engelbert Dollfuß über die Baustelle – und konnte ihn noch vor Ort vom Gegner zum Befürworter der Straße bekehren. Ende Juni beschloss der Nationalrat zumindest die Fertigstellung der begonnenen Teilstrecken. Anfang September war 1932 war schließlich die Nordrampe von Ferleiten bis Hochmais befahrbar: »Viele Hunderte von Autos«, so erinnerte sich Franz Wallack, »fuhren nun in langer Kette die an wunderbaren Ausblicken so reiche Straße ins Hochmais hinauf.« Einen Monat später wurde auch die Südrampe von Heiligenblut über das Glocknerhaus bis zur Franz-Josefs-Höhe eröffnet. Bevor Bundespräsident Wilhelm Miklas die Straße eröffnete, gedachte Franz Wallack auf dem kleinen Friedhof der Kirche in Heiligenblut mit Blick auf den Großglockner jener Arbeiter, die beim Bau der Straße ihr Leben gelassen hatten.

Ob und wie es im kommenden Jahr mit der Straße weitergehen sollte, hing nun von der Beschaffung der notwendigen Finanzierung für den Bau der Scheitelstrecke und der Lösung der Variantenfrage ab. Während am Berg die Gutachten gewälzt wurden, änderte sich in der von Massenarbeitslosigkeit immer stärker beeinträchtigten Republik Österreich erneut die politische Gemengelage: Im März 1933 nutzte Bundeskanzler Dollfuß eine Krise bei der Nationalratssitzung für einen Staatsstreich. Das Parlament war fortan ausgeschaltet, Dollfuß regierte per Notverordnung weiter – und verwandelte das Land schleichend in eine faschistische Diktatur konservativ-

If and how the road construction would continue the following year now depended on obtaining the necessary financing for building the crest route and settling the version issue. While the expert opinions were being pored over on the mountain, the political conflicts in the Austrian Republic were rekindled because of the mass unemployment that was affecting the country more and more adversely: in March 1933, Chancellor Dollfuß took advantage of a crisis during a National Assembly meeting to stage a coup d'état. The parliament was neutralized from then on, Dollfuß continued governing under an emergency decree – and gradually transformed the country into a fascist dictatorship marked by conservative Catholic influence. Inspired by the National Socialists in Germany and their policy of motorization, Dollfuß now also placed the car and the expansion of the road system at the center of his economic policy in Austria and made new funding available everywhere. The number of shares of the Grossglockner-Hochalpenstraßen AG was also increased so that the road construction could continue. At the end of July, the version dispute was also decided in favor of Wallack's Hochtor route – the construction cost of the alternative route could simply not be financed. The plan was to complete the road by 1935.

BILDER FOLGENDE SEITEN
MIT FREUNDLICHER GENEHMIGUNG
PICTURES FOLLOWING PAGES
COURTESY OF:
GROHAG ARCHIV

katholischer Prägung. Inspiriert von den Nationalsozialisten in Deutschland und ihrer Motorisierungspolitik rückte Dollfuß nun auch in Österreich das Automobil und den Ausbau des Straßennetzes ins Zentrum seiner Wirtschaftspolitik und stellte allerorts neue Mittel zur Verfügung. Auch bei der Großglockner Hochalpen AG wurden die Anteile erhöht, um den Bau der Straße fortsetzen zu können. Ende Juli wurde schließlich auch der Variantenstreit zugunsten von Wallacks Hochtorstrecke entschieden – die Baukosten der Alternativstrecke wären schlicht nicht finanzierbar gewesen. Die Fertigstellung war bis zum Jahr 1935 vorgesehen.

Im Laufe des Sommers 1933 ging die Arbeit weiter. Die Baraber verlegten die Baulager hinauf zur Scheitelstrecke, richteten auf Steilhängen und Felsabstürzen Güterseilschwebebahnen ein, bewegten tonnenweise Erde in Schubkarren und Feldbahnwagen, trugen bis zu 150 Kilogramm schwere Baumstämme in »Kraxen«, bearbeiteten den Fels des Hochtors mit ihren Presslufthammern – und entdeckten dabei am 14. September auf der Südseite des Tunnels jene kleine bronzene Statue eines in Löwenfell gehüllten Herkules', die nur zu gut in die mediale Aufbereitung eines historisch geradezu prädestinierten Straßenbaus passte. »Einst haben die Römer eine Straße über das Hochtor und das Fuscher Törl in unser Nordland gebahnt«, schwelgte Wallack im Sonderdruck der Zeitschrift *Bergland*, »jetzt bauen wir eine Straße über das Fuscher Törl und das Hochtor nach ihrem leuchtenden Südland.« Genau zwei Monate später war der »höchstgelegene Tunnel Österreichs« durchschlagen. Die Baustelle selbst war derweil ebenfalls zur Touristenattraktion geworden, auch wenn die Gäste aus Deutschland wegen der vom NS-Regime verhängten »1.000-Mark-Sperre« für Auslandsreisen nicht mehr wie bisher ins Salzburger Land pilgerten. Doch auch ohne deutsche Touristen gewann die nationalsozialistische Bewegung in Österreich merklich an Boden.

Während im Frühjahr 1934 die Finanzierung der Straße erst mal auf stabilen Füßen stand, musste man nun auf das Ende des Hochgebirgswinters jenseits von 2.000 Metern warten. Ende Mai nahmen die Tunnelarbeiter am Hochtor wieder ihre Arbeit auf, im Juni begannen die Aushubarbeiten des Mittertörltunnels, Mitte Juli begutachtete Bundeskanzler Dollfuß den Fortschritt der Arbeiten, Ende Juli war der Stollen durchschlagen. Zehn Tage nach seinem Baustellenbesuch wurde Dollfuß bei einem Putschversuch durch Österreichische Nationalsozialisten im Bundeskanzleramt ermordet. An seine Stelle an der Spitze des »Ständestaates« trat Kurt Schuschnigg. Derweil die österreichische Geschichte ihren unheilvollen Lauf nahm, feilte Franz Wallack an der Kür seiner Baukomposition: Sollte das 2.572 Meter hohe, direkt neben der Straße gelegene Poneck mit seinem atemberaubenden Rundumblick auf 37 Dreitausender und 19 Gletscherfelder den Autofahrern tatsächlich verschlossen bleiben? Um die finanzielle Rückendeckung

The work continued over the course of summer 1933. The laborers shifted the construction camps up to the crest route, set up material ropeways at steep slopes and rock falls, moved tons of earth in wheelbarrows and light train cars, carried up to 150-kilogram tree stumps on back frames, hacked at the Hochtor crag with their jackhammers – and on September 14, discovered the aforementioned small bronze statue of Hercules draped in a lion's pelt on the south side of the tunnel, which fit only too well into the media narrative of a historically preordained road construction. "The Romans once built a road to our northern lands via the Hochtor and the Fuscher Törl", Wallack rhapsodized in a special edition of *Bergland* magazine, "now we're building a road to their shining southern lands via the Fuscher Törl and the Hochtor". Exactly two months later, "Austria's highest-elevation tunnel" had been broken through. In the meantime, the building site itself had also become a tourist attraction, even though visitors from Germany didn't flock to the State of Salzburg as they had done previously, because the Nazi regime had imposed a "1000-mark restriction" on travels abroad. Yet even without the German tourists, the National Socialist movement began gaining ground noticeably in Austria.

While the financing of the road stood on firm ground to begin with in the spring of 1934, one now had to wait for the end of the high mountain winter above the 2,000-meter line. The tunnel laborers took up their work again at the end of May, the excavation of the Mittertörl tunnel began in June, Chancellor Dollfuß inspected the progress of the work in mid-July, and by the end of July the tunnel had been broken through. Ten days after his visit to the construction site, Dollfuß was murdered during a coup attempt by the Austrian National Socialists. Kurt Schuschnigg took his place as the head of the Corporative State. While Austrian history continued on its ominous course, Franz Wallack was fine-tuning the creative section of his construction composition: should the 2,572-meter high Poneck and its breathtaking panoramic view of 37 3000-meter peaks and 19 glaciers really remain closed off to car drivers? With the knowledge that there was financial backing from the authoritarian and car-loving Corporative State, Franz Rehrl let himself be persuaded of the necessity for a "modest drive" to the Poneck. Wallack was delighted that he had been able to assert himself once again – "if only the damned name Poneck had not existed". That was only a minor problem for the inventive councilor: quick as a flash he bestowed the peak with the more media-effective and marketable name of "Edelweiss-Spitze".

The maiden voyage Now it was Rehrl's turn to test the flexibility of his master builder. While Wallack was working feverishly on the finishing touches to the road on the Fuscher Törl and the Edelweiss-Spitze in den final days prior to opening the north ramp, the Salzburg governor gave a surprise announcement on September 19, 1934, stating that in three days he wanted to drive the entire

GROSSGLOCKNER HOCHALPENSTRASSE · PORSCHE DRIVE GESCHICHTE / HISTORY — 43

Begrüssung des Landeshauptmann Dr. Rehrl - durch das Söhnchen der Mautnerin von Heiligenblut.

des autoritären wie autobegeisterten Ständestaates wissend, ließ sich Franz Rehrl von der Notwendigkeit eines »bescheidenen Fahrwegs« auf das Poneck überzeugen. Wallack war höchst erfreut, sich erneut behauptet zu haben – »wenn nur der verdammte Name Poneck nicht gewesen wäre«. Für den findigen Hofrat freilich nur ein kleines Problem: Im Handumdrehen wurde dem Gipfel der werbewirksamere Name »Edelweiß-Spitze« verliehen.

Die erste Fahrt Nun war es wiederum an Rehrl, die Flexibilität seines Baumeisters zu testen. Während Wallack der Straße auf das Fuscher Törl und die Edelweiß-Spitze in den letzten Tagen vor der Eröffnung der Nordrampe fieberhaft den letzten Schliff verlieh, verkündete der Salzburger Landeshauptmann am 19. September 1934 überraschend, er wolle in drei Tagen mit einem Kraftwagen von Ferleiten über die gesamte Scheitelstrecke der Straße und bis hinab nach Heiligenblut fahren. Ein umgebauter Steyr 100 mit 158 Zentimeter Breite und 25 Zentimeter Bodenfreiheit stehe schon bereit. Ob das denn gehe? »Er soll nur kommen und wenn irgendwo nicht alles klappt, dann werden wir die Kiste tragen«, verkündete Wallack zunächst selbstsicher, stolperte dann aber doch eine Nacht lang besorgt über die Strecke, nahm Maß – und stellte schließlich beruhigt fest, dass die schmalste Stelle 165 Zentimeter breit war. Man hatte sieben Zentimeter Spiel.

Am 22. September stieg Wallack zu Rehrl und einem Chefingenieur der Steyrwerke in den modifizierten, mit Spruchbändern verzierten Wagen. Die halsbrecherische Erstüberquerung des Tauernmassivs entlang gähnender Abgründe, frisch gesprengter Felsen, notdürftig befestigter Stützmauern und durch den Hochtortunnel bis hinab nach Heiligenblut ging als Jungfernfahrt in die Geschichte der Großglockner Hochalpenstraße ein – dauerte allerdings stolze fünf Stunden, da unterwegs zahllose Arbeiter mit Zigaretten versorgt werden wollten. Retour benötigte das Trio in seinem alpentauglichen Leichtbaumobil nur noch eine Stunde und 56 Minuten. Die Bilder der skurrilen Fahrt gingen um die Welt.

Am kommenden Tag wurden schließlich die Nordrampe und die Edelweiß-Spitze mit einer Feldmesse beim Fuscher Törl offiziell eröffnet. Um 10 Uhr morgens setzte sich in Ferleiten eine Autokolonne in Bewegung. Im ersten Wagen saß wieder Franz Rehrl, es folgten der Bundespräsidenten, der Bundeskanzler, diverse Minister, Diplomaten, Würdenträger und schließlich 32 Autobusse und 318 Motorräder – die ersten Glocknertouristen waren an der Passhöhe angekommen. Um die Eröffnung der Straße mit dem Beginn der Salzburger Festspiele zu verbinden, war der geplante Termin um zweieinhalb Monate nach vorne auf Anfang August 1935 verlegt worden. »Auf Wiedersehen im August«, rief Rehrl den Eröffnungsgästen beim Fuscher Törl zu. »Auf Wiedersehen im elektrischen Lichte des Hochtortunnels und am sonnigen Eisstrom der Pasterze! Die Eröffnung des Verkehrs über

crest route of the road in an automobile, starting from Ferleiten all the way down to Heiligenblut. A modified Steyr 100 with a width of 158 centimeters and 25 centimeters ground clearance was already standing by. Would that be possible? "He should just go ahead and come, and if something goes wrong somewhere, then we'll just carry the thing," Wallack declared confidently at first, but then stumbled along the route a whole night long in the end, because he was worried about it. He took measurements – and was ultimately reassured because he determined that the narrowest point was 165 centimeters wide. There were seven centimeters of wiggle room.

On September 22, Wallack joined Rehrl and a chief engineer from the Steyr plant in the modified car that was decorated with banners. The highly risky debut drive across the Tauern Massif alongside yawning chasms, freshly blasted rock faces, provisionally braced supporting walls and through the Hochtor Tunnel and then descending to Heiligenblut was a maiden voyage for the Grossglockner High Alpine Road history books. However, it took a whole five hours as countless laborers along the way wanted to be supplied with cigarettes. The trio's return trip in the special lightweight vehicle adapted to the Alps only took one hour and 56 minutes. The photographs of the eccentric trip went around the world.

The next day the north ramp and the Edelweiss-Spitze were finally officially inaugurated with an open-air ceremony next to the Fuscher Törl. A convoy of cars set out from Ferleiten at 10 o'clock in the morning. Franz Rehrl was once again sitting in the first car, followed by the President, the Chancellor, various ministers, diplomats, dignitaries and bringing up the rear were 32 busses and 318 motorcycles– the first Glockner tourists had arrived at the top of the pass. In order to combine the opening of the road with the beginning of the Salzburg Festival, the scheduled dates had been moved up by two-and-a-half months to the beginning of August 1935. "Good-bye until August," Rehrl called out to the guests at the opening ceremony by the Fuscher Törl. "Until we meet again under the electric lighting of the Hochtor Tunnel and at the Pasterze Glacier's sunlit icy flow! The opening of the entire length of the Grossglockner High Alpine Road to traffic will be cause for a European celebration, and I hope that it will be a Festival of Peace for our dearly beloved Austria."

The laborers then concentrated on the crest route situated between 2,300 and 2,500 meters above sea level. In order to be able to keep to the timetable, work inside the Hochtor Tunnel continued in winter; a locomotive heated the air to a comfortable 0°C while the mercury in the outdoor thermometers sank to double-digit minus ranges. On December 9, the last ropeway car traveled from Hochtor into the valley for the final time, where from then on the northern access road was being worked on, starting at Bruck in the Salzach Valley – the new zero kilometer marker of the Grossglockner High Alpine Road – to the village

die ganze Großglockner Hochalpenstraße wird ein europäisches Fest sein, und ich hoffe, daß es für unser heißgeliebtes Österreich ein Fest des Friedens sein wird.«

Die Arbeiter konzentrierten sich nun auf die zwischen 2.300 und 2.500 Meter gelegene Scheitelstrecke. Um den Zeitplan einhalten zu können, wurde im Hochtortunnel auch im Winter weiter gearbeitet; eine Lokomotive heizte die Luft auf wohlige Null Grad, während das Quecksilber der Thermometer draußen in zweistellige Minusbereiche sank. Am 9. Dezember fuhr der letzte Seilbahnwagen vom Hochtor ins Tal, wo nun an der nördlichen Zufahrtsstraße von Bruck im Salzachtal – dem neuen Kilometer Null der Großglockner Hochalpenstraße – bis nach Dorf Fusch gearbeitet wurde. Im April 1935 begannen an der Baustelle die Schneeräumarbeiten. Nachdem die Hochtorbaustelle Ende Mai von einer Lawine verschüttet wurde, die fünf Arbeiter das Leben kostete, liefen im Juni und Juli bei Regen und Schnee die letzten Arbeiten mit Hochdruck. Schotterdecken wurden aufgebracht, Mauern fertiggestellt, Wehrsteine gesetzt, Telefonleitungen verlegt, die Strecke ein letztes Mal vom Salzburger Landeshauptmann begutachtet. Auf der Weltausstellung in Brüssel war die fertig gestellte Glocknerstraße zu diesem Zeitpunkt bereits Realität: Als Symbol des technischen Fortschritts, wirtschaftlichen Aufbaus und Ausbaus des alpinen Fremdenverkehrs schmückte ein zehn Meter breites Panoramabild der Alpenstraße den Österreichischen Pavillon.

Die Straße ist vollendet – und wird doch nie fertig Am 3. August 1935 wurde die Großglockner Hochalpenstraße schließlich nach 25 Monaten Bauzeit offiziell eröffnet. Im ersten Auto, dass die auf 48 Kilometer Länge von Bruck bis Heiligenblut mit Blumen, Girlanden und Fahnen geschmückte und von unzähligen Zuschauern gesäumte Straße überquerte, saßen Franz Rehrl, Bundespräsident Wilhelm Miklas und Franz Wallack. Händeschütteln, Schulterklopfen, Jubel, Böllerschüsse; es war geschafft. Wer von Salzburg nach Venedig fahren wollte, konnte sich fortan einen rund 150 Kilometer langen Umweg sparen. »Letzten Endes«, so philosophierte Wallack, »führt die Großglockner-Hochalpenstraße, um in der Sprache derer zu reden, die überall in der Welt zu Hause sind, von dem Salzburger Mozartdenkmal zu dem Standbild des Colleoni oder von dem Canal Grande zu dem Salzburger Festspielhaus, wo eben Toscanini den Taktstock schwingen mag.« Doch die meisten Automobilisten kamen nicht wegen Colleoni, sondern um die Straße selbst zu erleben: Noch im Eröffnungsjahr 1935 sollte die Großglockner Hochalpenstraße von über 19.000 Automobilen befahren werden – mit 13.000 österreichischen Kraftwagen besuchte sogar mehr als die Hälfte aller im Land zugelassenen Autos mindestens einmal die neue Straße.

Schon für den Tag nach der Eröffnung hatten die Automobil- und Touringclubs des Landes das »Erste Internationale Großglockner-Rennen« vom Dorf Fusch

of Fusch. In April 1935, the snow removal work began at the construction site. After the Hochtor construction site was buried by an avalanche at the end of May, which cost five laborers their lives, the last stages of work were undertaken at full steam through rain and snow in June and July. Gravel surfaces were applied, walls completed, stone barriers placed, telephone lines installed and the route inspected by the Salzburg governor one last time. By the time the International Exposition in Brussels took place, the completed Glockner Road had already become reality: a ten-meter wide panoramic photograph of the Alpine road adorned the Austrian pavilion as a symbol of technological progress, economic development, and the development of Alpine tourism.

The road has been completed– and yet will never be finished On August 3, 1935, the Grossglockner High Alpine Road was finally officially opened after 25 months of construction. Franz Rehrl, Federal President Wilhelm Miklas and Franz Wallack were seated in the first car that drove the 48-kilometer length of the route from Bruck to Heiligenblut, which was decorated with flowers, garlands, flags and lined with spectators. People were shaking hands, slapping each other on the back, there was cheering and gun salutes; they had done it. Anyone who wanted to drive to Venice from Salzburg could save themselves an approximately 150-kilometer detour from now on. "Ultimately," Wallack philosophized, "the Grossglockner High Alpine Road, to speak in the language of those who are at home anywhere in the world, leads from the Mozart monument in Salzburg to the Colleoni statue or from the Canal Grande to the Salzburg Festival Hall, where Toscanini might be wielding his conductor's baton". Yet most of the car enthusiasts didn't come because of Colleoni, but to experience the road itself: In its debut year of 1935, the Grossglockner High Alpine Road would be frequented by more than 19,000 cars – 13,000 Austrian cars meant that even more than half of all the cars registered in the country visited the new road at least once.

The Austrian automobile and touring clubs had already proclaimed the First International Grossglockner Race from the village of Fusch up to the Fuscher Törl for the day after the opening. And, as a matter of fact, 75 race drivers showed up on August 4, 1935, to start in the race on the 19.5-kilometer mountain route in spite of rain and foggy conditions. The drivers drove their vehicles there from England, France, Italy, the Netherlands, Spain and Switzerland. Their motorcycles and cars bore legendary names like Adler, Amilcar, Alfa Romeo, Austin, Austro Daimler, Bugatti, DKW, ERA, Frazer Nash, Maserati, MG and Nacional Pescara. The Italian machines by Alfa-Romeo, Fiat and Maserati were successful in the sports car class; in the category of racing cars with over 2,000 ccm displacement, Mario Tadini – a wealthy fashion house owner and co-founder of Scuderia Ferrari – set the first route record with an average speed of 79.58 km/h in his Alfa Romeo. Meanwhile, German drivers like Hans Stuck stayed away

MIT FREUNDLICHER GENEHMIGUNG
COURTESY OF:
GROHAG ARCHIV

Eröffnung einer neuen Alpenstraße
Vor kurzem ist die Nordrampe für den Automobilverkehr zum
Großglockner freigegeben worden

50 — GESCHICHTE / HISTORY

PORSCHE DRIVE · GROSSGLOCKNER HOCHALPENSTRASSE

GROSSGLOCKNER HOCHALPENSTRASSE · PORSCHE DRIVE
GESCHICHTE / HISTORY — 51

BILDER FOLGENDE SEITEN
MIT FREUNDLICHER GENEHMIGUNG
PICTURES FOLLOWING PAGES
COURTESY OF:
GROHAG ARCHIV

52 — GESCHICHTE / HISTORY

Wien, 8. August 1935   54. Jahrgang

Das interessante Blatt

Redaktion und Administration: Wien, III., Rüdengasse 11 (Telephon U-13-5-30 bis U-13-5-32).

Die Großglockner-Hochalpenstraße

Die feierliche Eröffnung des großen Werkes, das einen der schönsten Teile unserer Alpen dem internationalen Autoverkehr erschließt, fand unter ungeheurer Beteiligung Samstag statt; mehr als zweitausend Wagen fuhren am ersten Tag die Großglockner-Hochalpenstraße von Bruck-Fusch nach Heiligenblut. Bei der Feier am Hochtortunnel verkündet Rektor Prof. Kann die Ernennung des Landeshauptmanns von Salzburg Dr. Rehrl und des Erbauers der Straße Oberbaurat Ing. Wallack zu akademischen Ehrenbürgern der Technischen Hochschule. (S. S. 4.)   Phot. Ernst-Hilscher.

Im Innern des Blattes: Der Großglockner — historisch, bei der Eröffnung und dem Rennen.

hinauf zum Fuscher Törl ausgerufen. Und tatsächlich: Am 4. August 1935 starteten trotz Regen und Nebel 75 Rennfahrer auf der 19,5 Kilometer langen Bergstrecke. Die Piloten waren auf Achse aus England, Frankreich, Italien, den Niederlanden, Spanien und der Schweiz angereist. Ihre Motorräder und Autos hören auf mythische Namen wie Adler, Amilcar, Alfa Romeo, Austin, Austro Daimler, Bugatti, DKW, ERA, Frazer Nash, Maserati, MG und Nacional Pescara. In den Sportwagenklassen waren die italienischen Maschinen von Alfa-Romeo, Fiat und Maserati siegreich; bei den Rennwagen über 2.000 ccm stellt Mario Tadini – ein wohlhabender Modeunternehmer aus Modena und Mitbegründer der Scuderia Ferrari – auf seinem Alfa Romeo mit einem Tempo von durchschnittlich 79,58 km/h den ersten Streckenrekord auf. Deutsche Fahrer wie Hans Stuck waren dem Rennen derweil aus politischen Gründen fern geblieben.

Doch nicht nur der Grundstein für den Motorsport am Glockner – und den zweifelhaften Mythos der Hochalpenstraße als zivile Rennstrecke unter freiem Himmel – wurde bereits im Eröffnungsjahr 1935 gelegt. Auch der Erhalt der plötzlich so bequem erreichbaren Bergwelt rückte ins Zentrum der Aufmerksamkeit: das Gebiet um die Straße wurde erstmals unter Naturschutz gestellt. In den kommenden Jahren wurde immer wieder darüber nachgedacht, die Gipfelwelt rund um den Großglockner zum Nationalpark zu erklären. Auch die Nationalsozialisten, die das Salzburger Land zum »Erholungsgau« ihres Reiches erklären wollten, nutzten den Landschafts- und Naturschutzgedanken als Teil ihrer Propagandamaßnahmen. Bis der Nationalpark Hohe Tauern als größtes Schutzgebiet der Alpen entstehen durfte, sollten jedoch noch einmal 46 Jahre vergehen.

Im Frühjahr 1936 begann zum ersten Mal eine Prozedur, die bis heute die eindrücklichsten Bilder von der Großglockner Hochalpenstraße im kollektiven Gedächtnis verankert hat: die Schneefreimachung der gesamten Straße. Ganze 350 mit Schaufeln bewaffnete Arbeiter waren zehn Wochen im Einsatz, um die Straße zumindest einspurig von einer Viertelmillionen Kubikmeter Schnee zu befreien. Höhepunkt der Schneeräumung ist seit dieser Zeit der »Durchstich«, wenn sich die Salzburger und Kärntner Räumtrupps zum ersten Mal begegnen. Und auch an der Straße selbst gab es noch viel zu tun: Nach Ende der Bergwinters machten sich die Arbeiter daran, die Straßen durch neue Beläge oder Pflasterungen zu modernisieren – vorher waren es meist nur bessere Feldwege, auf denen die Autos ungeheuer viel Staub aufwirbelten. Auch die Edelweißstraße wurde weiter ausgebaut. Ab der Franz-Josefs-Höhe wurde die Fahrstrecke zudem bis zum Freiwandeck hoch über der Pasterze verlängert, von dort aus der Bau eines Panoramaweges zum Wasserfallwinkel-Gletscher begonnen. Gleichzeitig wurden die ersten privaten Gasthäuser wie die Edelweißhütte und der Gasthof Fuscherlacke errichtet, um die fast 150.000 Gäste, die allein schon in der ersten

from the race for political reasons. Yet it was not only the cornerstone for motor sports at the Glockner – along with the dubious myth of the High Alpine Road as a civil open-air race course – that was already laid in the opening year of 1935. The preservation of the mountain landscape that was suddenly so easily accessible also attracted attention: the area around the road was placed under protection as a nature preserve for the first time. In the following years, thoughts about declaring the peaks around the Grossglockner a national park came up time and again. Even the National Socialists, who wanted to turn Salzburg state into a "recreation area" of their Reich, used the landscape and nature preserve considerations as a part of their propaganda measures. However, another 46 years passed before the High Tauern National Park was able to become the largest protected area in the Alps.

In spring 1936, a procedure was initiated that has produced the most impressive images to date of the Grossglockner High Alpine Road, and which have become embedded in collective memory: the snow removal from the entire road. A total of 350 laborers armed with shovels worked for ten weeks to extricate at least one lane of road from a quarter of a million cubic meters of snow. The highlight of the procedure since that time is the "break-through", the moment the Salzburg and Carinthian snow removal crews first meet each other from opposite sides. And there was still a lot to do on the road itself: after the end of the mountain winter the laborers set to modernizing the roads with new coverings or surfaces – previously there were only dirt roads where cars would raise incredible amounts of dust. The Edelweissstrasse was also further upgraded. Starting at the Franz-Josefs-Höhe, the route was additionally extended to the Freiwandeck high above the Pasterze Glacier, and from there the construction of a panoramic path to the Wasserfallwinkel Glacier was begun. At the same time, the first private guesthouses, such as the Edelweisshütte and Gasthof Fuscherlacke were built, in order to feed and accommodate the nearly 150,000 guests who streamed to the Glockner Road in the first full summer season. In the meantime, Franz Wallack, the tireless master of the road, concentrated on the completion of his total art work. At his initiative, a Viennese graphics shop designed the toll-road sticker with the characteristic "G", which has been the distinguishing mark of the Grossglockner High Alpine Road to this day. Wallack later reminisced appreciatively about his own successes. "Soon there was no country on earth in which there weren't at least a few cars with a Glockner Road sticker on their windshield and so it became the cheapest and best advertising for the road." In addition, the respective country flag for each international visitor was raised as soon as the license plate was registered at the toll booth. The staging was perfect.

Germany's highest mountain While the national flags of the world peacefully fluttered in the wind on the Franz-Josefs-Höhe, the creeping Nazification of the Alpine republic was accelerated in 1936 with the July treaty

GROSSGLOCKNER HOCHALPENSTRASSE · PORSCHE DRIVE

GESCHICHTE / HISTORY — 57

Doppelerfolg der Auto Union auf dem Großglockner

Stuck und Kluge wurden Bergmeister

vollständigen Sommersaison auf die Glocknerstraße strömten, zu verköstigen und zu beherbergen. Franz Wallack als nimmermüder Herr über die Straße konzentrierte sich derweil auf die Vollendung seines Gesamtkunstwerks en detail. Auf seine Initiative gestaltete ein Wiener Grafikbüro die Mautvignette mit dem charakteristischen »G«, die bis heute als Erkennungszeichen der Großglockner Hochalpenstraße gilt. Wallack erinnerte sich später wohlwollend an die eigenen Erfolge: »Sehr bald schon gab es kein Land der Erde, in dem nicht zumindest einige Personenkraftwagen mit der Glocknerstraßenvignette auf der Windschutzscheibe herumfuhren und so die billigste und beste Reklame für die Straße machten.« Für internationale Besucher wurde zudem die jeweilige Landesflagge gehisst, sobald das Kennzeichen an der Mautstelle registriert worden war. Die Inszenierung war perfekt.

Der höchste Berg Deutschlands Während an der Franz-Josefs-Höhe die Nationen der Welt friedlich im Wind flatterten, wurde 1936 mit dem Juliabkommen zwischen Österreich und dem Deutschen Reich die schleichende Nazifizierung der Alpenrepublik beschleunigt. Franz Rehrl und Franz Wallack, nach der Vollendung ihrer Straße einer fordernden Aufgabe beraubt, wandten sich dem nächsten Ziel zu – dem Bau einer Personenseilbahn auf den Gipfel des Fuscherkarkopfes. Die Alpenvereine liefen Sturm, in der Presse kursierten Karikaturen, die sich über die immer neuen Erschließungspläne lustig machten: Was würde als nächstes folgen? Eine Autorutschbahn vom Glocknergipfel über den Gletscher ins Tal? Doch die Panoramastraße hatten sich zur wichtigsten Attraktion des Landes entwickelt, auch auf der Weltausstellung 1937 in Paris standen die Kurven und Kehren am Glockner im Zentrum der österreichischen Selbstdarstellung. Warum also aufhören, wenn es doch gerade so gut lief?

Was in der Luft gelegen hatte, wurde am 15. März 1938 Realität: Vom Balkon der Neuen Burg in Wien verkündete Adolf Hitler den auf dem Heldenplatz versammelten Massen den »Anschluss« Österreichs ans Deutsche Reich. Um den Einmarsch deutscher Truppen abzuwenden, hatte Schuschniggs Ständeregime wenige Tage zuvor abgedankt und den Nationalsozialisten die Macht überlassen. Vielerorts wurden die Besatzer freudig empfangen, nennenswerter Widerstand gegen die Annexion blieb zunächst aus. Der Großglockner war mit einem Mal der höchste Berg Deutschlands. Auf den Prospekten der Hochalpenstraße wurden die rot-weiß-rote Fahnen Österreichs kurzerhand gegen Hakenkreuzflaggen ausgetauscht, am Fuscher Törl erinnerte das Denkmal nicht mehr an Dollfuß, sondern den Anschluss ans Reich. Während Franz Rehrl seines Amtes enthoben, interniert und die Großglockner Hochalpenstraßen AG mit regimetreuem Personal umbesetzt wurde, blieb Franz Wallack Mitglied der Verwaltung und Herr über die Straße: Auch wenn er sich in seiner Glocknerstraßenbiografie später

between Austria and the German Reich. Franz Rehrl and Franz Wallack, the completion of their road having deprived them of a challenging task, turned to the next goal – construction of a passenger ropeway on the peak of the Fuscherkarkopf. The Alpine clubs were up in arms, caricatures disparaging the constant new development plans made the rounds in the press: What would be next? A slide for cars from the Glockner peak over the glacier down to the valley? Nevertheless, the panoramic road had become the country's most important attraction, the Glockner's curves and hairpin turns were the focal point of Austria's image cultivation at the 1937 International Exposition in Paris. So why quit when it was just going so well?

What had been in the air for some time became reality on March 15, 1938: standing on the balcony of Vienna's Neue Burg, Adolf Hitler proclaimed the "Anschluss", the annexation of Austria by the German Reich. To head off the invasion of German troops, Schuschnigg's government had stepped down a few days before and handed power over to the National Socialists. The occupying forces were joyfully welcomed in many places, and there was no notable resistance to the annexation at first. The Grossglockner suddenly became Germany's highest mountain. The red, white and red Austrian flags were summarily removed from the High Alpine Road brochures and replaced by swastika flags, the monument at the Fuscher Törl no longer commemorated Dollfuß, but the annexation by the Reich. While Franz Rehrl was ousted from office and imprisoned, the Grossglockner High Alpine Road AG was re-staffed with personnel loyal to the regime. Franz Wallack remained a member of the administration and master of the road: Even though he was quite critical of the new rulers later in his Glockner Road biography, he adapted to the new circumstances, became a member of the National Socialist Motor Corps, conducted snow research for the German roads authority, designed a first snow removal machine, drew up landscape conservation maps and worked on his road biography.

The "Anschluss" with the Nazi Reich also caused a rapid rise in the number of visitors in the entire Ostmark [the Nazi name for Austria] and thus also at the Glockner: while 147,994 visitors had been counted in 1937, in 1938 there were already 374,467 guests who drove on the Glockner Road in more than 76,000 cars and nearly 16,000 motorcycles. Bigger parking lots were built, the dust removal continued, and a second car race was also held. On August 28, 1938, the German marquee drivers competed in the serpentine, 12.6-kilometer International Grossglockner Hillclimb, the "great German mountain prize", in Ferleiten, which had previously been staged at the Schauinsland race course in the Black Forest. The class victory as well as the mountain champion title went to the "Mountain King" Hans Stuck for Auto Union against the young driver Hermann Lang for Mercedes-Benz. Ferdinand Porsche was also there as a design engineer and introduced the prototype of the KDF car – the first Volkswagen.

durchaus kritisch gegenüber den neuen Machthabern äußerte, passte er sich doch den neuen Verhältnissen an, wurde Mitglied des Nationalsozialistischen Kraftfahrerkorps, betrieb Schneeforschung für deutsche Straßenbehörden, konstruierte ein erstes Räumgerät, erstellte Landschaftsschutzkarten und schrieb an seiner Straßenbiografie.

Mit dem »Anschluss« ans NS-Reich stiegen die Besucherzahlen in der gesamten »Ostmark« und damit auch am Glockner rapide an: Waren 1937 noch 147.994 Besucher gezählt worden, waren es 1938 bereits 374.467 Gäste, die mit mehr als 76.000 Pkw und fast 16.000 Motorrädern über die Glocknerstraße fuhren. Größere Parkplätze wurden errichtet, die Staubfreimachung fortgesetzt, und auch ein zweites Automobilrennen wurde ausgetragen. Beim »Großen Bergpreis von Deutschland«, der bisher auf der Schauinsland-Rennstrecke im Schwarzwald veranstaltet worden war, starteten am 28. August 1938 die deutschen Vorzeigerennfahrer in Ferleiten auf der 12,6 Kilometer langen Kurvenstrecke. Den Klassensieg sowie den Bergmeister-Titel sicherte sich »Bergkönig« Hans Stuck auf Auto Union gegen den Jungfahrer Hermann Lang auf Mercedes-Benz. Auch Ferdinand Porsche war als Konstrukteur dabei und präsentierte den Prototypen des KDF-Wagens – den ersten »Volkswagen«.

Zu Beginn der Sommersaison 1939 hatte schließlich schon mehr als eine Millionen mautzahlender Besucher die Großglockner Hochalpenstraße befahren. Doch die Zeichen standen auf Krieg, und vielen Menschen war nicht mehr nach Urlaubsfahrten zumute. Am 6. August 1939, wenige Wochen bevor Deutschland sein Nachbarland Polen überfallen und die Menschheit in den Zweiten Weltkrieg reißen sollte, wurde am Glockner der vorerst letzte »Bergpreis« ausgetragen. Bei Nebel, Regen und Schnee fuhr Hermann Lang den Bergmeister-Titel ein. Ende August wurde auf der Straße noch die Internationale Sechs-Tage-Fahrt ausgetragen, wobei die Motorrad-Rennfahrer des britischen Militärs zur eigenen Sicherheit vorzeitig das Land verlassen mussten. Deutschland erklärte sich zum Gewinner, doch die Ergebnisse wurden nie international anerkannt.

Mit Ausbruch des Krieges brachen die Besucherzahlen am Glockner fast völlig ein. Auch für den Erhalt der Straße gab es weder Personal noch Treibstoff. Dafür lieferte sich nun die Bergjugend auf den leeren Serpentinen ihre Fahrradrennen. Im Gegensatz zu anderen Alpenstraßen war die Glocknerstraße jedoch nicht in Kampfhandlungen involviert und erlitt auch keine Kollateralschäden. Am 4. Mai befreiten amerikanische Truppen Salzburg, die Zweite Republik Österreich entstand, blieb aber unter Besatzung der alliierten Siegermächte Großbritannien, Frankreich, USA und der Sowjetunion. Im August 1945 kehrte der einstige Landeshauptmann Franz Rehrl aus Berliner Gefangenschaft nach Salzburg zurück.

At the beginning of the summer season of 1939, ultimately more than one million toll-paying visitors had already driven on the Grossglockner High Alpine Road. Yet the signs were all pointing to war, and many people were no longer in the mood for vacation trips. On August 6, 1939, a few weeks before Germany attacked its neighboring country Poland and embroiled humanity in World War II, the last "Mountain Prize" race for the time being was carried out at the Glockner. Hermann Lang won the Mountain Champion title in spite of fog, rain and snow. At the end of August, the International Six-Day-Drive still took place on the road, nevertheless, the motorcycles driven by British military personnel had to leave the country early for their own safety. Germany declared itself the winner, but the results were never recognized internationally.

With the outbreak of the war, the number of visitors to the Glockner collapsed almost completely. There was also neither personnel nor fuel for road maintenance. Instead, the mountain's youth conducted bicycle races on the empty serpentines. As opposed to other Alpine roads, though, the Glockner Road was not involved in battle action and didn't suffer any collateral damage. On May 4, American troops liberated Salzburg, the Second Austrian Republic came about, but remained under the occupation of the victorious allied powers Great Britain, France, the United States and the Soviet Union. In August 1945, the former governor Franz Rehrl returned to Salzburg after his imprisonment in Berlin.

The story continues Franz Wallack, still committed to the continued existence of his legacy even after the war, conducted an inspection of its condition, supervised the repair work, and began widening the road and upgrading the hairpin turns. He summarized it thus, "The road has now been completed for ten years and yet the predictions have held true. The Glockner Road will never be finished. It will always continue to be developed further, it will always have construction and improvements taking place, in order to adapt to emerging developments in regard to traffic and progress in means of transportation". In 1949, the Viennese Springer-Verlag published Franz Wallack's 216-page memoir about the road construction. The master builder had written the history of his own work of art.

To Franz Wallack – the tireless problem solver, his eye constantly on his complete Glockner composition – the work was still not finished, though. Even before the war he had begun working on building snow removal equipment to simplify and speed up the annual snow clearing work. In the early 1950s he finally presented the prototypes of his rotation snow plow. The gigantic blue Wallack plow with its chain crawler track and three engines is still in use today and can be inspected along the route in the summer months. Yet even while operating the roaring machines the laborers were not safe from Wallack's staging – while they worked they had to sing the song he composed, *The Snow Removers' Marching Song*. Always concerned about the

Die Geschichte geht weiter Auch nach dem Krieg war Franz Wallack um den Fortbestand seines Erbes bemüht, nahm den Zustand in Augenschein, leitete Ausbesserungsarbeiten an, begann mit der Verbreiterung der Straße und dem Ausbau der Kehren, resümierte: »Nun ist die Straße schon zehn Jahre fertig und doch hat die Vorhersage recht behalten. Die Glocknerstraße wird nie fertig werden. Sie wird immer weiter ausgestaltet werden, immer wieder wird an ihr gebaut und verbessert werden, um sie jederzeit der Entwicklung des Verkehrs und dem Fortschritt der Verkehrsmittel anzupassen.« 1949 erschienen im Wiener Springer-Verlag Franz Wallacks 216 Seiten starke Memoiren des Straßenbaus. Der Baumeister hatte seine eigene Werkgeschichte geschrieben.

Für Franz Wallack – den nimmermüden Problemlöser, seine Glockner'sche Gesamtkomposition stets im Blick – war die Arbeit jedoch immer noch nicht abgeschlossen. Schon vor dem Krieg hatte er mit der Konstruktion von Schneeräumgeräten begonnen, um die alljährlichen Räumarbeiten zu vereinfachen und zu verkürzen. Anfang der 1950er-Jahre präsentierte er schließlich die Prototypen seines Rotationsschneepflugs. Die gewaltigen blauen »Wallackfräsen« mit ihren Kettenfahrwerken und drei Motoren sind bis heute im Einsatz und können in den Sommermonaten entlang der Strecke begutachtet werden. Doch selbst in den dröhnenden Maschinen waren die Mitarbeiter nicht vor Wallacks Inszenierung sicher – musste doch bei der Arbeit das von ihm komponierte *Marschlied der Schneeräumer* angestimmt werden. Stets um die Öffentlichkeitswirkung der Straße bemüht, ließ Wallack die Strecke in den besonders milden Wintern 1955, 1957 und 1963 bereits zum Weihnachtsfest räumen und brauste in seinem offenen BMW Cabrio, den Christbaum und Geschenke für die tapferen Winterwächter auf der Rückbank drapiert, kurz vor Heiligabend über den Pass. Journalisten und Fotografen waren zuvor freilich alarmiert worden und berichteten folgsam.

Doch es gab auch andere, die ihre persönlichen Ambitionen auf der Glocknerstraße auslebten: Bei der ersten Österreichrundfahrt im Sommer 1949 erstrampelte sich

Nun ist die Straße schon zehn Jahre fertig und doch hat die Vorhersage recht behalten. Die Glocknerstraße wird nie fertig werden.

The road has now been completed for ten years and yet the predictions have held true. The Glockner Road will never be finished.

road's public image, Wallack saw to it that the snow was already cleared by Christmas in the particularly mild winters of 1955, 1957 and 1963, so he could zoom over the pass in his open BMW convertible shortly before Christmas Eve, loaded with a Christmas tree and gifts in the back seat for the brave winter wardens. Journalists and photographers had, of course, been alerted in advance and dutifully wrote their reports.

There were also others, though, who lived out their personal ambitions on the Glockner Road: At the first Tour of Austria in summer 1949, racing cyclist Richard Menapace pedaled to victory on the ascent to the Fuscher Törl, winning the title of Glockner King. The Glockner stage was also treated with awe by cyclists in the following decades, because they never knew what kind of surprises the high mountain weather had in store for them or if they would have to carry their bikes over a fresh avalanche deposit. Some racing cyclists who conquered the mountain by the sweat of their brows and didn't suffer heat stroke, went too fast on the cooling descent – and with a bit of luck were cushioned from a fall by the last remaining snow fields. The Giro d'Italia also featured the Glockner as an Alpine delicacy on numerous occasions.

With the advancing rebuilding of the country and withdrawal of the occupation forces in the mid-1950s, economic activity started up again – and soon tourists began to return in large numbers. Even so, travel behavior had changed – cars had become affordable and the vacationers from the north were attracted to the beaches of

BILDER FOLGENDE SEITEN
MIT FREUNDLICHER GENEHMIGUNG
PICTURES FOLLOWING PAGES
COURTESY OF:
GROHAG ARCHIV

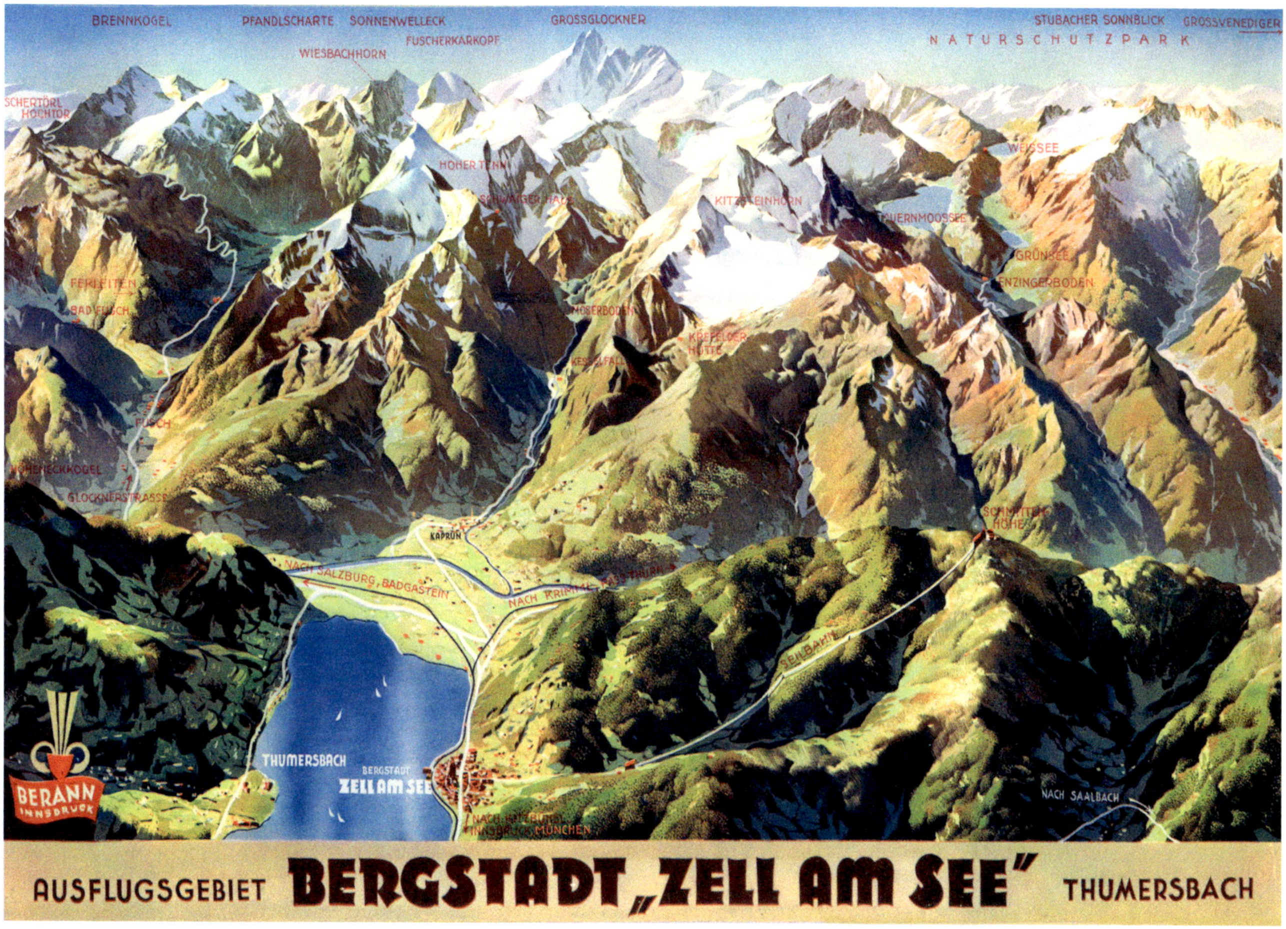
BRENNKOGEL
PFANDLSCHARTE
SONNENWELLECK
GROSSGLOCKNER
STUBACHER SONNBLICK
GROSSVENEDIGER
FUSCHERKARKOPF
WIESBACHHORN
NATURSCHUTZPARK
KITZSTEINHORN
KAPRUN
THUMERSBACH
BERGSTADT
ZELL AM SEE
NACH SAALBACH
BERANN
INNSBRUCK
AUSFLUGSGEBIET
BERGSTADT „ZELL AM SEE"
THUMERSBACH

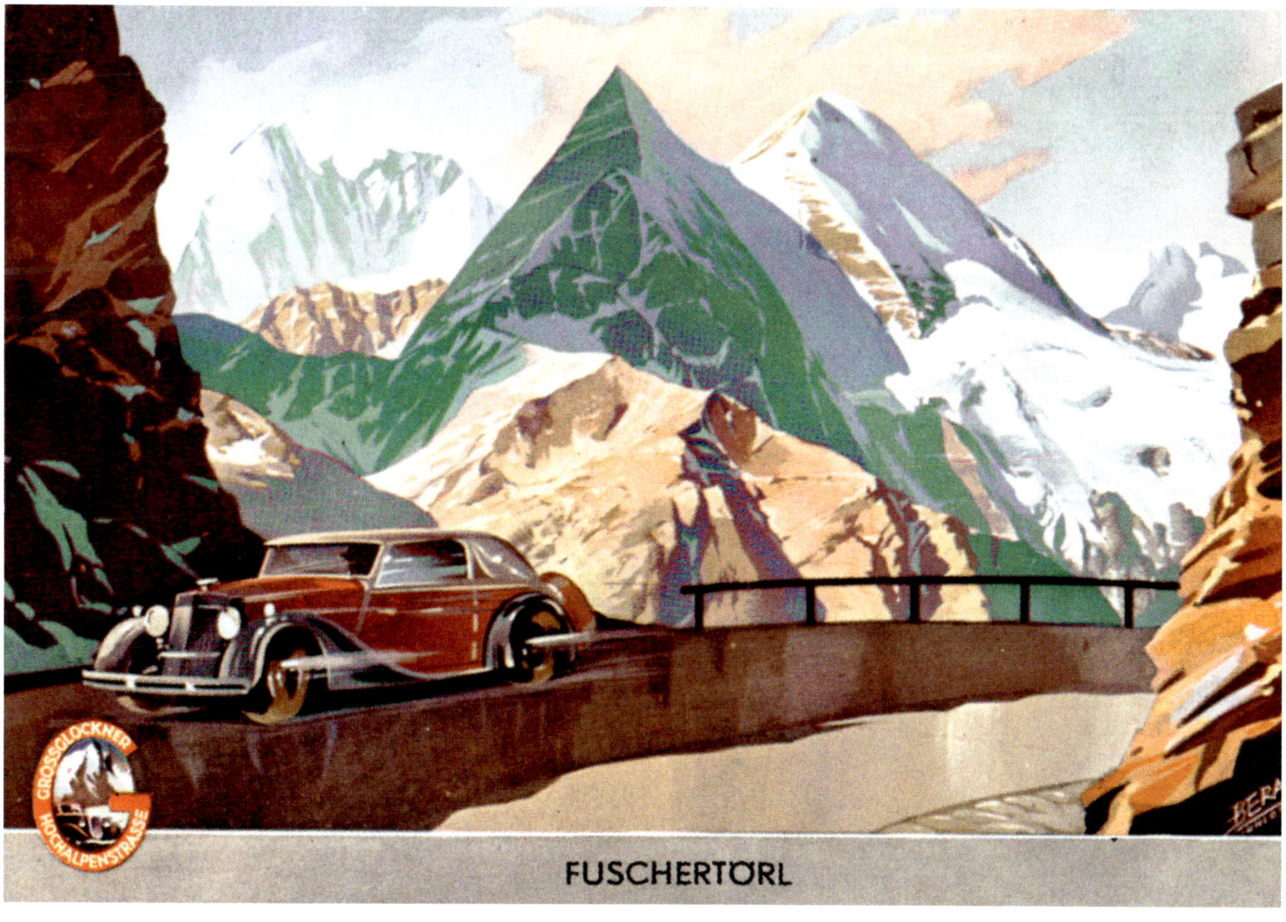
GROSSGLOCKNER
HOCHALPENSTRASSE
FUSCHERTÖRL

FRANZ JOSEFSHÖHE

AN DER FUSCHERLACKE

AUFFAHRT VON HEILIGENBLUT

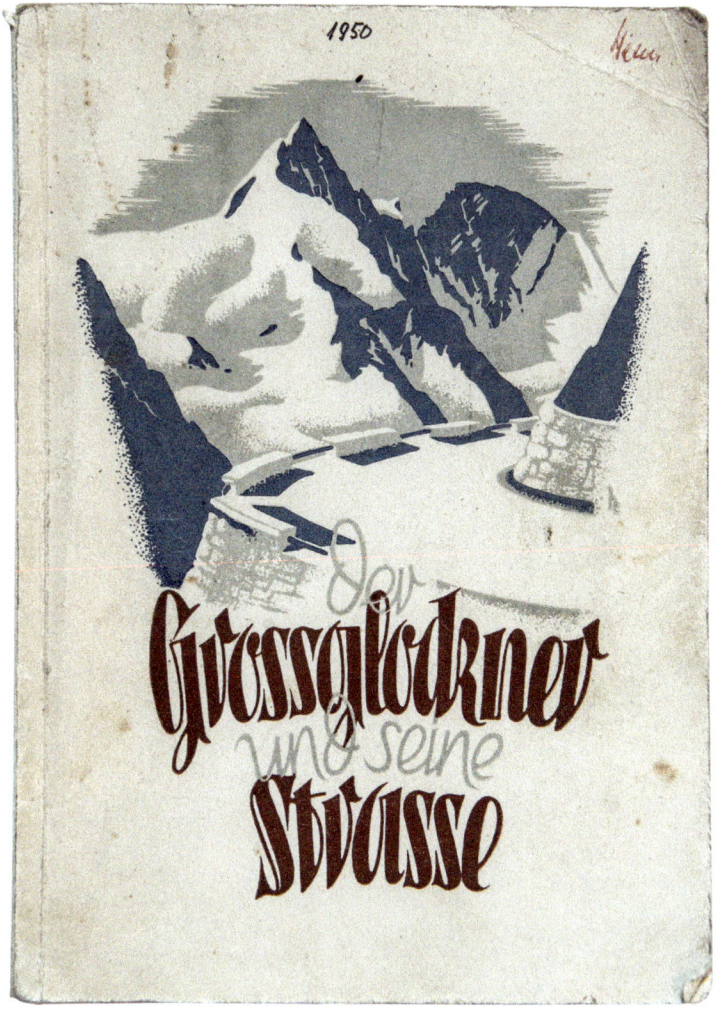

GROSSGLOCKNER HOCHALPENSTRASSE · PORSCHE DRIVE

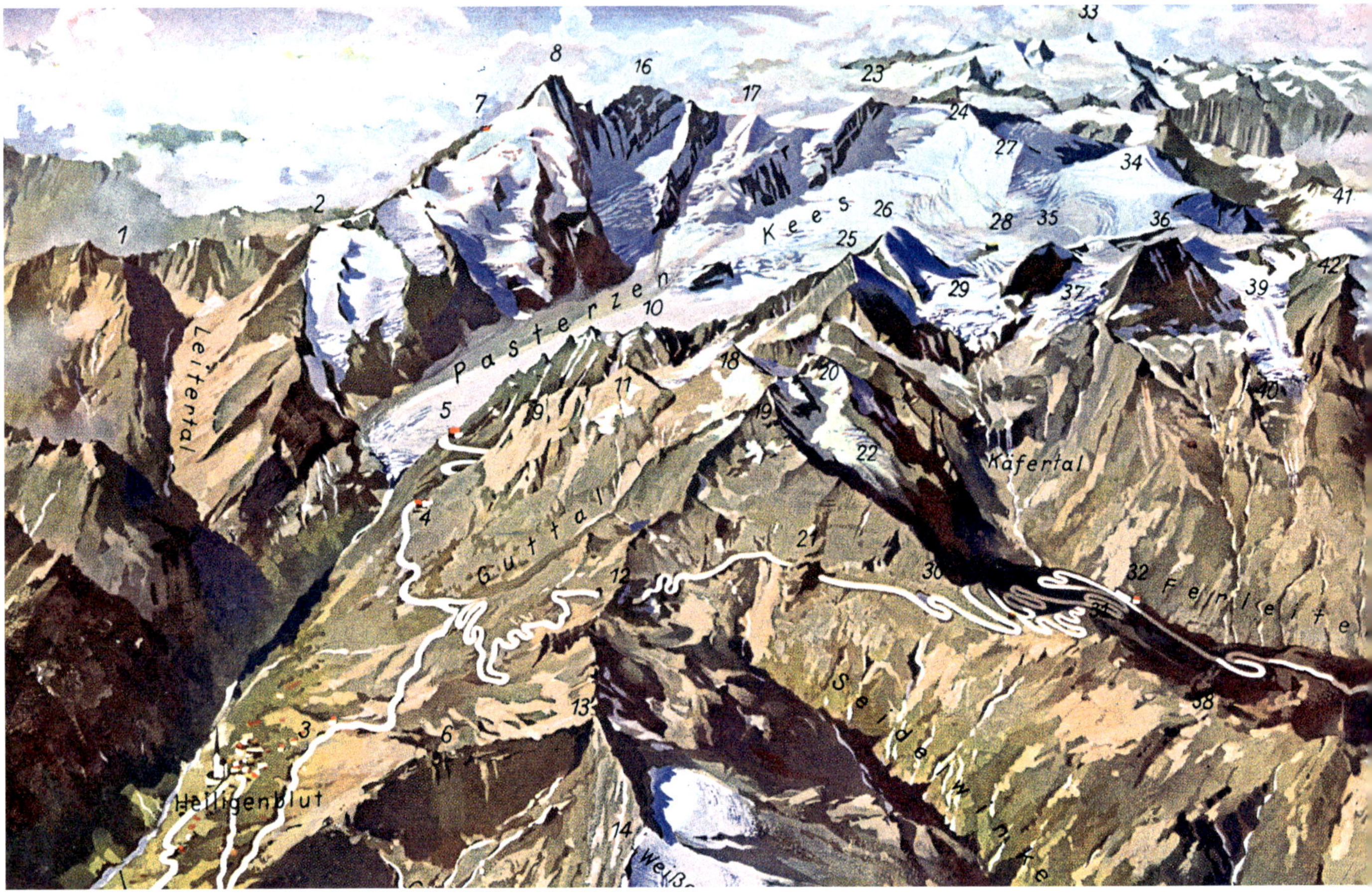

68 — GESCHICHTE / HISTORY

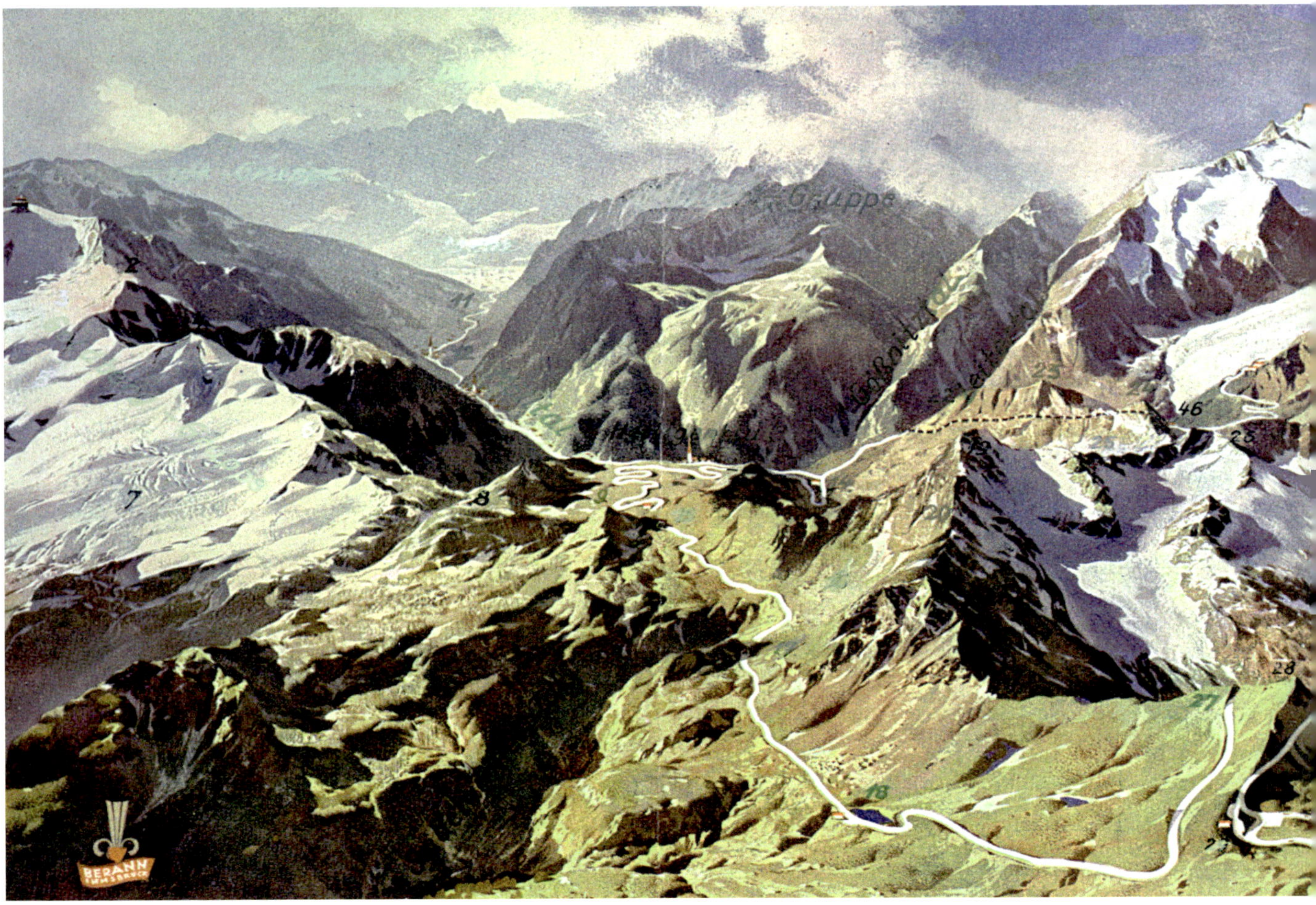

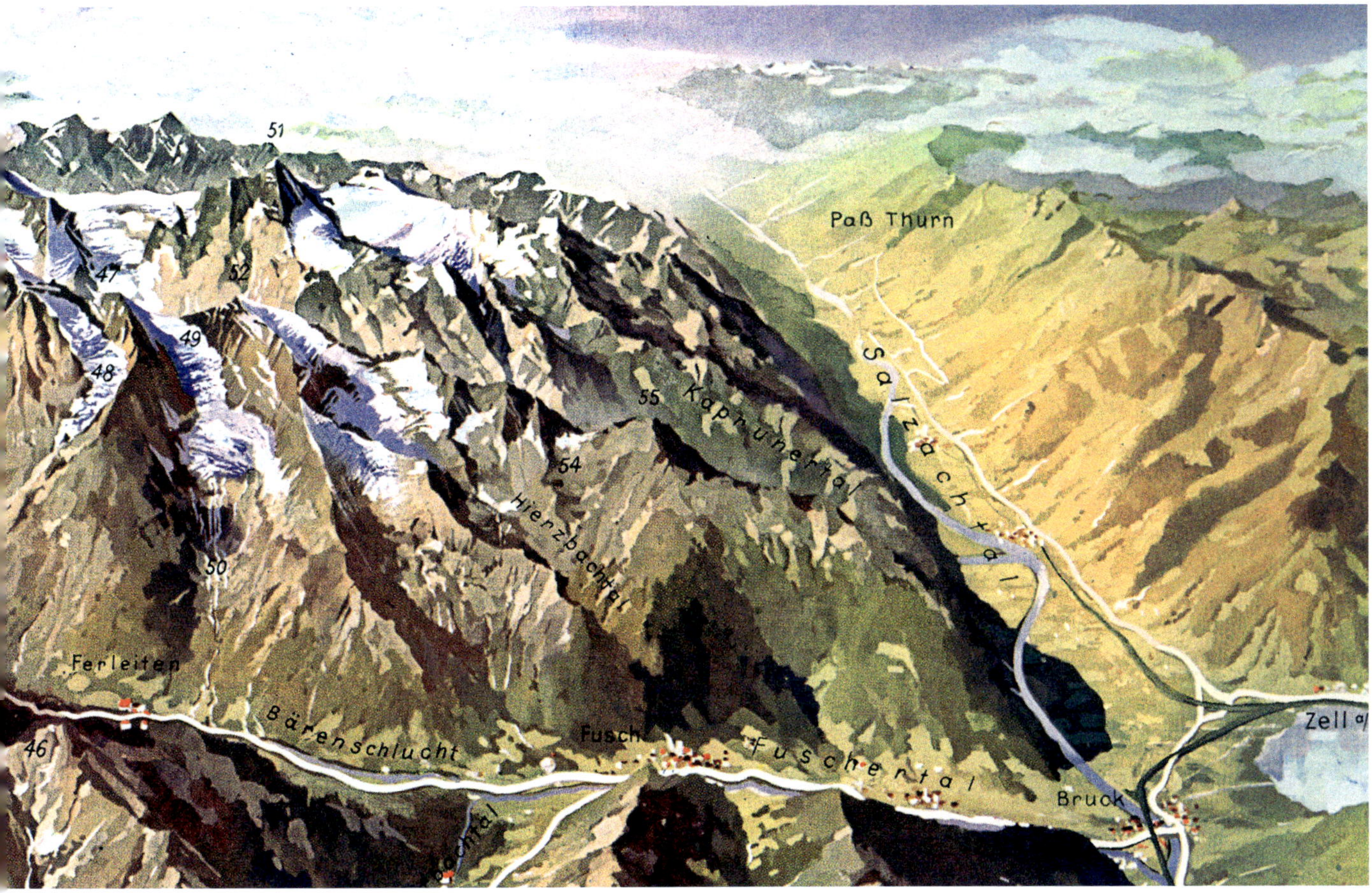

GESCHICHTE / HISTORY — 69

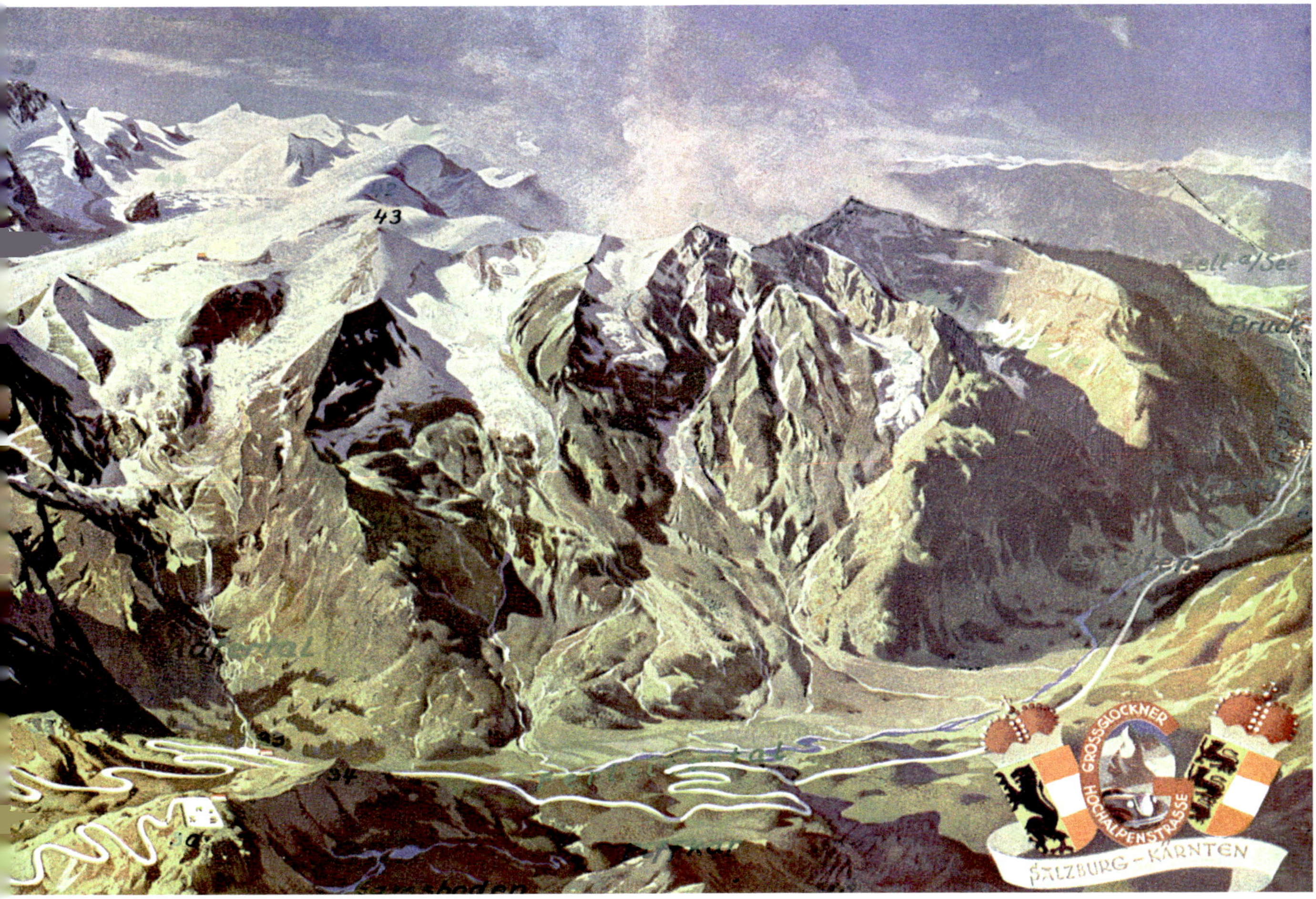

der Radrennfahrer Richard Menapace auf dem Anstieg zum Fuscher Törl den Titel des Glocknerkönigs. Auch in den kommenden Jahrzehnten wurde der Glockneretappe von Radsportlern mit Ehrfurcht begegnet, wusste man doch nie, welche Überraschungen das Hochgebirgswetter bereit hielt und ob man sein Velo nicht plötzlich über eine frisch abgegangene Lawine tragen musste. Mancher Rennfahrer, der den Berg im Schweiße seines Angesichts bezwungen und keinen Hitzeschlag erlitten hatte, ließ es auf der kühlenden Talfahrt zu schnell laufen – und wurde beim Fall mit etwas Glück von den letzten Schneefeldern gebremst. Auch beim Giro d'Italia stand der Glockner als alpines Schmankerl mehrfach auf dem Programm.

Mit dem fortschreitenden Wiederaufbau des Landes und dem Abzug der Besatzer setzte Mitte der 1950er-Jahre auch die Konjunktur wieder ein – und schon bald kehrten auch die Touristen in großer Zahl zurück. Doch das Reiseverhalten hatte sich verändert, das Auto war erschwinglich geworden und die Urlauber aus dem Norden zog es an die Strände der italienischen Riviera. Die Großglockner Hochalpenstraße war nicht mehr Ziel, sondern zur pittoresken Wegstation auf den Weg in die Ferien geworden. In der Sommersaison 1962 wurden mehr als 1,3 Millionen Besucher auf der Straße registriert – ein Rekord, der bis heute steht. Doch die Straße kam an ihre Grenzen, an schönen Tagen stauten sich Autos und Reisebusse praktisch von einer Mautstelle quer über den Berg zur anderen, an den Aussichtspunkten reihten sich jene Autos, denen das Kühlwasser übergekocht war, mit offenen Hauben. Neue Parkplätze entstanden, auch das Parkhaus am Freiwandeck wurde gebaut, konnte dem Ansturm jedoch kaum Stand halten. Für die Reisebusse wurden die Kurven zudem verbreitert, später an steilen Stellen von Stelzen gestützt. Entlastet wurde die Glocknerstraße schließlich 1967 durch die Eröffnung des Felber-Tauern-Tunnels und ab 1971 durch die Brenner-Autobahn. Die Panoramastraße war wieder in erster Linie ein Ausflugsziel. Der Erbauer Franz Wallack konnte dies nicht mehr erleben, er war im Herbst 1966 im Alter von 80 Jahren gestorben.

Interessant sind die historischen Nutzerzahlen der Großglockner Hochalpenstraße auch als Indikator des jeweiligen Zeitgeistes: Hatten 1955 noch 47.600 Motorradfahrer die Straße überquert, waren es 1968 – zur Hochzeit der Automobilisierung – nur noch etwas mehr als 2.000 gewesen. Erst mit dem Revival des Motorrads als Freizeitsportgerät um die Jahrtausendwende kamen die Biker zurück: 2013 wurden an den Mautstellen unfassbare 90.500 Maschinen gezählt. Auch die Reisebusse erlebten eine kurze Renaissance, als nach dem Fall des Eisernen Vorhangs die Besucher aus den Ländern des ehemaligen Ostblocks zum »heiligen Berg« Österreichs pilgerten. Einen weiteren automobilen Zeitzeugen der Wendejahre am Glockner kann man heute im Automuseum an der Franz-Josefs-Höhe bewundern: den Trabant. Mit viel Fürsorge

the Italian Riviera. The Grossglockner High Alpine Road was no longer the destination, but a picturesque way station en route to the vacation spots. More than 1.3 million visitors were registered on the road in the summer season 1962 – a record that still stands today. Yet the road reached its limits. On sunny days the cars and tour busses became backed up practically from one toll booth across the mountain to the next one, at the lookouts there were rows of cars with open hoods, whose cooling water had overheated. New parking lots and the parking garage at Freiwandeck was also built, but even then they could barely cope with the onslaught. In addition, the curves were made wider to accommodate the tour busses, and later supported by stilts at steep places. The Glockner Road was finally granted some relief in 1967 due to the opening of the Felber-Tauern Tunnel and the Brenner Autobahn from 1971 onward. The panoramic road was primarily a travel destination once more. The builder Franz Wallack was not able to experience these changes, he had passed away in fall 1966 at the age of 80.

It's interesting to also view the Grossglockner High Alpine Road's historic user numbers as an indicator of the respective Zeitgeist: whereas 47,600 motorcyclists had still traversed the road in 1955, in 1968 – at the height of the automobilization – there were only slightly more than 2,000. The bikers returned only with the revival of the motorcycle as a recreational vehicle around the turn of the millennium: in 2013, the toll booths counted an incredible 90,500 motorcycles. The tour busses also experienced a short renaissance, when the visitors from the former Soviet bloc countries traveled to Austria's "holy mountain" after the Iron Curtain fell. Another automotive witness to the transition years at the Glockner can be admired today in the car museum at the Franz-Josefs-Höhe: the Trabant. Starting in 1990, the Trabis had conquered the Fuscher Törl and the Hochtor with a lot of care from the road maintenance workers and by taking some curves in reverse for a better grip on the drive axle.

A new consciousness The oil crisis in the 1970s had already made the western world aware of their dependence on the Gulf states – and the number of visitors to the Glockner Road declined. At the same time, a new consciousness regarding the fragility of nature and the Alpine mountainscape had arisen. From 1981 onward, the largest protected area in the Alps was created: the High Tauern Nature Park encompassing over 1,800 km² and home to 300 three-thousand-meter peaks and 243 glaciers. These days, it is especially the sight of the Pasterze Glacier, located a few hundred feet from Franz-Josefs-Höhe, retreating by more than 50 meters yearly, that is a sign of the consequences of advancing climate change – and a good reason to fundamentally question one's own transportation habits as well as the common sense of the powerful racing cars standing in the sun only a few meters from the lookout point with the air shimmering above their hoods. It's hardly conceivable that you could once reach the

der Straßenwärter, manche Kurve für mehr Grip an der Antriebsachse gar im Rückwärtsgang erklimmend, hatten die Trabis ab 1990 das Fuscher Törl und das Hochtor erobert.

Ein neues Bewusstsein Schon in den 1970er-Jahren hatte die Ölkrise der westlichen Welt ihre Abhängigkeit von den Golfstaaten vor Augen geführt – auf der Glocknerstraße waren die Besucherzahlen zurückgegangen. Gleichzeitig hatte in Europa ein neues Bewusstsein für die Verletzlichkeit der Natur und der alpinen Bergwelt eingesetzt. Ab 1981 entstand mit dem über 1.800 km² großen Naturpark Hohe Tauern der größte Schutzraum der Alpen, in dem sich 300 Dreitausender und 243 Gletscher finden. Heute ist vor allem der Anblick des von der Franz-Josefs-Höhe einige Hundert Meter entfernten, pro Jahr um mehr als 50 Meter zurückweichende Pasterzen-Gletscher ein Zeichen für die Folgen des fortschreitenden Klimawandels – und ein guter Grund, die eigenen Fortbewegungsgeflogenheiten sowie die Sinnhaftigkeit der hubraumstarken Rennmaschinen, die wenige Meter vom Aussichtspunkt entfernt mit flimmernder Luft über den Hauben in der Sonne stehen, einmal grundsätzlich in Frage zu stellen. Kaum vorstellbar, dass man den Gletscher einst mit wenigen Schritten erreichen konnte. Gleichzeitig erinnert die Nationalparkausstellung an der Franz-Josefs-Höhe, dass der Gletscher Mitte des 19. Jahrhunderts zwar seinen Höchststand erreichte, aber in wärmeren Klimaperioden eben auch schon wesentlich kleiner war als heute: Der Stamm einer rund 9.000 Jahre alten Zirbelkiefer, die 1990 vom Gletscher freigegeben wurde, zeugt vom klimageschichtlichen Auf und Ab in den Alpen.

Neben den Gletschern, der Geologie und der Natur des Hochgebirges rückte um die Jahrtausendwende auch die Straße selbst ins Zentrum des politischen wie geschichtlichen Interesses: War das monumentale Bauwerk nicht ähnlich bedeutend für die österreichische Geschichte und entsprechend schützenswert wie etwa das Schloss Schönbrunn? Manifestierten sich in ihren Kurven nicht jener automobile Freiheitsgeist und Wunsch nach freizeitlicher Landschafts- und Naturerfahrung, die für den Zeitgeist der

> Ab 1981 entstand mit dem über 1.800 km² großen Naturpark Hohe Tauern der größte Schutzraum der Alpen, in dem sich 300 Dreitausender und 243 Gletscher finden.

> From 1981 onward, the largest protected area in the Alps was created: the High Tauern Nature Park encompassing over 1,800 km² and home to 300 three-thousand-meter peaks and 243 glaciers.

glacier in only a few steps. At the same time, the national park exhibit at the Franz-Josefs-Höhe reminds visitors that the glacier had reached its maximum size in the middle of the 19th century, but was then also already considerably smaller during warmer climate periods than today: the trunk of an approx. 9,000-year-old Swiss stone pine which was released by the glacier in 1990, was witness to the historical climate fluctuations in the Alps.

In addition to the glaciers, the geology and the high mountains' nature world, the road itself shifted to the center of political and historical interest: Wasn't the monumental construction work similarly significant to Austrian history and correspondingly worthy of protection like Schönbrunn Palace, for example? Weren't the curves a manifestation of the spirit of freedom provided by the automobile and desire for recreational experiences of the countryside and nature that were so typical of the Zeitgeist during the interwar period? In 2002, an application was submitted to UNESCO to declare the road and the national park a mixed World Heritage Site – but without success initially. In 2015, the Glockner Road ensemble, which was well-preserved in comparison to other Alpine passes, was finally placed under protection as a historical monument. It was a fine line for a high Alpine road important to traffic and travel to navigate, one which is visited annually by around a million people and must be constantly upgraded for the sake of safety, – nevertheless, the advantages outweighed the disadvantages and after years of

MIT FREUNDLICHER GENEHMIGUNG
COURTESY OF:
GROHAG ARCHIV

GROSSGLOCKNER HOCHALPENSTRASSE · PORSCHE DRIVE   GESCHICHTE / HISTORY — 73

Zwischenkriegsjahre so typisch waren? 2002 wurde bei der UNESCO der Antrag eingereicht, die Straße und den Nationalpark als gemischte Stätte zum Welterbe zu erklären – zunächst jedoch ohne Erfolg. 2015 wurde das im Vergleich zu anderen Alpenpässen gut erhaltene Ensemble der Glocknerstraße schließlich unter Denkmalschutz gestellt. Für eine verkehrsrelevante Hochalpenstraße, die jährlich von rund einer Millionen Menschen besucht wird und im Sinne der Sicherheit ständig ausgebessert werden muss, ein schmaler Grat – doch die Vorteile überwogen und nach jahrelangen Verhandlungen hatte sich die straßenbetreibende Aktiengesellschaft mit der Denkmalschutzbehörde auf die Zusammenarbeit geeinigt. Mit dem höchsten nationalen Schutz war auch der Weg frei für eine neue Bewerbung bei der UNESCO, dieses Mal mit alleinigem Fokus auf die Straße und ihre Elemente.

Auch wenn die Welterbe-Initiative bei den Menschen, die rund um die Großglockner Hochalpenstraße leben, nicht nur Beifall auslöste – brauchte es zwischen Franz-Josefs-Höhe und Fuscher Törl wirklich noch mehr Touristen aus aller Welt? –, führte sie doch nochmals deutlich vor Augen, was die 48 Kilometer lange Strecke so einzigartig machte: So fügte sich die Straße, von Tausenden Arbeitern in mühevollen Jahren errichtet, nicht nur sensibel in die Topografie ein, statt sie zu durchschneiden, sondern war als eine der ersten Alpenstraßen mit dem Ziel angelegt worden, Ausblicke von unvergleichlicher Schönheit zu gewähren und die Landschaftswahrnehmung möglichst eindrückliche zu inszenieren. Franz Wallack hatte die Autofahrt über die Hochalpenstraße durch seine sensible Komposition in ein wahrhaft mediales Erlebnis verwandelt. Auch was die touristische Erschließung betraf, hatten Wallack und Rehrl Pionierarbeit in Sachen Marketing und Public Relations geleistet – von der Umbenennung der Edelweißstraße über die Entwicklung einer zeitlosen »Corporate Identity« bis zur geschickten Positionierung der Mautvignette als Werbeträger. Schließlich war da noch das mehr als 80 Jahre alte Konstrukt einer einzigen, durchaus wirtschaftlich arbeitenden Betreibergesellschaft, die sich konstant dem Erhalt der Straße verschrieben, die Instandsetzung im perfektionistischen Geist Wallacks nachhaltig fortgesetzt und die Unterschutzstellung somit erst möglich gemacht hatte. Die Verwaltungen anderer Alpenstraßen, oft durch Zuständigkeiten und Ländergrenzen organisatorisch fragmentiert und durch verkehrspolitische Regelungen von der Einführung eines Mautsystems gehindert, können von solch einer Konstellation bis heute nur träumen.

Zuletzt war die Großglockner Hochalpenstraße mit ihrer wechselvollen Geschichte nicht nur ein wichtiger Teil der europäischen Tourismusgeschichte des 20. Jahrhunderts, sondern auch Sinnbild österreichischer Identitätsfindung nach dem Zusammenbruchs des Kaiserreichs, dem langsamen Weg einer Gesellschaft in Diktatur und Krieg – und die Rückkehr zur demokratischen Ordnung

negotiating, the stock company operating the road came to a cooperation agreement with the monument protection authority. With the highest national protection on hand, the path was cleared for a new application to UNESCO, but this time with the sole focus on the road and its elements.

Even though the World Heritage initiative didn't have the people living around the Grossglockner High Alpine Road exactly cheering for it – did there really need to be more tourists from around the world between Franz-Josefs-Höhe and Fuscher Törl? – it brought awareness again to what made the 48-kilometer route so unique: the road, built by thousands of laborers in years of hard work, not only was painstakingly adapted to the topography instead of slicing through it – but was one of the first Alpine roads to be planned with the goal of affording views of unparalleled beauty and to showcase the perception of the surroundings in the most impressive way possible. Franz Wallack made the car drive along the High Alpine Road into a genuine media experience through his finely-tuned sensibility for composition. In respect to tourist development, Wallack and Rehrl also did pioneering work regarding marketing and public relations – from renaming the Edelweissstrasse and the development of a classic corporate identity to the clever positioning of the toll sticker as an advertisement. Finally, there was still the more than 80-year-old construct of a single, absolutely economically functional operating company, that was dedicated to the constant preservation of the road, that continues sustainable maintenance in keeping with Wallack's perfectionistic spirit, which itself made the official protection measures possible to begin with. The administrations of other Alpine roads, which are often fragmented organizationally because of jurisdictions and state borders, and prevented from introducing toll systems due to transportation policy, can even now only dream of such a constellation.

Finally, the Grossglockner High Alpine Road and its colorful history are not only an important part of Europe's history of tourism in the 20th century, but also a symbol of Austria's quest for an identity after the collapse of the empire, the slow path of a society under a dictatorship and at war – and the return to a democratic order, including its reconstruction and economic growth. It has now been nearly 100 years since the idea of a road across the High Tauern was first announced on a political stage. After the journey into the past of the Grossglockner High Alpine Road, posing the question of how the story will continue becomes inevitable. Which social, political, ecological events and developments will leave their mark between Hochtor and Fuscher Törl, between Franz-Josefs-Höhe and Edelweiss-Spitze in the decades to come? Will only electric sports cars soon be humming around the curves? At the very least, the company has laid a symbolic cornerstone for the electrification of Alpine traffic with the introduction of a reduced toll and electric charging stations. The consequences of both the natural and man-made climate change at the Grossglockner will, of course,

samt Wiederaufbau und Wirtschaftswachstum. Fast 100 Jahre sind nun vergangen, seit die Idee einer Fahrverbindung über die Hohen Tauern erstmals auf politischer Bühne verkündet wurde. Nach der Reise in die Vergangenheit der Großglockner Hochalpenstraße stellt sich daher unvermeidlich die Frage, wie die Geschichte weitergeschrieben wird. Welche gesellschaftlichen, politischen, ökologischen Ereignisse und Entwicklung werden in den nächsten Jahrzehnten zwischen Hochtor und Fuscher Törl, zwischen Franz-Josefs-Höhe und Edelweiß-Spitze ihre Spuren hinterlassen? Werden bald nur noch Elektrosportwagen durch die Kurven surren? Mit einer reduzierten Maut und Elektrotankstellen entlang der Straße hat die Gesellschaft zumindest einen symbolischen Grundstein für die Elektrifizierung des Alpenverkehrs gelegt. Die Folgen des natürlichen wie menschgemachten Klimawandels am Großglockner werden die alternativen Antriebe freilich nicht mehr verhindern können – bis zum Jahr 2050 könnte der Pasterzen-Gletscher fast völlig verschwunden sein. Und doch bleibt zu hoffen, dass eine als architektonisches Wunderwerk geschützte Straße durch einen der imposantesten Nationalparks Europas auf ihre alten Tage zum Zeugen eines schonenderen, nachhaltigeren Tourismus werden wird. Die Ehre, sie mit offenen Augen für die Schönheit der Bergwelt, mit Rücksicht auf Menschen und Natur und ohne allzu große Eile zu befahren, sollte man ihr und ihren Erbauern erweisen.

> Die Ehre, sie mit offenen Augen für die Schönheit der Bergwelt, mit Rücksicht auf Menschen und Natur und ohne allzu große Eile zu befahren, sollte man ihr und ihren Erbauern erweisen.

> We should pay our respects to the road and its builders by keeping our eyes open to the beauty of the mountain landscape, by showing consideration for humanity and nature and by driving on it without too much haste.

not be prevented by the alternative engines – the Pasterze Glacier could have completely disappeared by the year 2050. And yet one can still hope that a road protected as an architectural masterpiece and which traverses one of Europe's most impressive national parks will become a witness to more thoughtful, sustainable tourism in its advancing years. We should pay our respects to the road and its builders by keeping our eyes open to the beauty of the mountain landscape, by showing consideration for humanity and nature and by driving on it without too much haste.

Die Großglockner Hochalpenstraße ist 48 Kilometer lang und verbindet die österreichischen Bundesländer Salzburg im Norden und Kärnten im Süden. Zählt man die beiden Panorama-Stichstraßen auf die Edelweiß-Spitze und zur Kaiser-Franz-Josefs-Höhe hinzu, misst die Straße rund 58 Streckenkilometer. Obwohl dies kein enorm langer Weg ist, kann man, seinem Verlauf folgend, in wenigen Stunden vier Klimazonen durchreisen. Den Alpenhauptkamm überquert man zwischen Fuscher Törl auf 2.431 Metern und Hochtor, das auf 2.504 Metern von einem Tunnel durchmessen wird. Der höchste befahrbare Punkt der Straße befindet sich auf der Edelweiß-Spitze auf 2.571 Metern. Auf der Fahrt zählt man 36 Kehren, die stärkste Steigung liegt etwa bei 12 Prozent. Meist ist die Straße von Mai bis Oktober geöffnet, wobei man stets den aktuellen Straßenbericht einsehen sollte – schließlich kann es in den Alpen auch im Hochsommer schneien.

Vom Kilometerstein »Null« in Bruck an der Großglocknerstraße im Pinzgau auf 756 Meter Höhe führt die Fahrt in Richtung Süden durchs wildromantische Fuscher Tal, das seinen Namen von den Römern bekam: Fuscus für dunkel oder düster. Dabei blühen hier im Frühjahr zwischen Bauernhöfen und Heustadeln die Blumenwiesen, während die weißverschneiten Gipfel des Sonnenwellecks und des Fuscherkarkopfes zwischen den dicht bewaldeten Talseiten verheißungsvoll am Horizont erscheinen. Die eigentlich Hochalpenstraße beginnt auf 1.145 Metern nach der Kassenstelle in Ferleiten: Auf der 12,9 Kilometer langen »Glocknerkönig-Strecke« bis zum Fuscher Törl gilt es, bei 8 bis 11 Prozent Steigung knapp 1.300 Höhenmeter zu bewältigen.

Bald schon werden die Bäume entlang der Straße weniger, die Landschaft alpiner. Man durchsteuert die ersten Kehren, blickt zur Piffalm, passiert das Straßenwärterhaus Piffkar und den Aussichtspunkt Hochmais mit seinem eindrucksvollen Blick ins Käfer- und Ferleitental, erklimmt die steilen Anstiege durch das Bergsturzgebiet der Hexenküche unterhalb der Edelweißwand, meistert die Kehren des Unteren und Oberen Naßfelds und erreicht schließlich den Parkplatz beim Gasthaus Fuschertörl, von wo aus die noch immer gepflasterte Stichstraße hinauf auf die Edelweiß-Spitze führt. Hier bietet sich bei klarer Sicht der schönste Blick der Strecke: 37 Dreitausender kann man sehen, dazu 19 Gletscher, den Gipfel des Großglockners und die Straße, auf deren ausladend über den Berg geschwungenen Kehren man gerade eben noch aus dem Tal heraufgefahren ist und die sich nun an der Flanke des Brennkogel durch einen aufgelassenen Goldbergbau, der im 16. Jahrhundert bis zu zehn Prozent der damals bekannten Weltgoldproduktion erreichte, hinüber zum Hochtor windet.

Zurück beim Gasthaus folgt man erneut der Hochalpenstraße, die nun in einer Panoramaschleife den Törlkopf elegant umkurvt. Jetzt führt die hochalpine Scheitelstrecke hinab zum Römerbogen und zur Fuscher Lacke auf 2.262 Metern, vorbei am Gasthof Mankeiwirt - Mankei ist Mundart für Murmeltier – durch den Mittertörl-Tunnel und den Elendbogen, bevor es wieder bergauf zum Hochtor-Tunnel geht, in dessen Mitte man die Landesgrenze zwischen Salzburg und Kärnten passiert. Hier ist die Landschaft nun weniger schroff als zuvor, die Südrampe windet sich in großzügigen Kehren über sanft geschwungene Almwiesen ins Mölltal. Man passiert den Berggasthof Wallackhaus auf rund 2.300 Metern sowie die Talstation der Großglockner Panoramabahn, bevor der Hang erneut steiler und die Kehren enger werden. Bei Guttal zweigt schließlich in einem Kreisverkehr die rund acht Kilometer lange Gletscherstraße ab, die zum Alpincenter Glocknerhaus, dem Margaritzen-Stausee, der Wasser durch den Alpenhauptkamm dem Kraftwerk Kaprun zuführt, und zu der auf 2.369 Metern gelegenen Kaiser-Franz-Josefs-Höhe führt. Der Ausblick auf den verschneiten Großglockner und die darunter liegende Pasterze ist beeindruckend, auch wenn der Gletscher selbst von Jahr zu Jahr zurückgeht. Wer sein Auto, Motorrad oder Fahrrad stehen lässt, kann die Gegend nun per Gletscherbahn oder zu Fuß auf einem der Panorama-Wanderwege weiter erkunden und Steinböcke in freier Wildbahn beobachten.

Zurück an der Abzweigung Guttal angelangt, geht es schließlich durch dichte Wälder weiter hinab ins Tal, zur Kassenstelle und schließlich bis nach Heiligenblut, wo die Großglockner Hochalpenstraße auf 1.288 Meter über dem Meer endet. Wer nun nicht weiter nach Süden fährt, sondern kehrt und den Pass erneut in umgekehrter Richtung überquert, wird erstaunt sein, wie sehr sich das Fahrerlebnis und die Aussicht unterscheiden.

The Grossglockner High Alpine Road is 48 kilometers long and links the Austrian provinces of Salzburg in the north and Carinthia in the south. If you include the two panoramic access roads to the Edelweissspitze and Kaiser-Franz-Josefs-Höhe, the road measures around 58 kilometers. While this is not a hugely long distance, by following the road's course you can travel through four climate zones in just a few hours. You cross the main Alpine ridge between Fuscher Törl at an altitude of 2,431 meters and at Hochtor, which has a tunnel running through it at the 2,504-meter point. The highest navigable point of the road is the Edelweissspitze located at an altitude of 2,571 meters. You meet 36 hairpin bends along the way, with the steepest gradient being around 12 percent. The road is usually open from May to October, although it's always advisable to check the latest road reports – it can, after all, snow in the Alps even in high summer.

Starting at the zero kilometer stone in the municipality of Bruck an der Grossglocknerstrasse in Pinzgau at an altitude of 756 meters, the road leads south through the wild and romantic Fuschertal valley, so named by the Romans, with fuscus meaning dark or somber. The flower meadows bloom here in spring between farms and haystacks, while the white snow-covered Sonnenwelleck and Fuscherkarkopf peaks appear auspiciously on the horizon between the densely wooded sides of the valley. The actual starting point of the High Alpine Road begins at 1,145 meters above sea level after the ticket booth in Ferleiten: The 12.9-kilometer section used for the Glocknerkönig cycling and running event involves climbing almost 1,300 meters at a gradient of 8 to 11 percent up to the Fuscher Törl.

Soon the trees along the road become fewer and fewer, as the landscape takes on a more alpine aspect. You drive through the first hairpin bends, looking at the Piffalm, passing the Piffkar roadman's house and the Hochmais viewpoint with its impressive view into the Käfertal and Ferleitental valleys, climb the steep ascents through the landslide area of the "Hexenküche" (witches' kitchen) section, below the side of the Edelweiss, negotiate the hairpin bends of the Lower and Upper Nassfeld, and finally reach the parking lot at the Fuschertörl Restaurant, from where the still cobbled access road leads up to the Edelweiss-Spitze. It is here at the top that, on a clear day, you have the best view of all from the road: 37 three-thousand-meter peaks are laid out before you, along with 19 glaciers, the Grossglockner's summit, and also the road itself, upon whose expansive, sweeping bends carving across the mountain you have just driven up from the valley, and which now winds its way up the flank of the Brennkogel through an abandoned gold mine, which produced up to ten percent of the world's existing gold back in the 16th century, up to the Hochtor mountain.

Back at the restaurant, you once again follow the High Alpine Road, now elegantly curving around the Törlkopf in a panorama loop. Now the high alpine mountain route leads down to the Römerbogen section and to Fuscher Lacke at a height of 2,262 meters, past the Mankeiwirt - 'Mankei' meaning 'marmots' in the local dialect – through the Mittertörl tunnel and the Elendbogen, before moving uphill again to the Hochtor tunnel, in the center of which you cross the border between Salzburg and Carinthia. The landscape is now less rugged here than before, the Südrampe road winding its way in generous curves over gently rolling alpine meadows into the Mölltal valley. You pass the Wallackhaus mountain inn at an altitude of about 2,300 meters, and the Grossglockner Panoramabahn valley lift station, before the slope steepens and the bends narrow again. Near Guttal the roughly eight-kilometer-long glacier road turns off at a roundabout, leading to the Alpincenter Glocknerhaus, the Margaritze reservoir, which supplies water through the main Alpine ridge to the Kaprun power station, and to Kaiser-Franz-Josefs-Höhe vantage point at a height of 2,369 meters. The view over the snow-covered Grossglockner and the Pasterze lying below is impressive, despite the glacier receding further year by year. If you leave your car, motorbike or bike you can now continue exploring the area by taking a glacier lift or on foot via one of the panorama hiking trails and observe ibex in their wild habitat. Back at the Guttal junction, the road finally descends through dense forests to the valley, to the ticket booth and finally to Heiligenblut, where the Grossglockner High Alpine Road ends, 1,288 meters above sea level. Anyone not driving on further south can turn around and cross the pass again in the opposite direction – and will be amazed at how different the driving experience and the view are this way round.

124 — DIE STRASSE / THE ROAD

PORSCHE DRIVE · GROSSGLOCKNER HOCHALPENSTRASSE

GROSSGLOCKNER HOCHALPENSTRASSE · PORSCHE DRIVE

DIE STRASSE / THE ROAD

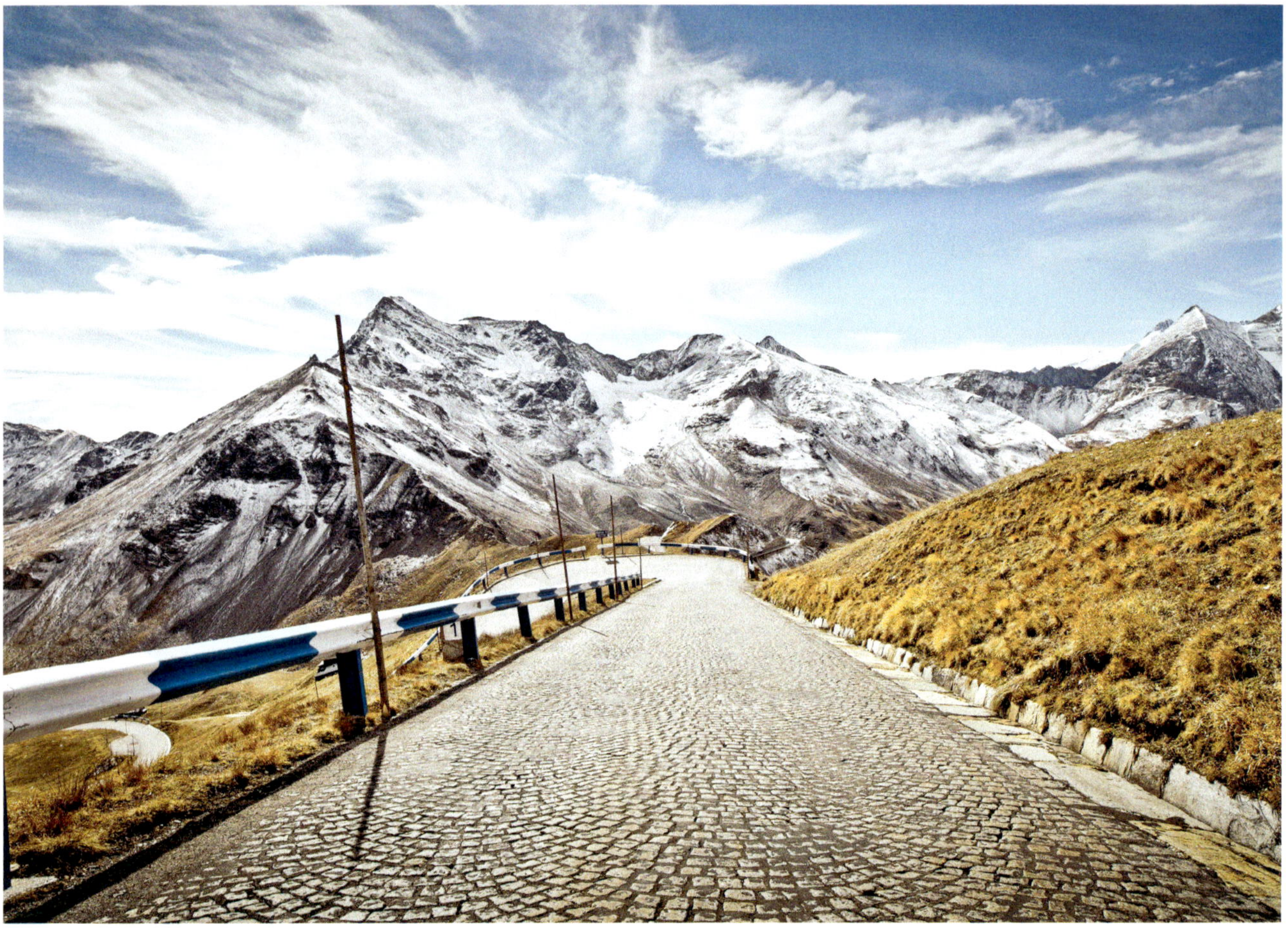

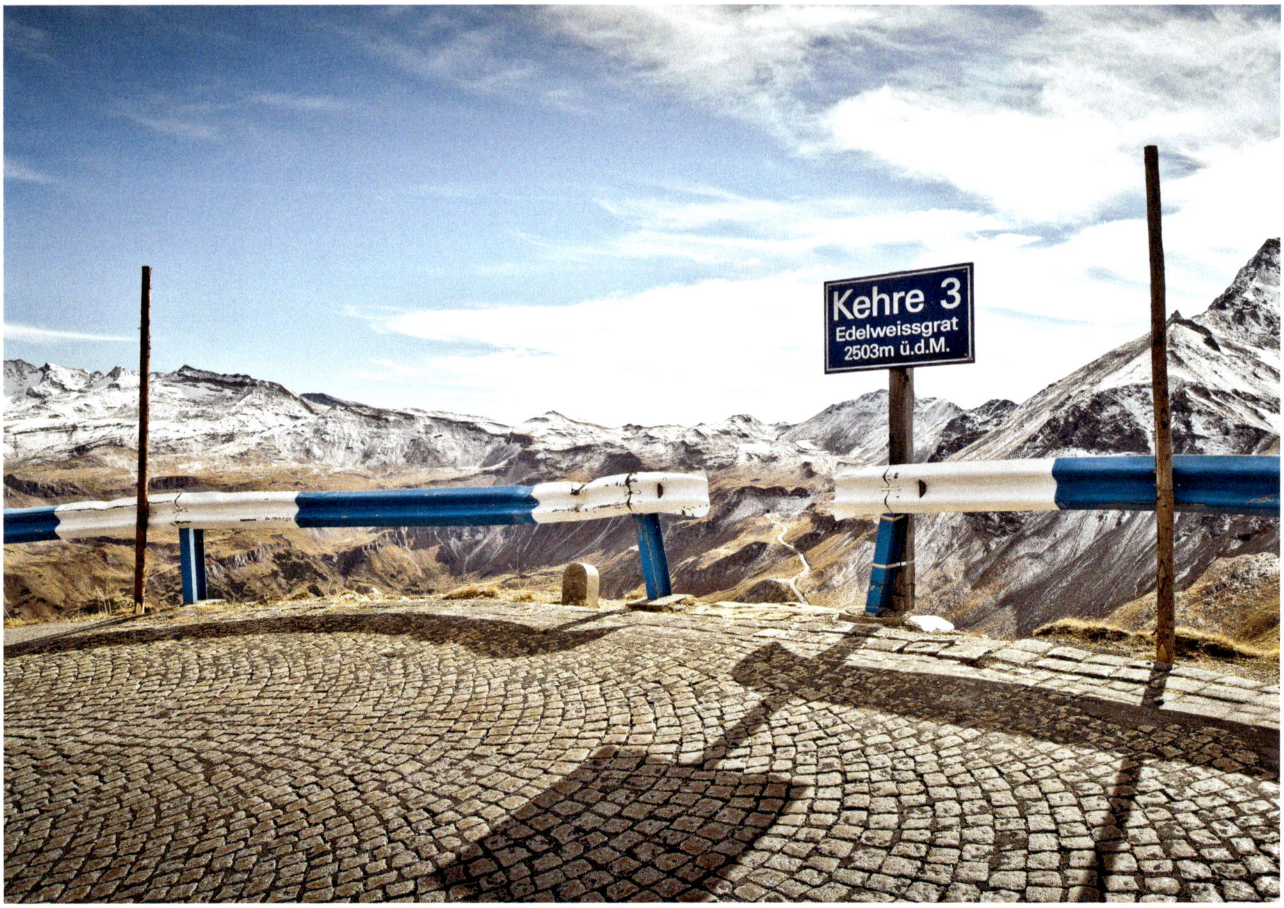
Kehre 3
Edelweissgrat
2503m ü.d.M.

GROSSGLOCKNER HOCHALPENSTRASSE · PORSCHE DRIVE

DIE STRASSE / THE ROAD — 145

GROSSGLOCKNER HOCHALPENSTRASSE · PORSCHE DRIVE

DIE STRASSE / THE ROAD — 155

PERSPEKTIVEN
PERSPECTIVES

DR. JOHANNES HÖRL

Die Großglockner Hochalpenstraße ist nicht nur ein Bauwerk von Weltrang, auch die organisatorische Konstruktion im Hintergrund ist einzigartig: Bis heute wird die Panoramastraße kontinuierlich und im Sinne ihrer Erbauer von jener Aktiengesellschaft verwaltet, die 1931 zu ihrer Planung und Umsetzung ins Leben gerufen wurde. Die im Mehrheitseigentum der Republik Österreich befindliche Großglockner Hochalpenstraßen AG mit Sitz in Salzburg wird seit gut einem Jahrzehnt von Dr. Johannes Hörl als Direktor und Vorstand geleitet. Ein Gespräch über Vergangenheit und Zukunft der Straße.

The Grossglockner High Alpine Road is more than just an internationally renowned work of engineering – the organizational design behind the scenes is also unique: The panoramic road has continued to be managed in the interests of its original builders by the same corporation that was founded in 1931 to plan and build it. Großglockner Hochalpenstraßen AG, which is headquartered in Salzburg, has been managed by Dr. Johannes Hörl as its director and chairman for a good decade now. A discussion centered on the road's past and future.

Worin liegt der außergewöhnliche universelle Wert der Glockner Hochalpenstraße? Warum gehört sie Ihrer Meinung nach zum Weltkulturerbe? Die Großglockner Hochalpenstraße ist die bekannteste und schönste Panoramastraße Europas sowie eine einzigartige Hochgebirgserlebniswelt. Als international – und vom Bundesdenkmalamt – anerkannter Monumentalbau österreichischer Ingenieurskunst ist die Großglockner Hochalpenstraße Symbolbild für die außerordentliche Leistungsfähigkeit Österreichs in »schwierigen Zeiten« und »Visitenkarte« der Republik. Aber es gäbe noch etliche Gründe mehr anzuführen, was hier den Rahmen sprengen würde …

Was macht die Straße im Vergleich zu anderen berühmten Alpenstraßen wie dem Stilfser Joch oder dem Gotthardpass so einzigartig? Der Erbauer, Ingenieur Franz Wallack, wollte die schönste Hochgebirgs-Panoramastraße der Welt erbauen, keine Serpentinenstraße, keine reine Transitroute, sondern sein Ziel war es, »der Natur nicht den Rang abzulaufen« – das ist ihm perfekt gelungen. Darüber hinaus ist sie die längste Hochgebirgsstraße Europas mit einer Scheitelstrecke von 10 Kilometer Länge auf über 2.300 Metern bis über 2.500 Meter Seehöhe, sie ist der Weg zu Österreichs höchstem Berg (dem Großglockner mit 3.798 Metern), dem längsten Gletscher der Ostalpen (der Pasterze, ca. 8 Kilometer lang) und befindet sich inmitten des IUCN-anerkannten Nationalpark Hohe Tauern, dem größten und bedeutendsten Schutzgebiet Mitteleuropas mit knapp 2.000 Quadratkilometern und 300 Dreitausendern.

Welchen Platz nimmt das Bauprojekt in der wechselvollen Geschichte Österreichs ein? Wie gesagt, die Großglockner Hochalpenstraße ist Symbolbild für die außerordentliche Leistungsfähigkeit Österreichs in

What gives the Grossglockner High Alpine Road its extraordinary universal value? Why does it, in your opinion, deserve recognition as a World Heritage Site? The Grossglockner High Alpine Road is the most famous, and most spectacular, panoramic route in Europe, and a unique way to experience the high Alpine world. As an internationally recognized monumental structure representing the epitome of Austrian engineering skill – an assessment shared by the Federal Monuments Office of Austria – the Grossglockner High Alpine Road symbolizes the extraordinary capacity of Austria to achieve greatness even in "difficult times", while also serving the Republic as its "calling card". There are numerous other reasons that I could list, however that would extend beyond the scope of our discussion here.

What makes the road so unique in comparison to other famous Alpine roads, such as Stilfser Joch or the Gotthard Pass? Its builder, the engineer Franz Wallack, wanted to build the most spectacular panoramic Alpine road in the world. It wasn't his intention to create a switchback road, or a route for transit purposes only; he instead aimed "not to outdo nature itself" – and he succeeded masterfully. Furthermore, it is the longest mountain road in Europe, with a summit section that is 10 kilometers in length which rises from more than 2,300 meters to more than 2,500 meters above sea level; it is the gateway to Austria's highest mountain (Grossglockner, measuring 3,798 meters) and to the longest glacier in the eastern Alps (Pasterze, around 8 kilometers long). It is right at the heart of the IUCN-recognized High Tauern National Park, which is the largest and most significant conservation area in Central Europe, measuring almost 2,000 square kilometers and encompassing 300 mountains more than three thousand meters in height.

»schwierigen Zeiten« und des Ständestaates, aber sie war im Verlauf der letzten Jahrzehnte stets auch stabiler Faktor als touristischer Partner und regionaler Wirtschaftsmotor, als verlässlicher Auftraggeber und Arbeitgeber in den Hohe Tauern-Bundesländern Kärnten, Salzburg und Tirol. Sie ist heute noch, vielleicht mehr als je zuvor, für jährlich Hunderttausende Besucher aus dem In- und Ausland »Visitenkarte« des alpinen Österreich.

Hätte die Straße auch ohne die Rückendeckung des Ständestaates realisiert werden können? Durch ihre Geschichte, ihre Aufgabenstellung und ihren rechtlichen Status unterscheidet sich die Betreiberin der Großglockner Hochalpenstraße, die Großglockner Hochalpenstraßen AG (GROHAG), von allen anderen Straßengesellschaften. Zweifelsfrei sind die Zeit des Ständestaates und die damals herrschende Not Mitauslöser für den bereits Jahre zuvor geplanten Bau dieses Großvorhabens gewesen. Die historisch feststellbaren Hauptgründe waren die Folgenden:

1. Der Bau eines neuen Verkehrsweges über den Tauernhauptkamm zwischen Brenner und dem Radstädter Tauern lag angesichts des stetig zunehmenden »Reise- und Kraftwagenverkehrs« im öffentlichen Interesse (Nord-Süd-Verbindung).
2. Die durch den Ersten Weltkrieg hervorgerufenen außerordentlichen Verhältnisse in Österreich machten eine Straßenverbindung zur »Förderung des Fremdenverkehrs« dringlich.
3. Der österreichischen Volkswirtschaft sollte dadurch entsprechender Nutzen gebracht werden, zumal die Straße weithin arbeitsstiftende und nachhaltige wirtschaftliche Impulswirkung haben konnte.

Alle diese Faktoren und Ziele sind vor dem Hintergrund der damaligen politischen Situation zu sehen, haben aber auch heute noch Gültigkeit.

Mit Franz Wallack und Franz Rehrl hat die Straße gleich zwei Väter mit starkem Willen. Wie lief die Zusammenarbeit dieser zwei »Sturköpfe« ab? Die Fragestellung ist berechtigt und – so ist es überliefert – die Zusammenarbeit zwischen dem »politischen Wegbereiter«, dem Salzburger Landeshauptmann Franz Rehrl, der sich unbeschreiblich für derlei Großprojekte und die Interessen der Landesbevölkerung eingesetzt hat, und dem »visionären Erbauer« Ingenieur Franz Wallack war auch nicht immer konfliktfrei. Doch hatte jeder seine Rolle, und nur durch das Zusammenwirken dieser beiden »Alphatiere« war es möglich, dieses Großprojekt politisch, finanziell und baulich zu bewältigen.

Franz Wallack war nicht nur ein genialer Baumeister, sondern auch ein Marketing-Vordenker. Welche seiner Leistungen imponiert Ihnen besonders? Auch hier gibt es so vieles, was heute kaum vorstellbar ist. Wallack war universalbegabt, er war nicht nur hervorragender

What significance does this building project assume within Austria's tumultuous history? As I mentioned, the Grossglockner High Alpine Road symbolizes the extraordinary capacity of Austria, and of the corporative state, to achieve greatness in "times of adversity", while also remaining a stable factor as a tourism partner over the course of the last century. It is an economic motor for the region, and a reliable contractor and employer in Carinthia, Salzburg and Tyrol, the states of Austria that span the High Tauern. And today it is, probably more than ever before, the "calling card" of Alpine Austria for the hundreds of thousands of visitors that come from Austria and overseas every year.

Could the road have been completed without the backing of the corporative state? Its history, its responsibilities and its legal status distinguish the operator of the Grossglockner High Alpine Road, Großglockner Hochalpenstraßen AG (GROHAG), from all other road building authorities. There can be no doubt that the era of the corporative state and the destitution that prevailed at the time played a role in contributing to this major project, the construction of which had already been planned years prior. The main historical reasons that could be ascertained are the following:

1 The construction of a new transit route across the main ridge of the Tauern between Brenner and Radstädter Tauern was a matter of public interest given the constantly growing "tourist and passenger vehicle traffic" (providing a north-south connection).

2 The extraordinary circumstances in Austria provoked by the First World War made a road link to "promote tourism" a matter of urgency.

3 The national economy of Austria was to draw the corresponding benefits from it, especially as the road would be able to continue to function as a vehicle for job creation and provide sustained economic stimulus.

All these factors and goals must be considered against the backdrop of the political situation at the time; however they do retain their validity today.

The road has two strong-willed founders in the form of Franz Wallack and Franz Rehrl. How did the collaboration between these two "stubborn" men proceed? The question is a good one and – as the story has been handed down – the collaboration between its "political pioneer" Franz Rehrl, the governor of Salzburg who made indescribable efforts to advocate major projects like this and the interests of the local population, and its "visionary builder", the engineer Franz Wallack, did not always proceed without conflicts. Yet each had his own specific role to play, and it was only the combined efforts of these two "alpha males" that made mastering this major project politically, financially, and structurally possible.

Techniker, er war auch Künstler, Fotograf, Maler, Komponist, erfolgreicher Sportler, Naturschützer, Gebirgsexperte, Marketinggenie und Ästhet. Beispielsweise hat er den Großglockner-Aufkleber schon in den Dreißigerjahren des vorigen Jahrhunderts entworfen und von Beginn an eingesetzt. Das »G« wurde auf etwa 7 Millionen Pkw aller Herren Länder geklebt und so zu einem der bekanntesten touristischen Markenlogos Europas. Das »Maut-Pickerl« wird noch heute an den Kassenstellen für jeden Fahrzeugbesitzer ausgegeben. Darüber hinaus war es ihm von Beginn an wichtig, was in der Satzung der Gesellschaft (GROHAG) seit dem Jahr 1931 vorgesehen ist: die adäquate Auflösung der sich aus den Spannungsfeldern Technik, Tourismus und Natur ergebenden Herausforderungen. Das fing an bei der naturschonenden Trassenführung auch vor dem Hintergrund einer optimalen Gestaltung als Panoramastraße im Hochgebirge und endete bei den Bautätigkeiten, indem er – ohne durch behördliche Auflagen dazu gezwungen zu sein – besonderen Wert auf eine bestmögliche Renaturierung gelegt hat.

Ist es kein Widerspruch, eine vielbefahrene Hochalpenstraße, die ständig ausgebessert und gesichert werden muss, unter Denkmalschutz zu stellen? Das oben genannte Spannungsfeld ist zweifelsohne unsere größte, aber auch tägliche Herausforderung. Es gelingt uns ganz gut, das »Monument« zu bewahren, es zu erhalten und gleichzeitig dieses auch für folgende Generationen und viele weitere Millionen Interessierte aus dem In- und Ausland zu sichern. Auch wenn aufgrund der Veränderung der Permafrostgrenze tendenziell mehr Kosten- und Sicherheitsthemen anstehen werden. Wir haben ein tolles Team von Technikern, Geologen, Alpinisten und Lawinenkundigen sowie insgesamt sehr verlässliche und erfahrene Mitarbeitende – wir werden die anstehenden Herausforderungen des Hochgebirges mit Sicherheit meistern.

Was versprechen Sie sich von einem Welterbe-Titel der UNESCO? Es geht nicht darum, was ich mir erwarte, aber sollte die UNESCO der Großglockner Hochalpenstraße das Prädikat »Welterbe« zuerkennen, können wir alle – als Österreich – schon stolz darauf sein, dieses Monument errichtet und »geschafft« zu haben und es mehr als ein Dreivierteljahrhundert lang über 65 Millionen Menschen, vorwiegend aus dem Ausland, präsentiert zu haben. Es ist davon auszugehen, dass wir dazu auch in Zukunft in der Lage sein werden, zumal die Sehnsucht, das Hochgebirge zu erleben und dabei den größten Nationalpark Mitteleuropas zu »erfahren« sicher ein Alleinstellungsmerkmal darstellt, das tendenziell einfach an Bedeutung gewinnt.

Die Glocknerstraße führt durch den größten Nationalpark der Alpen. Dennoch wird sie von vielen Auto- und Motorradfahrern als »Rennstrecke unter freiem Himmel« angesehen. Wie lässt sich das vereinbaren? Dazu kann und muss ich sagen, dass wir das Wort

Franz Wallack wasn't just an ingenious master builder, but also a trailblazer in terms of marketing. Which of his achievements impresses you the most? There's so much I could mention that is barely conceivable today. Wallack was universally gifted – not only was he an outstanding technician, but he was also an artist, photographer, painter, composer, successful athlete, conservationist, mountaineering expert, marketing genius and esthete. For example, he designed the Grossglockner sticker back in the 1930s, and utilized it right from the start. The "G" has been affixed to around 7 million cars from all different countries, making it one of the most recognized tourism brand logos in Europe. The toll road sticker is still issued to every vehicle owner at the tool booths. Moreover, what the articles of incorporation of the company (GROHAG) had envisioned since 1931 was, for him, important right from the start: Finding an adequate way of reconciling the challenges resulting from the conflicting priorities represented by technology, tourism and nature. This started with creating a route that would conserve nature while lending it an optimal design as a panoramic road in the High Alps, and ended with the construction activities, during which he – and without being forced to do so by official requirements – placed particular value on the best renaturalization possible.

Isn't it a contradiction to place a busy high Alpine road, which constantly needs repairs and safeguards, under heritage protection? The aforementioned conflict is undoubtedly one of the biggest we face, but it is also an everyday challenge. We are actually quite successful at retaining and maintaining the "monument" while simultaneously protecting it for the generations to come and the many more millions of interested visitors who come from Austria and overseas. Even though the changing permafrost line will tend to mean there are more cost and safety-related issues to tackle. We have a great team of technicians, geologists, mountain and avalanche experts, as well as employees who are extremely reliable and experienced overall – we are confident that we will be able to successfully master the upcoming challenges in the Alpine environment.

What do you hope that a UNESCO World Heritage listing will bring? This is not about what I am expecting, but should UNESCO award the Grossglockner High Alpine Road World Heritage status, then we all – as Austria – can be proud of having erected this monument and having succeeded in presenting it to more than 65 million people, most of whom came from other countries, over the last three-quarters of a century. We can only assume that we will also be in a position to do so in the future, especially as the desire to visit the mountains and to "experience" the largest national park in Central Europe definitely represents a distinguishing feature that will tend to gain significance.

**The Grossglockner High Alpine Road leads through the largest national park in the Alps. And yet many car drivers and motorcyclists consider it to be an "open-air

»Rennen« aus all unseren Gedanken und Werbemitteln gestrichen haben. Wir erlauben auch keine motorisierten Veranstaltungen, die sich mit dem Grundgedanken des Genussfahrens nicht identifizieren. Es ist ganz einfach: Wir arbeiten an der bestmöglichen Auflösung der Spannungsfelder Natur, Tourismus und Technik – und das erwarten wir auch von unseren Gästen. Wir klären auf und weisen darauf hin: in unseren Werbemitteln, auf der Homepage, in unserer täglichen Medienarbeit. Wir bitten aber nicht nur unsere Gäste, sich diesem Gedanken entsprechend bestmöglich zu verhalten, wir sind auch in engem Kontakt mit der Exekutive, die Verhalten und Geschwindigkeit kontrolliert und bei Bedarf auch abstraft.

Wie könnte ein nachhaltigerer Alpentourismus rund um die Glocknerstraße aussehen – und was tun Sie, um ihn zu fördern? Diese Frage ist spannend, denn sie ist das, was uns neben den Sicherheitsthemen des hochalpinen Gefildes am meisten beschäftigt, weil unser Erfolg in der Zukunft auch davon abhängt. Wie sieht es aus mit den Emissionen? Wie verändert sich die Mobilität? Immerhin sind wir im größten Schutzgebiet Zentraleuropas. Eine Studie der TU Wien mit dem Umweltbundesamt hat bestätigt, dass sich die Auswirkungen der Großglockner Hochalpenstraße auf die Umwelt in den maßgeblichen Schadstoffbereichen – Blei, Stickstoff, Schwefel, CO_2 und dergleichen – im Verhältnis von vor 40 Jahren bereits um etwa 80% und mehr reduziert (!) haben. Dies ist zum einen dem Fortschritt der Technik zu verdanken, aber wir haben auch mit eigenen Maßnahmen, wie dem Nachtfahrverbot, dem ökologischen (fahrzeugbezogenen) Tarifmodell, Vertriebssteuerung und ähnlichen Maßnahmen einen wesentlichen Beitrag leisten können und diese schönen Erfolge erzielt. Außerdem haben wir mit zehn Ausstellungen, die sich vorwiegend mit Bewusstseinsbildung von Natur und Umwelt in den Hohen Tauern sowie neuen Mobilitätsformen wie der E-Mobilität – 12 E-Lademöglichkeiten entlang der Straße – beschäftigen, schon einiges anstoßen können.

Was würden Sie einem Reisenden, der die Großglockner Hochalpenstraße zum ersten Mal besucht, empfehlen? Nehmen Sie sich Zeit! Das ist, was ich allen Interessierten sage. Es bringt wenig, einfach durch- oder drüberzufahren, man muss die Großglockner Hochalpenstraße im Herzen des Nationalparks im wahrsten Wortsinn erfahren! Aussteigen, verweilen, sich Plätze suchen, Infotafeln lesen, Ausstellungen besuchen, Wege begehen, jausnen, mit den Menschen reden und einfach eintauchen in die Hochgebirgswelt der Nationalpark Region Hohe Tauern.

Haben Sie rund um die Straße einen persönlichen Lieblingsort? Ja, das ist die Kaiser-Franz-Josefs-Höhe. Am Fuße des Großglockners zu stehen ist schon etwas ganz Besonderes und – aus meiner Sicht – der schönste Platz der Republik Österreich!

race track"? How can these two uses be reconciled?** On this topic, I can – and have to – say that we have eliminated the word "racing" from all of our ideas and advertisements. Nor do we allow any motorized events that do not identify with the basic tenet of driving for pleasure. It's really quite simple: We are working on reconciling the conflicting priorities of nature, tourism and technology in the best way possible – and we expect this of our visitors as well. We raise awareness of this and emphasize it in our advertising materials, on our website and in our daily media activities. However, not only do we ask our visitors to conduct themselves in a way that is harmonious with this idea, we also maintain close contact with the executive powers who police conduct and speed, and punish it when necessary.

What might a more sustainable approach to Alpine tourism involving the Grossglockner High Alpine Road look like – and what are you doing to promote it? This question is an interesting one, as this, along with issues related to protecting the High Alpine scenery, is what keeps us most occupied – because our future success depends on it. How are things looking when it comes to emissions? How will mobility change? After all, we are in the largest conservation area in Central Europe. A study by the TU Vienna and the Austrian Environment Agency confirmed that the effects of the Grossglockner High Alpine Road on the environment in terms of the most critical pollutants – lead, nitrogen, sulfur, CO_2 and similar emissions – have already been reduced by 80% and more (!) in relation to their levels 40 years ago. On the one hand, we owe this to advances made in technology, however we have also been able to make a huge contribution with measures of our own, such as the ban on driving at night, the ecological (vehicle-related) tariff model, distribution management and similar measures which have allowed these resounding successes to be realized. In additional, the ten exhibitions we have organized, and which predominantly focus on creating awareness of nature and environment in the High Tauern, as well as new forms of mobility such as electric mobility – 12 battery charging stations along the road – have been able to inspire some changes as well.

What would you recommend to a traveler who is visiting the Grossglockner High Alpine Road for the first time? Leave yourself plenty of time! This is what I tell everyone who is thinking of visiting. It's not worth simply driving through or driving across it, you need to discover the Grossglockner High Alpine Road at the heart of the national park, in the truest sense of the word! Get out of the car, linger, find places to sit, read the information boards, visit the exhibitions, walk the trails, have a snack, talk to the people and immerse yourself in the Alpine world of the High Tauern National Park region.

Do you have a personal favorite spot on the road? Yes, it's the Kaiser-Franz-Josefs-Höhe. Standing at the base of Grossglockner is something very special in itself and – in my opinion – the most beautiful spot in all of the Austria!

PETER EMBACHER

Peter Embacher ist technischer Betriebsleiter der Großglockner Hochalpenstraßen AG und verantwortlich für den Fuhrpark und die Werkstätten. Von der Basisstation in Fusch aus sorgt der »Herr über die Straße« dafür, dass die Strecke sich immer in gutem Zustand befindet – und organisiert die alljährliche Schneeräumung.

Peter Embacher is Technical Works Manager of Grossglockner Hochalpenstrassen AG and is responsible for the vehicle fleet and the workshops. From the base station in Fusch, the "master of the road" ensures that the route is always is top condition and organizes the annual snow clearing operation.

Wie sind Sie zur Großglockner Hochalpenstraße gekommen und wie lange arbeiten Sie schon hier? Ich bin jetzt im vierzigsten Betriebsjahr und habe eigentlich alle Abteilungen durchlaufen. Aufgewachsen bin ich 100 Meter von der Straße entfernt, ich kenne sie also schon aus Kindertagen, auch wenn ich damals mit meiner Familie nur selten heraufgefahren bin. Mein erlernter Beruf ist KFZ-Mechaniker. Gleich nach der Lehre im April 1979 habe ich im Straßendienst angefangen. Am ersten Tag war ich als Rotationspflugbeifahrer bei der Schneeräumung dabei. In den kommenden Jahren war ich Schneeräumer, Fräsenfahrer, bei der Absicherungsmannschaft oder habe Lawinen gesprengt. Später habe ich die KFZ-Meisterprüfung abgelegt, das Magazin verwaltet, und habe mich so Stück für Stück bis zum Betriebsleiter hochgearbeitet. Es ist ein vielseitiger und interessanter Beruf. Heute bin ich auch in die Durchführung vieler Veranstaltungen – vom Radlrennen bis zur Oldtimerausfahrt – und auch Filmproduktionen involviert. Manchmal hat man das Gefühl, hier ist mehr los als in Hollywood.

Die Straße ist meist von Anfang Mai bis Ende Oktober geöffnet. Womit beschäftigen Sie sich im Winter? Die Wintersaison beginnt bei uns meist schon Anfang Oktober, bevor der große Schnee kommt, wenn wir die Schneestangen setzen, um die Straße im Frühjahr bei der Schneeräumung überhaupt wiederzufinden. Dann beginnen wir damit, die Gebäude, die früher als Unterkünfte für die Arbeiter dienten und heute Ausstellungen und Geschäfte beherbergen, entlang der Strecke winterfest zu machen. Im Winter werden in den Werkstätten dann die Revisionen an den Maschinen und den alten Schneefräsen durchgeführt. Auch die Verwaltung hat das ganze Jahr zu tun.

What brought you to the Grossglockner High Alpine Road and how long have you been working here? I'm currently in my fortieth year at the company and I've worked in all of its departments. I grew up 100 meters from the road, so I've known it since I was a child even though my family only used it occasionally back then. I'm a qualified car mechanic. In April 1979, right after my apprenticeship, I started working with the road patrol. I spent my first day as a rotary plow co-driver on snow-clearing duty. In the years that followed I worked as a snow clearer, machine operator, a member of the safety team, and in avalanche blasting. I subsequently attained my mechanic's master certificate, managed the magazine, and gradually worked my way up to Works Manager. It's a varied, interesting job. I'm currently also involved in the organization of many events, from cycling races to vintage car meetings, and in film productions, too. Sometimes it feels as if there's more happening here than in Hollywood.

The road is usually open from the start of May to the end of October. What do you do during the winter? Our winter season usually begins at the start of October, before the first major snowfall, when we plant the snow stakes that enable us to find the road again in the spring when we're clearing the snow. Then we start winterproofing the buildings along the route that formerly housed our workers and are now used for exhibitions and businesses. Over the winter, the machines and the old slow blowers are repaired and maintained in the workshops. There's also administrative work to be done all year round.

So how exactly is the famous snow clearing carried

Wie läuft die berühmte Schneeräumung denn genau ab? Anfang April gehen wir meist auf einen ersten Kontrollflug, um die Schnee- und Lawinensituation zu beurteilen. Ab Mitte April wird dann auf beiden Seiten der Straße mit der Räumung begonnen. Dann wird die vom Schnee bedeckte Straße entlang der talseitig gesetzten Schneestangen von erfahrenen Bergführern, die auch die Lawinengefahr gut einschätzen können, vermessen. Die Schneefreimachung dauert ungefähr 15 bis 20 Tage, insgesamt sind zwei Räumtrupps, einer von der Nordseite und einer von der Südseite, mit vier Rotationspflügen im Einsatz. Vorweg fährt jeweils eine Pistenraupe, die den Weg für die Arbeiter und Schneefräsen frei schieben, sowie Traktoren immer wieder auch Unimogs, die für Versuchszwecke getestet werden.

Was macht die von Franz Wallack in den 1950er-Jahren konstruierten Rotationsschneepflüge so effizient, dass sie noch immer im Einsatz sind? In den ersten Wintern nach der Eröffnung wurde die Straße ja noch per Hand geräumt, 350 Mann haben da geschaufelt. Ab 1938 haben sie die ersten, damals noch sehr schwerfälligen Schneefräsen getestet und die Straße bis Mitte der 1940er-Jahre mit alten umgebauten Militärfahrzeugen geräumt. Das Besondere an den Schneepflügen von Hofrat Wallack ist das Kettenlaufwerk, mit dem man problemlos auf dem Schnee fahren kann. Schon der Prototyp hatte Messinstrumente an Bord, mit denen sich die einwirkenden Kräfte haben messen lassen. Die insgesamt fünf Fräsen wurden dann ab 1953 im Motormuliwerk, den heutigen Reformwerken, in Wels gebaut. Jede Maschine hatte drei Motoren – einen für die Vorwärtsbewegung und das Herunterschneiden des Schnees und zwei für das Auswerfen des Schnees zur Seite hin. Im Schnitt können wir eine Schneehöhe von 1,20 Meter und eine Breite von 2,40 Meter schichtweise fräsen. Wenn sich die Schneefräsen mit 1 km/h fortbewegt, werden rund 2.000 Kubikmeter Schnee pro Stunde durch die Auswurfkanäle geblasen. So leisten uns die Schneefräsen nach mehr als 60 Jahren noch immer beste Dienste. Jede Fräse trägt übrigens die Vornamen ihrer Erbauer im Reformwerk – nur der Name »Eisbändiger« geht auf den Spitznamen von Hofrat Wallack zurück.

Und die Schneeräumung läuft immer nach Plan? Nein. Es kommt auch vor, dass es während der Räumung einen Wettersturz gibt und wir uns sogar zurückziehen müssen, damit uns nicht von Lawinen der Weg zurück ins Tal abgeschnitten wird. 2017 hatten wir Ende April zwei Meter Neuschnee, aber eigentlich werden solche Wintereinbrüche mit dem Klimawandel immer seltener.

Ist eine Straße im Hochgebirgswinter nicht gewaltigen Kräften ausgesetzt, die an der Substanz zehren? Frostschäden gibt es fast nicht, weil die Straße ja vom Schnee geschützt wird. Meist etwas ausgebessert werden muss die Straße vor allem dort, wo Lawinen abgegangen sind. Wobei wir die Lawinenstriche natürlich kennen und

out? At the start of April, we usually perform a preliminary inspection flight to assess the snow and avalanche situation. From mid-April onwards, we start clearing on both sides of the road. Experienced mountain guides who are also skilled in judging the avalanche risk measure the snow-covered road along the snow stakes planted on the valley side. The snow clearing takes about 15 to 20 days with two clearing squads and four rotary plows in action, one from the north side and one from the south. A snowcat drives ahead of each squad, clearing a path for the workers and the snow blowers, along with tractors and occasionally also Unimogs that are used for test purposes.

What makes the rotary snow plows designed by Franz Wallack in the 1950s so efficient that they're still being used today? In the first winters after it was opened the road was cleared by hand, with 350 men working with shovels. In 1938 they began testing the first, initially very sluggish snow blowers, and up to the mid-1940s cleared the road with old, remodeled military vehicles. What is special about Counselor Wallack's snow plows is the crawler track that allows them to drive easily on snow. Even the prototype had instruments on board that could measure the acting forces. From 1953 onwards, all five blowers were built in the Motormuli plant in Wels, the present-day Reform factory. Each machine has three motors, one for forward motion and for cutting down the snow, and two for throwing the snow to the side. On average we can cut the snow in layers 1.20 meters high and 2.40 meters wide. When the snow blowers advance at 1 km/h, around 2,000 cubic meters of snow per hour is blown out of the chutes. Even after more than 60 years, these snow blowers do a great job for us. Incidentally, each blower was given the first name of the person who built it at the Reform factory, with the machine known as the "Ice Tamer" bearing Counselor Wallack's nickname.

And the snow clearing always goes according to plan? No. The weather can turn bad during the clearing and we may even have to pull out due to the risk of avalanches cutting off our path back down to the valley. In 2017 we had two meters of fresh snow at the end of April, although with climate change these returns of winter weather are becoming rarer.

Isn't a road high in the mountains exposed to the wear and tear of tremendous forces in winter? There's hardly any frost damage because the road is protected by the snow. Any repair work on the road is usually required in the places where avalanches have occurred. At the same time, we know the avalanche points, and during winterproofing we remove anything that could be swept off into the valley. And after the road has been opened and the sun gets stronger, there is a risk of slipping snow avalanches, especially on the southern slopes. Up to the end of May, we observe the snow situation closely and

MIT FREUNDLICHER GENEHMIGUNG
COURTESY OF:
GROHAG ARCHIV

beim Einwintern alles abmontieren, was mit ins Tal gerissen werden könnte. Auch nach Eröffnung der Straße, wenn die Sonne an Kraft gewinnt, besteht vor allem auf den Südhängen die Gefahr von Gleitschneelawinen. Bis Ende Mai beobachten wir die Schneesituation genau und sprengen, wo es nötig ist. Im Sommer sind wir dann damit beschäftigt, die Infrastruktureinrichtungen instand zu halten, Stützmauern zu sanieren und während der Betriebszeiten den Streckendienst durchzuführen. Jeden Tag fährt ein Mitarbeiter eine Stunde vor Straßenöffnung die Strecke ab, kontrolliert sie auf Schäden und gibt sie für den Verkehr frei.

Die Straße steht ja seit 2015 unter Denkmalschutz. Gleichzeitig muss die Straße ja ständig ausgebessert und gesichert werden. Wie verträgt sich das? Die Straße steht ja nicht nur unter Denkmalschutz, die Naturschutzauflagen des Nationalparks spielen ebenfalls eine Rolle, auch wenn rechts und links der Straße ein Geländestreifen vom Naturschutz ausgenommen ist. Wenn wir Elemente der Straße oder Gebäude sanieren, müssen sie so wieder hergestellt werden, wie sie zuvor gewesen sind. Verändert werden darf nichts. Das haben wir in der Betreibergesellschaft aber eigentlich immer so gehalten: Schon Hofrat Wallack hat den Naturschutz beim Bau der Straße sehr bedacht. Wiesenstücke wurden samt Wurzelwerk abgetragen, gelagert und vorsichtig wieder eingefügt. Für ihn musste alles stimmen. Die Betonabstützungen um Kehre 8 stammen derweil aus den 1980er-Jahren – das wäre nach heutigen Denkmalschutzbestimmungen nicht mehr möglich. Davon abgesehen ist Beton im Hochgebirge auch sehr wartungsintensiv und deshalb nicht ideal.

Würde der Welterbestatus Ihre Arbeit noch schwieriger machen? Die UNESCO-Bewerbung hat ja eher eine symbolische Bedeutung und schreibt nichts vor, sondern basiert vielmehr auf dem nationalen Denkmalschutz. Ich finde die Initiative nicht schlecht, solange der Tourismus nicht wie etwa in Hallstadt-Dachstein

> Schon Hofrat Wallack hat den Naturschutz beim Bau der Straße sehr bedacht. Wiesenstücke wurden samt Wurzelwerk abgetragen, gelagert und vorsichtig wieder eingefügt.

> Even Counselor Wallack was very cognizant of nature conservation when the road was being built. Areas of meadow, roots and all, were removed, put into storage and carefully reinstated afterwards.

blast wherever it's necessary. In the summer we're kept busy maintaining the infrastructure equipment, repairing the retaining walls and servicing the road during the operating hours. Every day, an hour before the road is opened, an employee drives the route, checks it for damage and approves it for traffic.

In 2015 the road was given protected historic status. At the same time, the road has to be continually repaired and secured. How are these things compatible? The road doesn't just have protected historic status; the nature conservation requirements of the national park also play a role, even though a strip of ground on the right and left of the road is excluded from this nature conservation. When we repair elements of the road or buildings, they have to look the same again afterwards. We're not allowed to change anything. But this has actually always been our approach in the operating company: Even Counselor Wallack was very cognizant of nature conservation when the road was being built. Areas of meadow, roots and all, were removed, put into storage and carefully reinstated afterwards. He wanted everything to be perfect. The concrete supports at bend 8 are from the 1980s; something like this wouldn't be possible under today's historical preservation requirements. Additionally, concrete requires a lot of maintenance in a high mountain region and is therefore less than ideal.

Would world heritage status make your job even more difficult? The UNESCO application is mainly of symbolic significance and does not prescribe anything,

Rotationspflug
Bauart Wallack

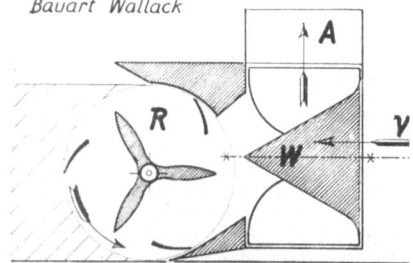

R = Rotationspflug
W = Wurfrad
A = Auswurfkamin

Schleuderpflug „Crosti"

V = Vortriebsrichtung
W = Wurfrichtung

Schleuderpflug „Schneekönig"

V: Vortriebsrichtung
W: Wurfrichtung

Peterfräse
Bauart Schallert

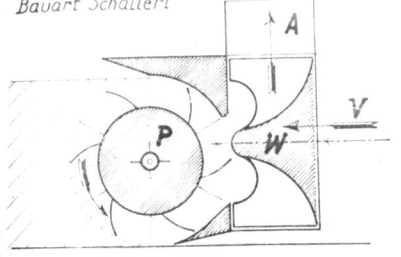

P = Peterfräse
W = Wurfrad
A = Auswurfkamin
V = Vortriebsrichtung

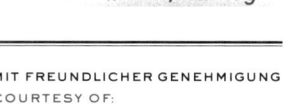

MIT FREUNDLICHER GENEHMIGUNG
COURTESY OF:
GROHAG ARCHIV

GROSSGLOCKNER HOCHALPENSTRASSE · PORSCHE DRIVE

PERSPEKTIVEN / PERSPECTIVES — 267

Überhand nimmt. Bei uns konzentriert sich ja immer alles auf die Schönwettertage, bei schlechtem Wetter und schlechter Sicht ist die Straße leer. Dabei haben wir entlang der Straße viele interessante Ausstellungen, da kann man auch mal ein Wochenende in der Region bleiben.

Auf der Straße sind ja nicht nur Touristen unterwegs, man sieht auch fast immer Prototypen neuer Autos. Die Glocknerstraße war immer schon eine Versuchsstraße für die Automobilhersteller. Der Motor und das Getriebe des VW Käfer sind ja hier am Berg entwickelt worden. Bis heute kommen Hersteller aus der ganzen Welt zum Testen zu uns. Vor allem die Elektromobilität rückt in den Fokus, und der Energiebedarf auf einer Hochalpenstraße ist natürlich besonders groß. Momentan haben wir drei Ladestationen entlang der Straße.

Die Großglockner Hochalpenstraße gilt vielen sportlichen Fahrern als Rennstrecke unter freiem Himmel. Was halten Sie davon? Ich fahre auch gerne zügig, aber ich kenne die Straße und weiß: die erlaubten 100 km/h sind am Berg einfach zu schnell, zu gefährlich und auch zu laut. Die Bergsteiger an den gegenüberliegenden Hängen fallen vor Schreck ja fast aus der Wand, wenn ein Sportwagen auf der Straße beschleunigt. Auch Sportwagentouren haben stark zugenommen, und die Fahrer überholen im Pulk in schlecht einsehbaren Kurven ohne Kenntnis der Straße, Kopf und Verstand. Die Behörden begrenzen das Tempo aber nicht auf 70 km/h, da die allermeisten Autofahrer ihrer Ansicht nach sowieso langsamer unterwegs sind. Aber wir haben mittlerweile die Befugnis, besonders dreiste Raser aufzuhalten, zu ermahnen und anzuzeigen. Auch Radarmessungen führen wir durch. Wir haben seit einigen Jahren auch immer mehr Motorradfahrer. Denn wenn ein Unfall passiert, ist meist ein Motorrad beteiligt. Wir haben jetzt in den Kurven Ellipsen auf den Asphalt aufgezeichnet, die die Motorradfahrer vom Kurvenschneiden abhalten. Das funktioniert. Generell gilt: Wer Vollgas geben und sich austoben will, sollte zum Salzburgring fahren und nicht auf die Glocknerstraße.

Zu welcher Jahreszeit ist es hier oben am schönsten? Die Schneeräumung und Eröffnung der Straße nach einem langen Winter ist natürlich ein Highlight. Dann ist es schön zu beobachten, wie Höhenschicht für Höhenschicht die Vegetation aus dem Winterschlaf erwacht und die Murmeltiere aus ihren Bauten kommen. Am schönsten ist es für mich aber im Herbst, wenn es wieder ruhiger wird, die Lärchen in den Wäldern ihre Farbe wechseln, die Sicht aufklart und man selbst die entferntesten Gipfel am Horizont erkennen kann.

Und von wo hat man den schönsten Blick? Von der Edelweiß-Spitze, eindeutig. Wenn man zeitig in der Früh aufsteht und dort oben noch vor Sonnenaufgang seinen Tag beginnt, das ist schon etwas ganz Besonderes.

being based on the national historical preservation order. I think the initiative is fine as long as the tourism doesn't get out of hand, like in Hallstatt-Dachstein, for example. In our case, we're always busiest when the weather is good. If the weather's bad and the view is poor, the road is empty. Having said that, we have a lot of interesting exhibitions along the route, making a weekend in the region an attractive option, too.

You don't just see tourists driving on the road; there are almost always prototypes of new cars out there. The Glocknerstrasse has always been a test road for car manufacturers. The engine and transmission of the VW Beetle were developed up here on the mountain. Manufacturers from all over the world still come here to do their tests. The focus is increasingly on electromobility, and the energy requirements on a high alpine road are particularly stringent. At present we have three charging stations along the road.

Many sports drivers see the Grossglockner High Alpine Road as an outdoor racing circuit. What do you think about this? I also like driving fast, but I know the road and know that the permitted 100 km/h is too much in the mountains, too dangerous and too loud as well. The climbers on the opposite slopes nearly fall off the mountain in shock when a sports car accelerates on the road. There has also been a big increase in sports car tours, with the drivers overtaking wholesale on curves with little visibility, without any knowledge of the road, and without thinking. However, the authorities haven't lowered the speed limit to 70 km/h because they reckon that the majority of drivers go slower than this anyway. But we're now authorized to stop, caution and charge particularly brazen speeders. We also conduct radar measurements. In recent years we've also had more and more motorbike riders. When an accident happens, a motorbike is involved in most cases. We've put ellipses on the asphalt on the bends to keep the motorbike riders from cutting corners. And this is working. The general rule is that if you want to go full throttle and let off some steam, you go to the Salzburgring, not the Glocknerstrasse.

What part of the year is the most beautiful up here? The snow clearing and the opening of the road after a long winter is naturally a highlight. It's lovely to see how from one altitude level to the next the vegetation awakens from its winter sleep and the marmots emerge from their burrows. However, my favorite season is fall, when things calm down again, the larches change color in the woods, the view clears, and you can see the very farthest peaks on the horizon.

And where is the most beautiful view to be had? On the Edelweiss-Spitze, most definitely. If you get up early and start your day up there before the sun has risen, that's a really special experience.

MIT FREUNDLICHER GENEHMIGUNG
COURTESY OF:
GROHAG/SVEN SIMON

WALTER RÖHRL

Walter Röhrl gilt als bester Rallyefahrer aller Zeiten und hat sein Leben vorzugsweise im Drift verbracht. Was weniger bekannt ist: Der Rallyemeister und Porsche-Versuchsfahrer ist auch ein begeisterter und beeindruckend rasanter Radfahrer. In den Achtziger- und Neunzigerjahren saß Walter Röhrl jedes Jahr als Konditionstraining bis zu 10.000 Kilometer auf dem Sattel und fuhr in den Ferien sogar mit Profi-Radrennfahrer Eddy Merckx und anderen Helden der Tour de France über französische und italienische Alpenpässe. Die Großglockner Hochalpenstraße hat Walter Röhrl sowohl mit dem Sportwagen als auch mit dem Rennrad bezwungen. Und noch eine Erkenntnis: Walter Röhrl hat keine Zeit mit langen Antworten zu verlieren. Der Mann folgt auch bei Interviews präzise der Ideallinie!

Walter Röhrl is considered the best rally driver of all time – and has happily devoted most of his life to drifting around bends in a rally car. A lesser known fact about this rally champion and Porsche test driver is that he is also an enthusiastic and impressively fast cyclist. In the 1980s and 1990s, Walter Röhrl spent up to 10,000 kilometers every year in the saddle to keep fit, and even biked over French and Italian Alpine passes in the holidays with professional cyclist Eddy Merckx and other heroic Tour de France riders. Walter Röhrl has mastered the Grossglockner High Alpine Road in both a sports car and on a racing bike. And another realization we had is that Walter Röhrl has no time to waste giving long answers to questions. Even in interviews, the man opts for the ideal racing line.

Herr Röhrl, Sie haben die Großglockner Hochalpenstraße sowohl mit dem Auto als auch auf dem Rennrad oft befahren. Gibt es ein Erlebnis, dass Ihnen eindrücklich in Erinnerung geblieben ist? Mit dem Auto bin ich im Rahmen einer Classic Rallye den Glockner von der Nordseite gefahren, die Sicht war maximal zehn bis 20 Meter! Mit dem Rennrad bin ich 1987 als Geburtstagsgeschenk mit einem Freund (langsam) gefahren. Nachdem ich zwei Wochen vorher beim Pikes Peak Bergrennen in Colorado war, wo ich täglich mit dem Rennrad in der Höhe von 3.000 Metern circa 100 Kilometer trainiert hatte, stellte sich die Supercompensation anscheinend genau an diesem Tag ein und ich fuhr den Glockner mit der Übersetzung 42:21.

Die Strecke von Ferleiten bis zum Fuscher Törl gilt als »Königsetappe« der Österreichrundfahrt. Ist der Aufstieg per Rennrad wirklich so hart? Ja! Man sollte am Anfang mit einer guten Einteilung angehen, sonst wird's oben eng.

Was ist ihre persönliche Rekordzeit mit dem Rad? Eine Stunde und sechs Minuten.

Die Glocknerstraße gilt als eine der schönsten Panoramastraßen der Alpen. Ist sie auch für einen Rallyemeister wie Sie fahrerisch interessant? Ja, die schnellen Kurven zwischen den Kehren sind das Sahnestück.

Haben Sie einen bevorzugten Straßenabschnitt? Den schnellen Anfang und das Mittelstück mag ich gern.

Die Glocknerstraße ist sanfter geschwungen als etwa das Stilfser Joch. Haben Sie Tipps, wie man sie mit den Sportwagen optimal fährt? Kehren zu fahren ist nicht schwer. Spaß machen die mittelschnellen Kurven, welche man weich und auf Zug fahren sollte.

Welcher Porsche wäre ihr Favorit für eine sportliche Glocknerausfahrt an einem schönen Sommertag? Ein Porsche Carrera GT von 2003.

Mr. Röhrl, you have negotiated the Grossglockner High Alpine Road both in a car and on a racing bike. Is there any one experience that particularly sticks in your mind? I drove the Glockner from the north during one Classic Rally – visibility was ten to 20 meters at most! I rode my racing bike there with a friend (slowly) as a birthday present in 1987. After being at Pikes Peak Hill Climb race in Colorado two weeks previously where I had trained about 100 kilometers a day on the road bike at an altitude of 3,000 meters, the supercompensation seemed to kick in on precisely that day and I rode the Glockner with a 42:21 gear ratio.

The route from Ferleiten to Fuscher Törl is regarded as the "crowning stage" of the tour of Austria. Is this ascent on a racing bike really that hard? Yes! You have to get well up the classification at the beginning, otherwise it gets tight at the top.

What is your personal best time with the bike? One hour and six minutes.

The Glockner Road is one of the most stunning panoramic roads in the Alps. As a rally car champion, do you find it interesting to ride the road on a bike? Yes, the fast curves between the hairpin bends are the real deal.

Do you have a favorite section of the High Alpine Road? I like the fast start and the middle section.

The Glockner Road has gentler curves than those of the Stelvio Pass for example. Do you have any tips on how to drive the Glockner in a sports car? It's not difficult to drive along the curves. The medium-fast curves are fun, you have to drive these smoothly while keeping the speed on.

Which Porsche – the vintage and model – would be your favorite pick for a sporty ride along the Glockner Road on a beautiful summer's day? A 2003 Porsche Carrera GT.

FRANZ SCHWARZ

Was ist Ihre erste Erinnerung an die Großglockner Hochalpenstraße? Die noch vorhandenen Gletscher.

Was macht die Straße so besonders? Sehr gut ausgebaut und der grandiose Panoramablick.

Sie waren auf der Glocknerstraße schon mit dem Rennrad, dem Motorrad und dem Sportwagen unterwegs. Wie unterscheidet erlebt man die Straße – und mit welchem »Gerät« ist das Fahrerlebnis am schönsten? Mit dem Motorrad und Sportwagen ist man eher sportlich unterwegs und dann aufs Fahren orientiert. Mit dem Rennrad ist das Fahrerlebnis am schönsten man bekommt mehr von der Aussicht, Natur und Tierwelt mit.

Welche Tipps würden Sie einem Radfahrer geben, die die Strecke zum ersten Mal fährt? Sehr früh losfahren, nicht zu schnell am Anfang und die richtige Übersetzung, z.B. 34:29

Nimmt man die grandiose Landschaft als Rennradler in den letzten Kehren vor dem Hochtor überhaupt noch wahr? Ganz besonders sogar weil man es fast geschafft hat.

Ihre persönliche Bestzeit? Von Fusch aus 1 Stunde und 35 Minuten

Wie fühlt man sich, wenn man oben angekommen ist? Es ist immer ein sehr gutes Gefühl wieder einen Paß geschafft zu haben.

Welche Kurven und Streckenabschnitte machen mit dem Motorrad am meisten Spaß? Eher die engeren oberen mit noch Gletscherblick.

Mit welchem »Sportgerät« würden Sie die Glocknerstraße gern einmal befahren? Mit einem Singlespeed Rad, widerspricht aber der obigen Übersetzung.

Stimmt es, dass man Alpenpässe wie die Glocknerstraße mit klassischen Autos, Motorrädern und Fahrrädern intensiver erleben kann? Das stimmt, man nimmt die Landschaft und das Fahrerlebnis bewusster war, besonders mit offenen Old-/Youngtimern und Fahrrädern.

Was wünschen Sie sich für die Zukunft der Alpenstraßen? Weniger Massentourismus mit Reisebussen und Wohnmobilen und mehr Autofreie Wochenende wie es schon in Südtirol praktiziert wird.

What's your first memory of the Grossglockner High Alpine Road? The glaciers that still existed back then.

What makes the road so special? It's very well-developed and has spectacular panoramic views.

You've already been on the Glockner Road on a racing bike, a motorcycle and a sports car. How differently do you experience the road – and which vehicle makes the driver's or rider's experience most enjoyable? You are more likely to be into the sports aspect with a motorcycle or sports car and then more focused on the driving. The rider's experience is best on a racing bike because you take in more of the scenery, nature and wildlife.

What tips would you offer a cyclist who will be riding the route for the first time? Get a very early start, don't go too fast at first and make sure you have the right gear ratio, 34:29, for instance.

As a racing cyclist, are you even aware of the awe-inspiring countryside by the final hairpin turns before the Hochtor? Yes, even more so because you have almost made it.

Your personal best time? An hour and 35 minutes starting at Fusch.

How do you feel when you have reached the top? It's always a very good feeling to have reached a pass again.

Which curves and stretches are the most fun on a motorcycle? The tighter ones higher up that still have views of the glacier.

Which kind of sports vehicle would you like to use to drive or ride the Glockner Road that you haven't used yet? A single speed bicycle, but that contradicts the gear ratio mentioned above.

Is it true that you can experience Alpine passes like the Glockner Road more intensively with classic cars, motorcycles and bicycles? That's true, you can experience the countryside and the driving feeling more consciously, especially with convertible classic cars, modern classics and bicycles.

What is your wish for the future of the Alpine roads? Less mass tourism with tour busses and campers and more car-free weekends, as they already have put into practice in South Tyrol.

ERIKA SALLABERGER & HARTMUT HENKEL

Hartmut Henkel war 24 Jahre alt, als er 1964 das Restaurant Fuschertörl auf 2.430 Meter Seehöhe als Hüttenwirt pachtete. Der Glocknertourismus erlebte damals gerade seinen Höhepunkt, unzählige Touristen auf dem Weg nach Italien machten an der Passstraße Station. Das Leben der vierköpfigen Familie am Berg war nicht einfach, und doch hätten Hartmut Henkel und seine Frau an keinem anderen Ort leben und arbeiten wollen. Denn die Bergluft hält fit: Hartmut Henkel sieht man seine 76 Jahre wirklich nicht an! Seit Ende der Neunzigerjahre betreiben nun seine Tochter Erika Sallaberger gemeinsam mit ihrem Mann Robert das Restaurant. Sie leben im Tal und fahren von Mai bis Oktober jeden Morgen die Straße hinauf. Ihre Kurven kennen sie im Schlaf.

Hartmut Henkel was 24 years old when he signed the lease that made him the innkeeper at the Restaurant Fuscher Toerl, situated at an altitude of 2,430 meters. At the time, the Grossglockner was at the peak of its popularity as a tourist destination, with innumerable tourists on their way to Italy stopping off at the pass. Life on the mountain wasn't easy for the four-member family, and yet there's no other place in the world that Hartmut Henkel and his wife would have wanted to live and work. After all, the alpine air keeps you fit: Hartmut Henkel really doesn't look like he's 76! His daughter, Erika Sallaberger, has been running the restaurant with her husband Robert since the end of the nineties. They live in the valley and drive up the mountain road every day between May and October. They could master its curves in their sleep.

Ein nebeliger Nachmittag im Mai, auf Besuch in der gemütlichen Gaststube. Im Radio läuft Ziehharmonikamusik, es gibt Kaffee und Kuchen. Neben uns zeigt ein ausgestopftes Murmeltier seine Zähne. Die Berghänge vor den Fenstern sind noch tief verschneit. Wir blättern in einem alten Fotoalbum: alte Autos, Kindergesichter, die Kurven der Straße, Erinnerungen.

Herr Henkel, Sie haben die alte Hütte am Fuscher Törl Mitte der Sechzigerjahre gepachtet. Wie kann man sich das Leben am Berg zu dieser Zeit vorstellen? *Hartmut Henkel:* Es war alles noch ganz primitiv: Kein Wasser, kein Strom, beleuchtet wurde mit Gaslampen, und der Kühlschrank wurde mit Eis vom Gletscher gekühlt. Im Frühjahr sind wir meist schon zwei Wochen vor der Eröffnung der Straße auf Ski hier heraufgestiegen und haben das Haus und die Quelle freigeschaufelt. Den Sommer über haben wir dann mit unseren beiden Kindern sechs Monate lang hier oben gelebt und gearbeitet, jeden Tag zwölf bis 15 Stunden. Wenn man morgens um sechs Uhr aufgestanden ist, musste man erst einmal den Kohleofen einheizen. Wir haben uns im Keller auch mit einem Schlauch eine Dusche selbst gebaut, die Temperatur musste aber oben in der Küche geregelt werden: Einmal an die Decke klopfen hieß »zu heiß«, zweimal Klopfen »zu kalt«. Die Gäste aus dem Tal konnten oft nicht verstehen, dass wir kein Wasser hatten, wenn die Quelle noch zugefroren war, und dass wir unseren Strom selbst generieren mussten. Für uns war das ganz normal. Irgendwann wurde dann der Kanal gebaut und Stromleitungen verlegt, das machte das Leben natürlich einfacher. Später hatten wir das erste und lange Zeit auch einzige Telefon am

It's a misty May afternoon when we stop in for a visit to the cozy restaurant. Accordion music is playing on the radio, and coffee and cake are being served. We sit next to a stuffed marmot which seems to be gnashing its teeth at us. The mountainsides outside the window are still covered in deep snow. We leaf through an old photo album: Old cars, children's faces, the winding road, memories.

Mr. Henkel, you signed the lease for the old hut at Fuscher Toerl in the mid-sixties. What was life on the mountain like back then? *Hartmut Henkel:* Everything was still really primitive: No water, no electricity, we used gas lamps for lighting, and the refrigerator was cooled using ice from the glacier. We usually came up here on skis in the spring, two weeks before the road was opened, and shoveled the house and the well free from snow. We stayed here all summer long, living and working up here for six months with both our children, spending twelve to 15 hours a day on the job. When you start the day by getting up at six o'clock, then the first thing you need to do is light the coal stove. We used a hose to make ourselves a shower in the basement, the temperature of which was controlled upstairs from the kitchen: Banging on the ceiling once meant "too hot", banging twice meant "too cold". The guests coming up from the valley couldn't understand why we didn't have water when the well was still frozen, and that we had to generate our own power. That was all routine for us. At some point in time, water mains were built and power lines installed up here, which, of course, made life a lot easier. Later on, we also had the first, and for a long time, the only telephone on Grossglockner. If someone called to speak

Großglockner. Wenn jemand für den Wirt auf der Edelweiß-Spitze angerufen hat, bin ich hochgefahren und habe Bescheid gegeben.

Wie haben sich Haus und Gäste denn über all die Jahre verändert? *Hartmut Henkel:* Das alte Haus diente zu Zeiten des Straßenbaus als Baubaracke. Meine Urgroßeltern haben kurz nach der Eröffnung im Sommer 1935 ein Restaurant daraus gemacht – mit Silberbesteck, Kaviar, dem Besten vom Besten. Nur höher gestellte Leute konnten es sich damals leisten, mit dem eigenen Auto hier heraufzufahren. Der Glockner war damals die größte Attraktion des Landes. Das Hauptgebäude mit 40 Fremdenbetten und Tankstelle war etwas weiter unten gelegen. In den Bergen zu übernachten, war noch bis in die späten Sechzigerjahre sehr beliebt. Die Autos waren ja auch noch nicht so schnell und zuverlässig wie heute, und viele Reisende auf dem Weg nach Italien sind bei uns abgestiegen. Auch die Gäste aus dem Tal kamen schon in der Früh, um den Sonnenaufgang zu sehen, und haben dann bei uns gefrühstückt. Das hatte Tradition. Vor 40 Jahren haben wir das alte Haus dann abgerissen und ein neues gebaut.

Frau Sallaberger, wie ist es, als Kind im Hochgebirge aufzuwachsen? *Erika Sallaberger:* Nicht lustig. Hier oben geht oft der Wind. Viele Möglichkeiten zum Spielen gibt es auch nicht, also waren wir nur selten draußen. Als Kind will man auch nicht ständig Wandern gehen oder im Restaurant mithelfen. Wenn die Freunde im Tal ins Schwimmbad gingen, saßen wir hier oben auf dem Berg – wenn wir Pech hatten, im Schnee. Die Zeit, in der es hier oben wirklich schneefrei ist, beträgt vielleicht vier Wochen im Jahr. Deswegen war ich mir immer sicher, dass ich das Restaurant niemals übernehmen würde und habe einen anderen Berufsweg eingeschlagen. Doch als mein Vater in Pension ging, fand ich die Vorstellung, das von ihm aufgebaute Haus einfach aufzugeben, doch zu schade – und habe es ausprobiert. Im ersten Sommer hier oben habe ich meinen Mann kennengelernt. Er war sehr gerne in den Bergen und sagte: Ich komme mit dir da rauf. Das ist jetzt 19 Jahre her.

Was hat sich seit Ihren Kindertagen hier oben verändert? *Erika Sallaberger:* Ich erinnere mich noch an die unzähligen Busreisenden, die bei uns früher zu Kaffee und Kuchen einkehrten. Die gibt es heute so gut wie gar nicht mehr – und wenn, dann beehren sie uns höchstens noch als Klotouristen. Spektakulär waren auch die Jahre nach dem Fall des Eisernen Vorhangs – die Gäste aus den Ostblockländern sind hier fast überfallartig eingefallen: Wir haben morgens Dutzende Teller mit Torten vorbereitet und Hunderte Kaffee vorgekocht, um gegen den täglichen Ansturm gewappnet zu sein. In den letzten Jahren haben dann die Motorrad- und Rennradfahrer massiv zugelegt. Außerdem haben wir immer mehr Gäste aus Asien, die haben wohl gerade den Glockner für sich entdeckt.

to the innkeeper on the Edelweissspitze peak, then I'd drive up there and let him know.

How has the building, and its guests, changed over all the years? *Hartmut Henkel:* The old building was used as a builder's shack back when the road was being built. My great-grandparents turned it into a restaurant just after the road was opened in the summer of 1935 – with silverware, caviar, the finest of the finest. Only the well-to-do could afford to drive up here with a vehicle of their own back then. Grossglockner was the country's biggest drawcard at the time. The main building with 40 beds for guests and a gas station was located a bit further down. Spending the night in the mountains remained a popular thing to do until the end of the sixties. After all, the cars weren't as fast and reliable as they are today, and many travelers stopped here for the night on their way to Italy. The guests used to come up from the valley early in the day to see the sun rise, and then have breakfast in our restaurant. That was a tradition. 40 years ago we tore down the old building and built a new one.

Mrs. Sallaberger, what is it like to spend your childhood high up in the mountains? *Erika Sallaberger:* It wasn't much fun. There's often a lot of wind up here. And there aren't many opportunities to play, so we didn't get outside very much. And as a kid, you don't really want to go hiking all the time, or help out in the restaurant. When our friends went to the pool down in the valley, we were sitting up here on the mountain – and if we were really unlucky, stuck in the snow. The period in which there isn't any snow at all up here only adds up to maybe four weeks a year. This is why I was always certain that I would never take over the running of the restaurant, and I chose a different career. And yet when my father retired, I found the idea of simply giving up the establishment that he set up too much of a shame – and I gave it a go. The first summer I spent up here I met my husband. He loved being in the mountains, and said: I'll join you up there. That's 19 years ago now.

What has changed up here since you were a child? *Erika Sallaberger:* I still remember all those tourists coming up here by coach, who used to stop off here for coffee and cake. That really doesn't happen anymore – and when they do come, then they only grace our restrooms with their presence. The years following the fall of the Iron Curtain were also spectacular – it was almost like an invasion when the guests from the Eastern Bloc arrived here: We used to prepare dozens of plates with cakes in the morning, and made hundreds of coffees in advance to prepare for the daily onslaught. In the last few years, the number of motorcyclists and cyclists has increased massively. And we have more and more visitors from Asia, who have only just discovered Grossglockner for themselves.

Wie gefällt Ihnen das Leben am Berg heute? *Erika Sallaberger:* Mittlerweile weiß ich es zu schätzen. Wenn man um fünf Uhr in der Früh von der Edelweiß-Spitze auf die Berge schaut, ist das unvergleichlich. Aber man arbeitet eben für sechs Monate im Jahr sieben Tage die Woche. Für die Familie bleibt da wenig Zeit. Das habe ich lernen müssen, und das erleben jetzt auch unsere Kinder. In der anderen Jahreshälfte hat man dann aber umso mehr Zeit und kann gemeinsam verreisen – in den Süden, um den Sommer nachzuholen. Es ist ein anderes Leben. Aber, wie ich finde, ein schönes.

Hatten Sie früher viel Kontakt zu den anderen »Bergmenschen«? *Hartmut Henkel:* Wenn es neblig war, kamen keine Gäste, dann saß man hier oben und hat mit den anderen Wirten tagelang Karten gespielt. Und man hat sich geholfen: Der Wirt von der Edelweiß-Spitze ist Mechaniker; wenn wir ein Problem mit dem Stromaggregat hatten, hat er es repariert. *Erika Sallaberger:* Es gab damals ein viel stärkeres Gemeinschaftsgefühl. Da gab es keinen Fernseher. Abends sind wir oft mitsamt dem ganzen Personal in den Bus gestiegen und auf die andere Seite zum Wallackhaus gefahren, weil da ein Fernseher stand. Ich erinnere mich noch, wie es einmal angefangen hat zu schneien und wir nachts fast nicht mehr zurückkamen. Herbert Haslinger, der heute als Mankeiwirt die Fuscherlacke betreibt, kam mit 15 Jahren als junger Koch zu meinem Vater. Meine Mutter ist Schwedin, und wir hatten immer schwedische Kindermädchen – eines ist jetzt mit dem Mankeiwirt verheiratet. Er war übrigens damals schon so tierlieb, er hatte Hunde, Papageien und auch Murmeltiere, die liefen hier frei herum. Mein Bruder und ich haben immer gerne mit den Murmeltierbabys gespielt. Wir hatten auch einmal einen Kellner, der sich einen Luchs gehalten hat. Das war manchmal schon skurril.

Gab es besondere Gäste, die Ihnen in Erinnerung geblieben sind? *Hartmut Henkel:* Einmal gab es Mitte Juli drei Tage am Stück Schneesturm, und die Straße war gesperrt. Bei uns haben dann zwanzig Motorradfahrer, die nicht mehr ins Tal herunterkamen, im Speisesaal übernachtet. Das war eine Gaudi. Auch die Testfahrer von BMW und von anderen Automarken haben für Stimmung gesorgt. Damals hatten wir dreimal in der Woche eine Hüttenparty, da wurde abends der Glühwein und der Jagertee getestet. Das hat sich aber wohl rumgesprochen, die Testfahrer haben dann nur noch rationierte Essensgutscheine bekommen. Vor 30 Jahren gab es auch einen Radfahrer, der jedes Wochenende von Salzburg zu uns herauf gefahren ist – der Mann war eine Attraktion. Sogar der Hundertwasser hat einmal bei uns übernachtet. Er meinte, wenn wir neu bauen, sollten wir alles mit Gras zuwachsen lassen, dann müssen wir nicht so viel heizen. Wir haben schon viel erlebt.

Wie lebt es sich mit dem Hochgebirgswetter? Und hat es sich über die Jahrzehnte verändert? *Hartmut Henkel:*

How do you like living on the mountain today? *Erika Sallaberger:* I've now learned to appreciate it. There's nothing that compares to taking in the view of the mountains from the Edelweiss-Spitze peak at five o'clock in the morning. You do, however, work seven days a week for six months of the year. There's not much time left for the family. That's something I had to learn, and now our children are also experiencing what it's like. But we have all the more time for the other half of the year, and can go traveling together – somewhere in the south, where we can catch up on summer. It's a different kind of life. But, for me, it's a good life.

Did you used to have a lot of contact with other "mountain people"? *Hartmut Henkel:* If it was foggy, then no guests would come, and we'd sit up here and play cards with the other innkeepers for days on end. And we helped each other out: The innkeeper from the Edelweissspitze peak is a mechanic; if we had problems with the power generator he'd repair it. *Erika Sallaberger:* We had a much stronger sense of community back then. We didn't have television. In the evening, we often got the bus, together with our entire staff, and drove to the Wallackhaus on the other side of the valley, because they had a television. I still remember when it once began to snow and we almost didn't make it back at night. Herbert Haslinger, who now runs the Fuscherlacke guesthouse and is known as the "marmot" innkeeper, first worked for my father as a 15-year-old cook. My mother is from Sweden, and we always had Swedish nannies – one of them is now married to the "marmot" innkeeper. He has, by the way, always had a love of animals, and kept dogs, parrots and marmots, which were always running around at large here. My brother and I always liked playing with the baby marmots. We once also had a waiter who kept a lynx. It was sometimes quite bizarre.

Were there any particular guests you still remember? *Hartmut Henkel:* Once there was a blizzard in the middle of July which lasted for three days, and the road was closed. There were twenty motorcyclists who couldn't get back down into the valley and who spent the three nights in our dining room. That was huge fun. The test drivers for BMW and other automotive brands were also very entertaining. Back then we had a party at the hut three times a week, where the evening was spent testing mulled wine and hot toddies. Word must have gotten around, because the test drivers then only received vouchers for meals, which were rationed. And 30 years ago there was a cyclist who used to ride up here to us from Salzburg every weekend – the man was a tourist attraction in himself. Even Friedensreich Hundertwasser once spent a night at our hotel. He said that if we were to build a new building, we should let grass grow on everything so we wouldn't have to heat as much. We really have seen a lot.

What is life like with the Alpine weather? And has it changed over the decades? *Hartmut Henkel:* The

Er war übrigens damals schon so tierlieb, hatte Hunde, Papageien und auch Murmeltiere, die liefen hier frei herum. Mein Bruder und ich haben immer gern mit den Murmeltierbabys gespielt. Wir hatten auch einmal einen Kellner, der sich einen Luchs gehalten hat. Das war manchmal schon skurril.

He has, by the way, always had a love of animals, and kept dogs, parrots and marmots, which were always running around at large here. My brother and I always liked playing with the baby marmots. We once also had a waiter who kept a lynx. It was sometimes quite bizarre.

Das Wetter hier oben ist schon extrem. Die Tage im Jahr, an denen man auf der Terrasse sitzen kann, kann man an einer Hand abzählen. Meist ist es zu windig oder zu kalt. Einmal gab es ein so starkes Gewitter, dass durch den Hagel alle Fenster zu Bruch gegangen sind. Früher war es so: Wenn es unten im Tal regnete, schneite es hier oben. Das ist heute nicht mehr unbedingt der Fall, es ist generell wärmer geworden. Als ich hier in den Sechzigerjahren angefangen habe, haben wir bis Mitte Juni Schnee geschaufelt. Anfang September war die Straße dann meist schon das erste Mal wieder derart zugeschneit, dass man nicht hochfahren konnte. Das passiert heute meist erst Mitte Oktober. Aber man stellt sich darauf ein: In einem Jahr mit einem besonders milden Winter haben sie auf der Straße um die Weihnachtszeit eine Rodelbahn eröffnet, die von hier oben bis Ferleiten ins Tal ging. Mit dem Postauto kamen die Leute hier rauf und sind mit dem Schlitten wieder runtergefahren. Das war ein Erlebnis. *Erika Sallaberger:* Mein Vater hat sein Leben lang Wetteraufzeichnungen betrieben – und immer wenn Schaltjahr war, hat es zwischen dem 10. und 20. Juli so geschneit, dass auch die Straße geschlossen wurde. Die Gäste hier oben müssen dann auf den Schneepflug warten und hinter ihm zurück ins Tal fahren. Die meisten Besucher unterschätzen die Höhe und stehen dann in Sandalen frierend im Schnee. Generell werden die Sommer aber tatsächlich immer wärmer. 2017 war es so heiß, dass man nicht mehr draußen sitzen konnte. Auch die Schneemenge war vor 20 Jahren deutlich größer

weather up here really is extreme. You only need one hand to count the number of days a year on which you can sit out on the terrace. It's usually too windy, or too cold. Once there was a thunderstorm so violent that the hail broke all the windows. It used to be the case that when it rained down in the valley, it was snowing up here. But that's not necessarily how it works these days, as it's generally become warmer. When I first started out here in the sixties, we were shoveling snow until the middle of June. And by early September the road was usually covered in so much snow for the first time that you couldn't drive up here. That usually doesn't happen until mid-October now. But you get used to everything: There was one year with a particularly mild winter when they opened a toboggan run on the road at Christmas time, which ran from up here down to Ferleiten in the valley. People came up here with the mail van and used a toboggan to make the descent. That was a great experience. *Erika Sallaberger:* My father has spent his life recording the weather – and every time there was a leap year, then it snowed so much between July 10 and 20 that the road was closed. The guests up here had to wait for the snow plough, and drive behind it to get back down to the valley. Most visitors underestimate the altitude, and end up standing around freezing in the snow in their sandals. In general, the summers are, in fact, getting warmer. In 2017 it was so hot that you couldn't sit outside any more. And the amount of snow was significantly higher 20 years ago than it is today. All

als heute. Durch die Webcams hat auch der Schönwettertourismus noch zugelegt: Ist es morgens bedeckt, haben wir auch keine Besucher. Bricht dann die Sonne durch, ist eine Stunde später alles voll.

Was ist die schönste Jahreszeit rund um die Glocknerstraße? *Hartmut Henkel:* Die Berge sehen ja jeden Tag anders aus. Anfang Mai, wenn die Straße aufgesperrt wird und die hohen Schneewände noch stehen … das ist schon imposant. Morgens steigt man dann auf den Brennkogel und den Kloben und fährt mit den Ski wieder runter, bevor man das Restaurant aufschließt – Frühsport. Mein Schwiegersohn Robert macht das heute jeden zweiten Tag. Das schönste Wetter hat man aber im September und Oktober. Es ist ein Paradies, aber auch das wird irgendwann alltäglich, wenn man darin lebt. *Erika Sallaberger:* Schön ist es im Frühling, wenn hier oben noch alles weiß und ruhig ist. Dann kommen aber schon bald die Rennfahrer, die sich im Tal ihre Sportwagen ausleihen und hier morgens in aller Frühe wie die Verrückten die Straße hoch rasen – das ist mühsam. Im Hochsommer ist es natürlich auch schön, aber da gibt es einfach zu viel Verkehr. Ab Mitte Juli bis Mitte August stauen sich die Autos ja manchmal von der Mautstelle bis zu uns herauf. Dann haben wir natürlich volles Haus. Mir persönlich gefällt auch der Herbst am besten, wenn die Autos weniger werden und sich die Natur gelb und orange färbt. Da sieht es hier oben manchmal aus wie im Märchen.

Und dann kommt der Winter … *Erika Sallaberger:* Ja, im Oktober beginnen wir damit, das Haus winterfest zu machen. Im Frühjahr kommt dann die große Überraschung. Jedes Jahr ist anders. Vor etwa 18 Jahren rief mich der Wirt der Edelweiß Spitze im Winter an, weil der Sturm unser Dach fortgeweht hatte. Wir mussten dann mit dem Helikopter einen neuen Dachstuhl auf den Berg fliegen. Silvester 2000 haben einige Leute die Fenster eingeschlagen und den Jahrtausendwechsel hier gefeiert. Im Frühjahr die Überreste der Party zu entsorgen war dann weniger witzig.

Was sind Ihre Lieblingsorte entlang der Großglocknerstraße? *Erika Sallaberger:* Ich mag das Panorama bei uns am Restaurant, natürlich die Edelweiß-Spitze mit ihrem Blick bis Zell am See, und die Aussicht nach Kehre 6 ins Käfertal hinein. Als Kinder haben wir oben am Brennkogel nach Bergkristallen gesucht, auch diese Bilder sind mir auch stark in Erinnerung geblieben.

Es sind diese persönlichen Erinnerungen und Bilder aus den privaten Fotoalben, in denen man der Geschichte der Großglockner Hochalpenstraße am nächsten kommt und die einem wiederum selbst noch lange lebhaft im Gedächtnis bleiben. Wenige Wochen nach unserem Gespräch ist Hartmut Henkel leider verstorben. Der besondere, von ihm und seiner Familie geschaffene Ort an der Glocknerstraße besteht fort.

the webcams mean that fair-weather tourism is on the rise: If it's cloudy in the morning, then we don't have any guests. If the clouds part and the sun starts shining, then everything's full an hour later.

What is the best time of year to be around the Grossglockner High Alpine Road? *Hartmut Henkel:* Well, the mountains do look different every day. In early May, when the road is first opened and there are still big banks of snow… that's an impressive sight. You can climb up Brennkogel and Kloben in the morning and ski back down again before opening up the restaurant – some early morning exercise! My son-in-law Robert now does that every other day. However, the best weather comes in September and October. It's a paradise, but even that becomes routine sooner or later when you're living right in the middle of it. *Erika Sallaberger:* It's lovely in spring, because everything up here is still so white and peaceful. Though that's when the racing drivers start coming, who rent their sports cars down in the valley in the morning and then speed up the road like maniacs – that can be tiresome. At the height of summer it is, of course, also beautiful, but there's simply too much traffic. Between mid-July and mid-August there's sometimes a traffic jam that starts at the tollbooth and only ends up here. Then, of course, we have a full house. I personally like fall the best, when there are fewer cars and nature starts turning yellow and orange. Sometimes it looks like a fairytale up here.

And that's followed by winter… *Erika Sallaberger:* Yes, in October we start winter-proofing the building. And in spring we always get a big surprise – every year is different. Around 18 years ago, the innkeeper from Edelweiss-Spitze called me, because a storm had blown off our roof. We then had to fly a new truss up to the mountain with a helicopter. On New Year's Eve 2000 there were some people who broke the windows and celebrated the new millennium here. Having to clean up the remnants of the party in spring wasn't nearly as much fun.

What are your favorite spots along the Grossglockner High Alpine road? *Erika Sallaberger:* I like the panorama from our restaurant, and of course the peak of Edelweiss-Spitze with its view extending all the way to Zell am See, as well as the vista down into Kaefertal you get after hairpin bend number 6. As kids we used to search for quartz crystals up on Brennkogel, and these images have also remained strong in my memory.

It is exactly these personal memories and the pictures from private photo albums that really make the history of the Grossglockner High Alpine Road come alive, and which will, in turn, remain vivid in our own memories for years to come. Sadly, only a few weeks after we talked, Hartmut Henkel passed away. Yet the special place that he and his family created on the Grossglockner High Alpine Road will live on.

DR. WOLFGANG PORSCHE

Die Geschichte von Porsche und die der Großglockner Hochalpenstraße sind seit jeher verbunden. Schon der Firmengründer Ferdinand Porsche erprobte auf der Alpenstraße seine automobilen Konstruktionen und erwarb 1941 am Fuße der Schmittenhöhe in Zell am See – nur wenige Fahrminuten vom Kilometer Null der Panoramastraße entfernt – einen alten Gutshof für seine Familie. In der Nachkriegszeit führte sein Sohn Ferry Porsche die Tradition der Bergtestfahrten mit wegweisenden Modellen wie dem Porsche 356 und dem 911 fort. Auch Ferrys Sohn Wolfgang, Jahrgang 1943, war als Bub oft als Beifahrer bei den Erprobungsfahrten auf den Glockner dabei. Heute wacht Dr. Wolfgang Porsche als Vorsitzender des Aufsichtsrats der Porsche AG und wichtigster Botschafter der Marke über die Geschicke des Konzerns. Die Fahrt vom Schüttgut, dem Familiensitz der Porsches in Zell am See, bis hinauf zum Hochtor gehört noch immer zu seinen liebsten Strecken.

Was ist Ihre früheste Erinnerung an die Glocknerstraße? Meine früheste Erinnerung sind die Fahrten mit meinem Vater über den Großglockner nach Gmünd in Kärnten, wohin unser Betrieb wegen der Kriegswirren

The histories of Porsche and the Grossglockner High Alpine Road have long been intertwined. Company founder Ferdinand Porsche tested his automotive designs on the Alpine road and in 1941 bought an old estate for his family at the foot of the Schmittenhöhe in Zell am See – just a few minutes' drive from the starting point of the panoramic roadway. In the postwar period, his son Ferry Porsche continued the tradition of mountain test drives with groundbreaking models such as the Porsche 356 and the 911. And even Ferry's son Wolfgang, who was born in 1943, came along on the Glockner test drives as a youngster. Today, Dr. Wolfgang Porsche keeps watch over the company as the Chairman of the Supervisory Board of Porsche AG and is its most important brand ambassador. The drive from Schüttgut, the Porsche family estate in Zell am See, up to Hochtor is still one of his favorite routes.

What is your earliest memory of the Glockner? My earliest memory is the drives with my father over the Grossglockner to Gmünd in Carinthia, where our operation had been moved due to the war. As a child I was

ausgelagert war. Ich war als Kind nicht unbedingt ein unerschütterlicher Beifahrer, manchmal wurde mir schon in den ersten Kehren schlecht.

Welchen Stellenwert hatte die Straße für Ihren Großvater, Ihren Vater – und die Geschichte der Sportwagen von Porsche? Die Straße über den Großglockner hatte eine große verkehrspolitische und auch touristische Bedeutung. Sie war im Sommer die Verbindung der beiden österreichischen Bundesländer Salzburg und Kärnten und lockt bis heute unzählige Touristen an. Für meinen Großvater und Vater war wichtig, dass sie praktisch vor der Haustür lag. Auf derartig herausfordernden Bergstraßen kann man sehr viel über die Eigenschaften eines Fahrzeugs herausfinden, in unserem Fall über Agilität, Traktion und Bremsen. Ein Fahrzeug, das in den Vierziger- und Fünfzigerjahren des vorigen Jahrhunderts die Glocknerstraße bezwang, bestand auch auf allen anderen Berg- und Passstraßen der Welt.

Vor 55 Jahren unternahmen Sie zusammen mit Ihrem Vater die erste Fahrt mit einem Porsche 911 über die Großglockner Hochalpenstraße. Was ist Ihnen von diesem Tag in Erinnerung geblieben? Ich bin mit meinem Vater oft über den Glockner gefahren, in allen möglichen Modellen: VW Käfer, Porsche 356, Porsche 911, Porsche 928. Unsere damalige Erkenntnis war: Der Elfer ist deutlich besser als der 356, was natürlich auch am neuen Sechszylinder-Boxer-Motor lag.

Gibt es ein weiteres Erlebnis, das Ihnen im Zusammenhang mit dem Großglockner und der Straße besonders im Gedächtnis geblieben ist? Anfangs, als Kind, war ich immer Beifahrer. Am liebsten sind mein Vater und ich im 356 Speedster gefahren, offen und frühmorgens, wenn die Luft noch ganz frisch war. Wir fuhren im Tal im Schatten los und dann immer höher hinauf ins Licht, bis oben dann die Sonne strahlend am blauen Himmel stand. Mein Vater hat mich dann, nachdem ich den Führerschein hatte, selbst fahren lassen, und später habe ich dies von ihm übernommen und bin mit meinen Kindern ebenfalls über den Glockner gefahren, immer auch gern in den diversen 911-Speedster-Modellen oder auch anderen.

Welche sind Ihre liebsten Orte entlang der Straße? Wo und zu welcher Tageszeit hat man den schönsten Blick? Naja, es gibt ja nicht viele Ortschaften an der Straße, aber viele wunderschöne Stellen. Auf meiner, also auf der Salzburger Seite, geht's ja praktisch im Wald los, und dann erschließt sich Kehre für Kehre dieses einzigartige hochalpine Panorama. Ich mag eigentlich jede einzelne Kehre bis hinauf zum Hochtor. Dort oben, auf der Passhöhe, hat man bei schönem Wetter einen extrem weiten Blick in alle Richtungen. Drum herum diese kargen, felsigen Gipfel und Berge. Von oben hat man nach dem zweiten Tunnel einen sehr schönen Blick auf die Kärntner Seite, nicht mehr ganz so schroff und steil, mit vielen

not exactly an unflappable passenger; sometimes I felt ill as soon as we started going around the first hairpin bends.

How important was the road for your grandfather, your father – and the history of the sports cars from Porsche? The road over the Grossglockner was very important in terms of transport policy and also tourism. In the summer, it was the connection between the two Austrian states of Salzburg and Carinthia and still draws countless tourists today. For my grandfather and father, it was important because it was practically right outside the front door. One can learn a lot about the characteristics of a vehicle from such challenging mountain roads; in our case, it was agility, traction and brakes. A vehicle that could master the Glockner in the 1940s and 1950s could pass muster on any mountain or pass road in the world.

55 years ago, you and your father undertook the first drive over the Grossglockner High Alpine Road in a Porsche 911. What do you remember about that day? I often drove over the Glockner with my father, in all kinds of different models: VW Beetle, Porsche 356, Porsche 911, Porsche 928. What we learned then was that the 911 was significantly better than the 356, which was naturally due, in part, to the new flat-six engine.

Is there another experience that you remember particularly in relation to the Grossglockner and the road? In the beginning, as a kid, I was always the passenger. My favorite thing was when my father and I drove the 356 Speedster with the top down in the early morning when the air was still fresh. We took off in the shade of the valley and then ascended upwards into the light until we were up at the top and the sun shone brightly in the blue sky. Once I got my driver's license, my father let me drive, and later I adopted the practice from him and drove over the Glockner with my kids as well, which we also enjoyed in the various 911 Speedster models, among others.

What are your favorite places along the route? Where and at what time of day do you have the best view? Well, there aren't many towns along the route, but there are a lot of gorgeous vistas. On my, that is the Salzburg side, it essentially starts in the woods and you gradually emerge into this unique Alpine panorama with each passing bend. I actually really like every single hairpin turn on the way up to Hochtor. Up at the top of the pass, you can see extremely far in every direction if the weather is good. All around you you have these rugged, rocky peaks and mountains. From up there, after the second tunnel, you have a very beautiful view of the Carinthian side, which is not quite so austere and steep, with a lot of nicely sweeping curves. The most beautiful, indeed the only town, is Heiligenblut in Carinthia.

> Die ganze Komposition und die Architektur sind sehr beeindruckend. Die Straße hat einen markanten Rhythmus und schwingt sich beschaulich, aber präzise in hochalpine Regionen.

> The entire composition and architecture are exceptionally impressive. The road has a striking rhythm and rises with great beauty, but also precision, into the high-Alpine regions.

schön geschwungenen Kurven. Der schönste, und ja auch der einzige Ort ist Heiligenblut in Kärnten.

Können Sie uns ein Restaurant zur Einkehr empfehlen? Die meisten Restaurants entlang der Glocknerstraße sind touristisch orientiert, da gibt es alles, Souvenirs, Trachtenhüte, Murmeltiersalbe. In Heiligenblut sind einige gute Lokale. Am liebsten ist mir aber das Restaurant Mayer's in Zell in meinem Schlosshotel Prielau, in dem früher der Dichter Hugo von Hofmannsthal gelebt hat.

Sie besitzen eine ansehnliche Sammlung historischer Porsche-Sportwagen. Mit welchem Auto lässt sich die Glocknerstraße mit ihren Kurven, Anstiegen und Alpenpanoramen am schönsten erfahren? Meine eigenen Porsche-Fahrzeuge sind alle bergerprobt. Meine Auswahl hängt also sehr vom Wetter und von meiner Stimmung ab und auch davon, welches Fahrzeug gerne bewegt werden will. Für Oldtimer-Veranstaltungen nehme ich aber am liebsten mein 356 Carrera Coupé.

Die Straße ist nicht nur ein österreichisches Monument – sie könnte bald auch von der UNESCO zum Welterbe gezählt werden. Was macht die Straße so einzigartig? Die ganze Komposition und die Architektur sind sehr beeindruckend. Die Straße hat einen markanten Rhythmus und schwingt sich beschaulich, aber präzise in hochalpine Regionen. Man kann unten bei Sonnenschein losfahren und oben Schneefall erleben.

Was wünschen Sie sich für die Zukunft der Straße und der Region? Unsere Region ist touristisch inzwischen sehr gut erschlossen und längst kein Geheimtipp mehr, also haben die Fremdenverkehrsverbände alle gut gearbeitet. Für meine persönlichen Fahrten über den Glockner wünsche ich mir – aber nur für diese wenigen Momente – keine Autobusse und Wohnwagengespanne vor mir. Und dass jeder beim Runterfahren auf die Bremsen aufpasst. Es ist ja kein Zufall, dass die Autoindustrie viele Bremsentests auch hier am Großglockner fährt.

Can you recommend a restaurant to stop at? Most of the restaurants along the Glockner road are geared toward tourists. They have everything: souvenirs, traditional hats, marmot ointment. There are several nice places in Heiligenblut. My favorite, however, is Restaurant Mayer's in Zell in my Schlosshotel Prielau, where the writer Hugo von Hofmannsthal used to live.

You have a splendid collection of historic Porsche models. What's the best car in which to experience the curves, ascents and Alpine panoramas of the Glockner? All of my own Porsche vehicles are mountain-tested. So my choice depends very much on the weather and my mood, as well as which vehicle needs a good drive. For classic car events, I prefer to take my 356 Carrera Coupé.

The road is not just an Austrian monument – it may soon be recognized as a World Heritage site by UNESCO. What makes the road so unique? The entire composition and architecture are exceptionally impressive. The road has a striking rhythm and rises with great beauty, but also precision, into the high-Alpine regions. You can set off amid bright sunshine and encounter snowfall up top.

What do you wish for the future of the road and the region? Our region is now very well developed in terms of tourism and is by no means an insider tip anymore, so the tourism associations have all done good work. For my personal drives over the Glockner – but only for these few moments – I hope to avoid having buses and mobile homes lined up in front of me. And that everyone minds the brakes on the way down. It's no coincidence that the automotive industry does a lot of brake tests on the Grossglockner.

HERBERT HASLINGER

Schon als Schuljunge kam Herbert Haslinger in den Sommerferien zum Arbeiten an die Großglocknerstraße – und entdeckte dabei die Murmeltiere für sich. Heute betreibt er als »Mankeiwirt« das Gasthaus Fuscherlacke und wird dabei nicht müde, den Gästen seine Murmeltiere vorzustellen und ihre Geschichten zu erzählen.

Even as a schoolboy, Herbert Haslinger came to work on the Grossglockner High Alpine Road on his summer vacation – where he got to know the Alpine marmots first-hand. The guests at his Gasthaus Fuscherlacke inn call him the "Marmot Innkeeper." He never tires of showing his guests his marmots and telling their story.

Was ist ihre erste Erinnerung an die Glocknerstraße? 1970 war ich das erste Mal am Großglockner. Ich bin unten im Tal zwischen Bruck und Fusch aufgewachsen. Wir waren neun Kinder und haben schon früh angefangen zu arbeiten. Ab meinem 12. Lebensjahr bin ich in den Ferien zum Arbeiten ins Restaurant Fuschertörl gegangen und habe den ganzen Sommer über dort oben gewohnt. Mein Schulzeugnis haben meine Geschwister für mich mitgenommen, damit ich früher auf den Berg konnte, und den ersten Schultag nach den Ferien habe ich auch noch gearbeitet. Das war früher ganz normal. Ich habe dann bei Hartmut Henkel, dem Gastwirt vom Fuschertörl, meine Lehre zum Koch gemacht und auch meine Frau kennengelernt, die aus Schweden kam und dort als Kindermädchen gearbeitet hat.

Haben Sie damals schon Ihre Liebe zu den Murmeltieren entdeckt? Ja genau. Vorher wusste ich gar nicht, was ein Murmeltier ist. Wir hatten nicht viel Freizeit, aber wenn ich nicht arbeiten musste, bin ich eben in den Bergen herumgeschlichen und habe dabei diese Tiere entdeckt. Ich habe dann damit angefangen, Murmeltier-Findelkinder aufzuziehen und wieder freizulassen. Wie bei allen Nagetieren werden kleine Tiere, die zu schwach sind, aus der Familie ausgestoßen. Ich habe auch ausgewachsene Exemplare gefangen und Gehege für sie gebaut, doch am nächsten Tag waren sie meistens wieder weg. So habe ich gelernt, dass Murmeltiere gute Kletterer und Gräber sind.

Heute sind Sie allerorts als »Mankeiwirt« bekannt, Ihr Gasthaus ist wegen der Murmeltiere eine Attraktion. Wie kam es dazu? Hier stand schon immer eine

What is your earliest memory of the Grossglockner High Alpine Road? My first time on the Grossglockner was in 1970. I grew up down in the valley between Bruck and Fusch. I had eight brothers and sisters and I started working early. From the age of eleven, I worked at Restaurant Fuschertörl during the vacations and I stayed up there the whole summer. My siblings used to pick up my report card so that I could leave for the mountain earlier, and I always worked on the first school day after the vacation, too. Back then, that was quite normal. I then trained as a chef under Hartmut Henkel, the owner of the Fuschertörl. I also met my future wife there, who was an au pair from Sweden.

Did you discover your love for Alpine marmots back then? Yes, exactly. Before then, I didn't even know what a marmot was. We didn't have a lot of time off, but when I didn't have to work I would wander around in the mountains, which is where I came across these creatures. I started raising marmot orphans and then releasing them back into the wild. As with all rodents, the runts are rejected by the family. I also caught mature marmots and built enclosures for them, but they were usually gone by the next day. That taught me that marmots are good climbers and diggers!

Everyone now calls you the "Marmot Innkeeper" and your inn is an attraction thanks to the marmots. How did that come about? There was always a cabin here, but it burned down in 1980. It was then rebuilt, but the work was never finished. When we took over Gasthof Fuscherlacke, my brother and I came up here in spring 1991 on skis to renovate the cabin and make it ready for the

Hütte, die allerdings 1980 abgebrannt ist. Sie wurde dann neu aufgebaut, ist aber nie fertig geworden. Als wir den Gasthof Fuscherlacke übernommen haben, sind mein Bruder und ich im Frühjahr 1991 mit den Ski hier hochgekommen, um die Hütte auszubessern und für die Saison vorzubereiten. Oberhalb vom Haus saß ein Murmeltier allein im Schnee. Es konnte nicht richtig laufen und ist vor uns den Hang hinuntergekugelt. Ich habe das Tier dann unter meinen Anorak genommen, da es schon sehr unterkühlt war, und mitgenommen. Im Haus habe ich ein Nest gebaut, und es hat dann zwei Jahre bei uns gewohnt. Auch mit meinem Hund hat es sich bestens verstanden, die beiden haben zusammen gespielt. Eines Tages ist es hinter dem Haus in die Schlucht gestürzt, aber auch das hat es überlebt. Leider wurde es später vom Jagdhund eines Gastes totgebissen. Für meinen Sohn, der damals vier Jahre alt war, musste natürlich ein neues Murmeltier her. Die Gäste begannen sich zu interessieren, und ich habe begonnen, über die Murmeltiere zu erzählen. Tiergeschichten sind beliebt, bald waren die Medien hier und haben es in die Welt getragen. Heute kann ich hinfahren wo ich will, irgendwann erkennt mich jemand: Sie sind doch der Mankeiwirt vom Großglockner. Wir leisten schon Herzensarbeit. Gerade wenn hier ältere Leute mit ihren Bussen kommen und die Murmeltiere sehen und streicheln ... die zergehen wie Butter, die Leute. Das freut einen.

Aber es gibt bestimmt auch Menschen, die es kritisch sehen, wenn Sie Wildtiere in einem Gehege halten. Freilich leben die Tiere im Gehege. Aber das sind Familientiere, die sind es gewohnt, bei ihren Verwandten zu bleiben und ein begrenztes Territorium zu haben. Ich habe die Tür schon oft offen gelassen, die Tiere wollen gar nicht weg. Wir haben immer Tiere gehabt - Hunde, Katzen, Papageien, eine Schildkröte. Aber wenn ich ein Murmeltier als Baby mit der Flasche aufziehe, habe ich natürlich eine besondere Bindung. Im Herbst nehmen wir die Murmeltiere mit ins Tal, damit sie den Winterschlaf bei uns in Sicherheit halten können. Die Tiere haben Vertrauen zu mir und umgekehrt. Das größte Tier, der Moritz, ist fünf Kilo schwer, aber er sitzt gerne auf meiner Schulter. Wenn er mich mit seinen nachwachsenden Nagezähnen und seiner gewaltigen Kraft in den Hals beißen würde, könnte man nur noch den Hubschrauber rufen. Die Tiere haben aber auch einen Selbstwillen und lassen mich wissen, wenn sie ihre Ruhe haben möchten. Man braucht einfach das richtige Feeling, um die Murmeltiere zu verstehen. In der Wildnis werden Murmeltiere etwa acht bis zehn Jahre alt. Mein Ältestes war über 14 Jahre alt. Heute habe ich zwei Pärchen.

Gibt es noch etwas Interessantes, das wir von Ihnen über Murmeltiere lernen können? Murmeltiere sind sehr hitzeempfindlich, sie können nicht schwitzen. Oft denken die Besucher, wenn sie früh am Morgen ein Murmeltier auf einem Stein oder der Straße liegen

season. Above the house, a marmot sat in the snow. It couldn't walk properly and tumbled down the hill right before our eyes. I picked up the creature and placed it under my anorak, because it was already clearly suffering from hypothermia, and took it home. I built a nest for it in the house and it lived with us for two years. It even got on great with my dog – the two of them used to play together. One day it fell into a gorge behind the house, but it survived. Unfortunately, it was later bitten to death by a guest's hunting dog. My son, who was four at the time, had to have a new marmot, of course. The guests began to take an interest, and I started telling people about marmots. People love animal stories and, soon, the media started spreading it around. Now wherever I can go somebody will recognize me and say, "you're the Marmot Innkeeper of the Grossglockner!" People really take what we do to heart. Especially when older people arrive by bus and see and stroke the marmots – they really melt. That's lovely to see.

I am sure there are people who aren't pleased to see that you keep wild animals in an enclosure. It's true that the animals live in an enclosure, but they are family animals and they are used to staying with their relatives and having a limited territory. I have often left the door open and the animals didn't want to leave. We have always had animals - dogs, cats, parrots, a tortoise. But when I bring up a baby marmot with a bottle, I naturally have a special connection with it. In fall, we bring the marmots down into the valley with us so they can hibernate safely in our home. The animals trust me, and vice versa. The biggest animal, Moritz, weighs five kilos, but he loves to sit on my shoulder. If he bit me in the neck with his regrowable front teeth and his extraordinary strength, all we could do would be to call the emergency helicopter. The animals do have their own free will, however, and they let me know when they want to be left alone. You just need the right feeling to understand marmots. In the wild, marmots live to be about eight to ten years old. The oldest one I had was over 14. At the moment I have two pairs.

Is there anything else interesting you can tell us about marmots? Marmots are very heat-sensitive; they can't sweat. Our visitors often think, when they see a marmot lying on a stone or on the road early in the morning, that it's eaten too much and is relaxing. But a stone is colder than the meadow in the morning; it stores the cold for longer. Marmots lie prostrate on the stone in order to cool as much of the surface of their bodies as possible, and to get rid of parasites. There are no trees to give shade. But, of course, marmots could just stay in their den.

What are the nicest times of year up here on the Grossglockner High Alpine Road? Every day is different because the weather changes its mood so often. The peace and quiet in the mornings and evenings is really special. I also like the first week in spring. I come up here with my wife and we're all alone. We get the house heated up and

sehen, es ist vollgefressen und entspannt sich. Der Stein ist morgens ja noch kühler als die Wiese, er speichert die Kälte länger. Das Murmeltier macht sich lang, um möglichst viel Körperfläche durch das Gestein zu kühlen und dabei auch Parasiten loszuwerden. Schatten durch Bäume gibt es ja nicht. Aber klar, es könnte natürlich auch einfach im Bau bleiben.

Was sind die schönsten Zeiten hier oben an der Glocknerstraße? Jeder Tag ist anders, weil die Wetterstimmungen sich so schnell verändern. Die Ruhe am Abend und am Morgen ist wirklich besonders. Schön ist auch die erste Woche im Frühjahr, in der ich mit meiner Frau hier hoch komme und wir ganz alleine sind, das Haus einheizen und uns höchstens Peter Embacher von der Straßenverwaltung besucht – auf Ski. Wenn später im Jahr dann die Schneeräumer kommen, bekommen sie bei mir ein warmes Essen. Dafür helfen mir die Arbeiter dann, wenn ich ein Werkzeug oder eine Schraube zum Ausbessern brauche. Dieser Zusammenhalt ist hier oben besonders wichtig.

Die Sommer am Berg sind kurz, das Wetter ist mitunter hart. Könnten Sie sich vorstellen, einmal nicht mehr hier oben zu leben? Das Panorama hier oben bei guter Sicht ist unschlagbar. Aber es gibt auch schlimme Momente. Gewaltige Gewitter, die sich hier oben entladen. Eisregen im Sommer. Auch die Winde werden immer stärker und aggressiver. Wir müssen unsere Dächer doppelt so gut befestigen wie im Tal unten. Wenn man so lange hier oben verbracht hat wie ich – bei meiner Pensionierung werden es 50 Jahre sein –, gehört das Bergwetter einfach zum Leben dazu. Gleichzeitig merke ich aber auch, dass ich es vermisse, einmal einen wirklichen Sommer zu erleben. Rad zu fahren, durch Wälder zu spazieren, Schwimmen zu gehen, den Duft von frisch gemähten Wiesen zu riechen – das kennen wir ja alles gar nicht mehr. Und das fehlt uns jetzt.

Aus Ihrer Sicht als Gastwirt: Was hat sich an der Glocknerstraße über die Jahre verändert? Früher haben die Gäste erst mal einen Kaffee bestellt, heute fragen sie zuerst nach dem WLAN-Passwort. Auch ging es hier oben früher etwas ruhiger zu. Das größte Handicap am Berg ist heute aber, dass man kaum noch Leute zum Arbeiten findet. Dabei haben meine Angestellten in der Woche zwei Tage frei und arbeiten von halb neun Uhr morgens bis abends um sechs. Wir haben auch schöne Zimmer hergerichtet. Klar gibt es stressige Tage, aber dann ist es auch wieder ruhiger. Ich habe überall annonciert, in den regionalen Zeitungen, beim Arbeitsamt – nicht ein einziges Mal hat das Telefon geläutet. Dabei muss man nur etwas tüchtig sein, um hier oben ein gutes, glückliches und zufriedenes Leben zu haben. Aber Arbeit lohnt sich wohl nicht mehr.

Gehört die Großglockner Hochalpenstraße für Sie zum Weltkulturerbe? Und wie lässt sich die Berg-

the only visitor we might have is Peter Embacher from the road management department – on skis. When the snowplows arrive later in the year, we give the drivers a hot meal. But, in turn, they help me if I need to borrow a tool or a screw to perform a small improvement. Sticking together is particularly important up here.

The summers on the mountain are short and the weather can sometimes be very tough. Could you imagine not living up here anymore one day? The panoramic views up here are unbeatable on a clear day. But there are hard moments too. Powerful storms right over our heads. Sleet in the summer. And the winds are getting stronger and more aggressive. We have to make our roofs twice as strong as down in the valley. Once you've spent as much time up here as I have – and when I retire, it will have been 50 years –, the mountain weather is just a part of life. At the same time, however, I have noticed that I miss having a real summer. Cycling, walking in the woods, swimming, enjoy the fragrance of a freshly mown meadow – these are all things that we don't get to experience anymore. And we miss them.

From the point of view of an inn owner, what would you say has changed on the Grossglockner High Alpine Road over the years? Guests used to order a coffee when they arrived, now they ask for the Wi-Fi password! It also used to be quieter up here. The biggest hindrance to working on the mountain today is not being able to find staff. But I do give my employees two days off a week and they work from 8:30 in the morning until 6 in the evening. We also have some lovely rooms. Of course, some days are stressful, but then you also get quieter periods. I advertised for staff everywhere – in regional newspapers and at the employment bureau –and the phone didn't ring once. But you only need to be somewhat industrious to lead a good, happy and satisfying life up here. But I guess people no longer think that work is worth it anymore.

Do you think that the Grossglockner High Alpine Road is a world heritage site? And how can this mountain environment and its marmots be preserved for future generations? Everything that UNESCO declares a world heritage site is an attraction. And of course, people expect to make money out of it because, nowadays, everything has to be bigger and better. Our business has grown fivefold since we started here. But that also means that we have to work more and more and have less and less free time. I don't think it would be such a bad thing if it was a bit quieter up here. Nobody would die and people would have better quality of life and more time for their families. That could only be positive. Of course, a landscape like this should be protected. People are also becoming a lot more conscious. There are some environmentalists who say that the Grossglockner High Alpine Road should be completely closed to cars. But I think that's stupid. It's better to show people the fragile nature up here so that they learn how to look after it. That's the only way to preserve it.

Ich finde, es würde gar nicht schaden, wenn hier einmal ein bisschen weniger los wäre. Keiner würde umkommen, man hätte mehr Lebensqualität und mehr Zeit für die Familie. Das wäre doch positiv. Natürlich sollte eine Landschaft wie diese geschützt werden. Die Menschen werden ja auch wesentlich bewusster.

I don't think it would be such a bad thing if it was a bit quieter up here. Nobody would die and people would have better quality of life and more time for their families. That could only be positive. Of course, a landscape like this should be protected.

welt mit ihren Murmeltieren für zukünftige Generationen erhalten? Alles was von der UNESCO zum Kulturerbe erklärt wird, ist eine Attraktion. Man verspricht sich natürlich ein Geschäft, heute muss ja immer alles mehr werden. Seit wir hier angefangen haben, hat sich unser Geschäft verfünffacht. Das heißt aber auch, dass wir immer noch mehr arbeiten müssen und noch weniger Freizeit haben.

Ich finde, es würde gar nicht schaden, wenn hier einmal ein bisschen weniger los wäre. Keiner würde umkommen, man hätte mehr Lebensqualität und mehr Zeit für die Familie. Das wäre doch positiv. Natürlich sollte eine Landschaft wie diese geschützt werden. Die Menschen werden ja auch wesentlich bewusster. Freilich gibt es auch Umweltschützer, die sagen, man sollte die Glocknerstraße ganz für Autos sperren. Aber das halte ich für eine Dummheit. Man sollte den Menschen diese fragile Natur lieber zeigen und nahe bringen, damit sie lernen, wie man damit umgehen muss. Nur so kann man sie erhalten.

D
DRIVE

DRIVE

Unzählige Sportwagen sind seit der Eröffnung der Großglockner Hochalpenstraße im Jahr 1935 durch ihre Kurven und Kehren gebraust, haben Steinchen wegspritzen lassen, Staub aufgewirbelt und die Menge zum Jubeln gebracht – und doch gibt es keine andere Automobilmarke, deren Geschichte so eng mit der Straße über die Hohen Tauern verbunden ist, wie Porsche. Schon der Konstrukteur und Firmengründer Ferdinand Porsche erprobte und demonstrierte Ende der Dreißigerjahre seine ersten Prototypen des KdF-Wagens, der später als VW Käfer zum Symbol der Automobilisierung in der Nachkriegszeit werden sollte, auf der Glocknerstraße.

Sein Konstruktionsbüro betrieb Ferdinand Porsche zu dieser Zeit zwar in Stuttgart, doch 1941 erwarb er auf einer Alm am Fuße der Schmittenhöhe in Zell am See – und gerade einmal vier Kilometer vom nördlichen Ausgangspunkt der Glocknerstraße in Bruck entfernt – das 600 Jahre alte Schüttgut als Rückzugsort für seine Familie. Nachdem die Porsches das Konstruktionsbüro 1944 kriegsbedingt von Stuttgart nach Gmünd in Kärnten verlegt hatte, entstand im dortigen Werk auch der erste Sportwagen unter dem Namen des Firmengründers und seines ähnlich talentierten Sohnes. Die Nummer 1, ein Porsche 356 Roadster, war von Ferdinand Anton Ernst »Ferry« Porsche und seinem Team, wie dem Chefkonstrukteur Karl Rabe, aus VW-Teilen von Hand zusammengebaut worden und hat am 8. Juni 1948 die allgemeine Betriebserlaubnis erhalten.

Nur 53 Porsche-Sportwagen wurden in Gmünd gefertigt, doch die fast 150 Kilometer lange Strecke vom Werk über die Großglockner Hochalpenstraße bis zum Familiensitz in Zell am See dürften eine ebenso aufregende wie aufschlussreiche Teststrecke abgegeben haben. Schon 1949 zog Porsche zurück nach Stuttgart, doch »Ferry« Porsche hielt den Glocknerkurven auch weiterhin die Treue und testete zahlreiche der neuen Modelle weiterhin am Berg zwischen Fuscher Törl und Hochtor. Denn egal ob Motor, Fahrwerk oder Bremsen – was beim Härtetest am Großglockner überzeugt hatte, musste auch anderswo funktionieren. So verewigte Porsche die berühmten Kehren zumindest indirekt in seinen kompakten und leichten Sportwagen, die wie gemacht zu sein schienen für die Bergstraßen dieser Welt.

Was gäbe es also für eine bessere Hommage an die nunmehr 70 Jahre währende Automobilgeschichte von Porsche, als einige der schnellsten, sportlichsten, schönsten und seltensten Sportwagen aller Jahrgänge für eine Jubiläumsfahrt auf der Großglockner Hochalpenstraße zu versammeln? Bei den Besitzern aus der Porsche Community

Since the Grossglockner High Alpine Road opened in 1935, innumerable sports cars have sped round its curves and hairpin bends, sending stones flying, churning up dust, and making the crowds cheer – but no other automobile brand has a history that is so closely linked to the road across the High Tauern mountain range as Porsche. Designer and company founder Ferdinand Porsche was using the Glockner Road back in the 1930s, testing and demonstrating his first prototypes of the KdF car which would later become the VW Beetle – the symbol of post-war Germany's mass motorization.

Ferdinand Porsche ran his engineering office out of Stuttgart at that time. However, in 1941 he bought the 600-year-old Schüttgut estate as a retreat for his family, located on an Alpine pasture at the foot of the Schmittenhöhe mountain in Zell am See – and just four kilometers from the northern starting point of the Glockner Road in Bruck. After the events of the war forced Porsche to move the engineering office in 1944 from Stuttgart to Gmünd in Carinthia, the first sports car was built in the works there under the name of the company founder and his equally talented son. The "Number 1", a Porsche 356 Roadster, was made by hand using VW parts by Ferdinand Anton Ernst "Ferry" Porsche and his team, including chief designer Karl Rabe, and received its general operating permit on 8 June 1948.

Only 53 Porsche sports cars were produced in Gmünd. But the almost 150-kilometer-long stretch of road from the works via the Grossglockner High Alpine Road to the family home in Zell am See must have been a test route that was as exciting as it was instructive. Porsche moved its offices back to Stuttgart in 1949, but "Ferry" Porsche stayed loyal to the Glockner bends, continuing to test many of the new models on the mountain between Fuscher Törl and Hochtor. Engine, chassis or brakes – any component that passed the endurance test on the Grossglockner was sure to function anywhere else. Porsche thus immortalized these famous bends, at least indirectly, in its compact and lightweight sports cars, which seemed born to take on mountain roads anywhere in the world.

So what better way to pay homage to Porsche for writing what are now 70 years of automotive history than by lining up some of the fastest, sportiest, most beautiful and rarest sports cars of all vintages for a commemorative sprint out on the Grossglockner High Alpine Road? The owners from the Porsche community were swift to

PORSCHE DRIVE · GROSSGLOCKNER HOCHALPENSTRASSE

stießen wir mit unserer Idee auf offene Ohren. Und tatsächlich reichte das Aufgebot, das wir an einem verhangenen Junitag ziemlich genau sieben Jahrzehnte nach dem Stapellauf der »Nummer 1« auf der Panoramastraße versammelten, von einer so weit wie möglich originalgetreuen Kopie des mythischen Berlin-Rom-Wagens bis hin zur futuristischen Konzeptstudie des Porsche Mission E, mit dem die Marke derzeit die Zukunft der Mobilität neu definiert.

Neben diesen zwei so unterschiedlichen automobilen Erscheinungen gab es an diesem Tag noch einige weitere Gründe, sich mitunter in den Arm zu zwicken, um nicht an der eigenen Wahrnehmung zu zweifeln: Denn war der kanariengelbe Porsche 911 ST 2.5, der da mit sattem Dröhnen über das Kopfsteinpflaster in Richtung Edelweiß-Spitze beschleunigte, nicht jener Le-Mans-Klassensieger von 1972, der im Nebenjob als Kamerawagen für den Kultfilm *The Speed Merchants* im Einsatz gewesen, fast in der Schrottpresse gelandet und jüngst von Porsche aufwändig restauriert worden war? Und der ältere Herr, der da am Steuer eines Porsche 904 Platz nahm – war das etwa der einstige Porsche-Werksfahrer, Bergspezialist und Europameister Rudi Lins, der da nach mehr als 50 Jahren ein Wiedersehen mit seinem alten Rennwagen feierte? Und konnte es sich bei den drei Rennwagen, die sich so selbstverständlich durch die Kehren zum Fuscher Törl hinauf arbeiteten, tatsächlich um einen Porsche Carrera 6, einen Porsche 962 und einen Porsche 718 RSK Spyder mit Pikes-Peak-Historie handeln – oder hatte den Beobachter dieser Szenerie bloß die Höhenkrankheit übermannt? Dass sich in dieses Gefolge auch legendäre Porsche-Sportwagen wie ein 911 ST Repsol, ein 550 Spyder, ein 911 Safari, ein 911 (964) Carrera RS sowie moderne Raritäten wie ein Porsche 918, der jüngste 911 GT2 RS sowie die Monte-Carlo-Rallyeversion des neuesten 911 T gemischt hatten, – allesamt von einem Polizei-Porsche 911 aus Zell am See eskortiert –, ließ die Szenerie schließlich völlig ins Land der Träume abgleiten. Doch Träume zu erfüllen und Realität werden zu lassen, das hat Porsche in den letzten 70 Jahren schließlich immer wieder geschafft – und dabei eine weltweite Fangemeinde aufgebaut, die mit der Aussprache von Zungenbrechern wie Gmünd, Zell am See und Großglockner Hochalpenstraße zwar mitunter ihre Probleme haben dürfte, die österreichischen Sehnsuchtsorte ihrer Porscheliebe aber mit Hingabe verehrt und auf ihren Pilgerfahrten besucht. Und tatsächlich ist die Region rund um die Glocknerstraße bis heute »Porscheland«. Auch Ferrys Sohn Ferdinand Alexander Porsche, der Anfang der Sechzigerjahre die Gestaltung des Porsche 911 verantwortet hatte, blieb dem Salzburger Land verbunden und verlegte das von ihm 1972 in Stuttgart gegründete Porsche Design Büro 1974 nach Zell am See. Hier werden von Uhren, Sonnenbrillen und Smartphone bis hin zu Superyachten anspruchsvolle Produkte entworfen und produziert. Sogar die Seilbahngondeln der lokalen Schmittenhöhenbahn wurden von dem Designstudio entworfen – und bieten den Besuchern die momentan noch etwas ungewohnte Möglichkeit, in einem fliegenden, fahrerlosen Porsche durch die alpine Bergwelt zu schweben.

sign up to our idea. And so it was, that a cloudy June day, almost precisely seven decades after the launch of the "Number 1", saw us gather together on the panorama road. The models present ranged from a replica as true as possible to the original mythical Berlin-Rome car to the futuristic Porsche Mission E concept car, the brand's current answer to redefining the future of mobility.

In addition to these two manifestations of automotive ideas from opposite ends of the spectrum, the day provided plenty of other reasons to pinch yourself to make sure your eyes weren't deceiving you. For instance, wasn't the canary-yellow Porsche 911 ST 2.5 accelerating with a roar across the cobblestones towards the Edelweiss-Spitze actually the Le Mans class winner of 1972 which also moonlighted as a camera car for the cult film *The Speed Merchants*, and which almost landed in the car crusher before recently being extensively restored by Porsche? And the older gentleman getting behind the wheel of a Porsche 904 – was that not the former Porsche works driver, mountain specialist, and European champion Rudi Lins, celebrating being reunited with his old racing car after over 50 years? And could the three racing cars so self-assuredly swinging their way round the curves up to Fuscher Törl really be a Porsche Carrera 6, a Porsche 962, and a Pikes Peak legend Porsche 718 RSK Spyder – or had the scene in front of us brought on a touch of altitude sickness?

What finally took everything into true dreamland territory was that this entourage was then joined by legendary Porsche sports cars such as a 911 ST Repsol, a 550 Spyder, a 911 Safari, a 911 (964) Carrera RS and modern rarities such as a Porsche 918, the latest 911 GT2 RS and the Monte Carlo Rally version of the latest 911 T – all escorted from Zell am See by a Porsche 911 police car. But fulfilling dreams and making them a reality time and again is actually precisely what Porsche has succeeded in doing over the past 70 years. It has simultaneously established a global fan community that may have its problems pronouncing tongue twisters like Gmünd, Zell am See and Grossglockner High Alpine Road, but which adores the Austrian place of longing deep at the heart of its love for Porsche with devotion and visits it on its pilgrimages.

And indeed, the region around the Glockner Road remains "Porsche country" to this day. Ferry's son, Ferdinand Alexander Porsche, in charge of designing the Porsche 911 in the early 1960s, retained his links to the Salzburg region and moved the Porsche Design offices he founded in Stuttgart in 1972 to Zell am See in 1974. It is here that sophisticated products are designed and made, from watches, sunglasses and smartphones to super yachts. Even the cable cars at the local Schmittenhöhe complex were created by the design offices – offering visitors the still slightly unusual chance to float in an airborne, driverless Porsche through the alpine landscape.

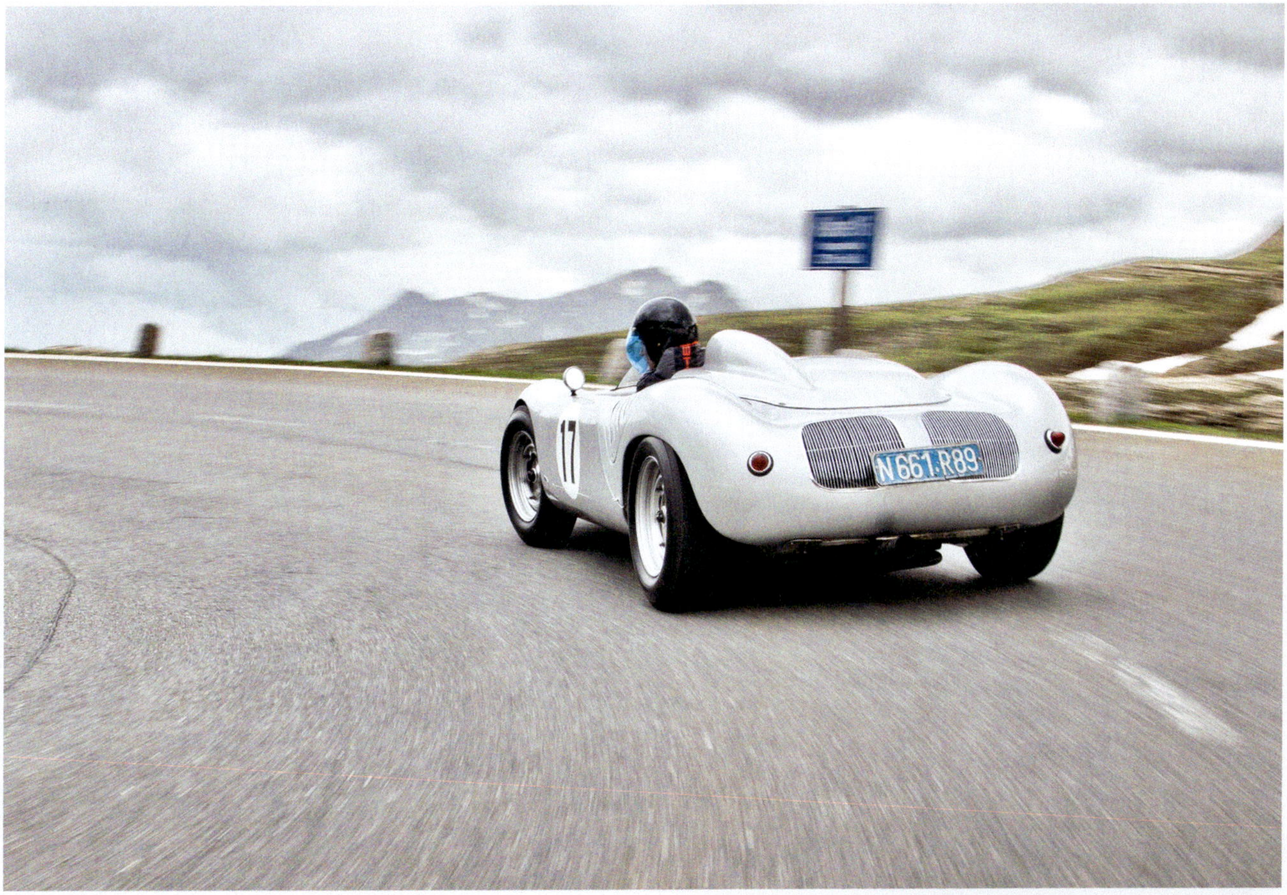
17
N 661 R 89

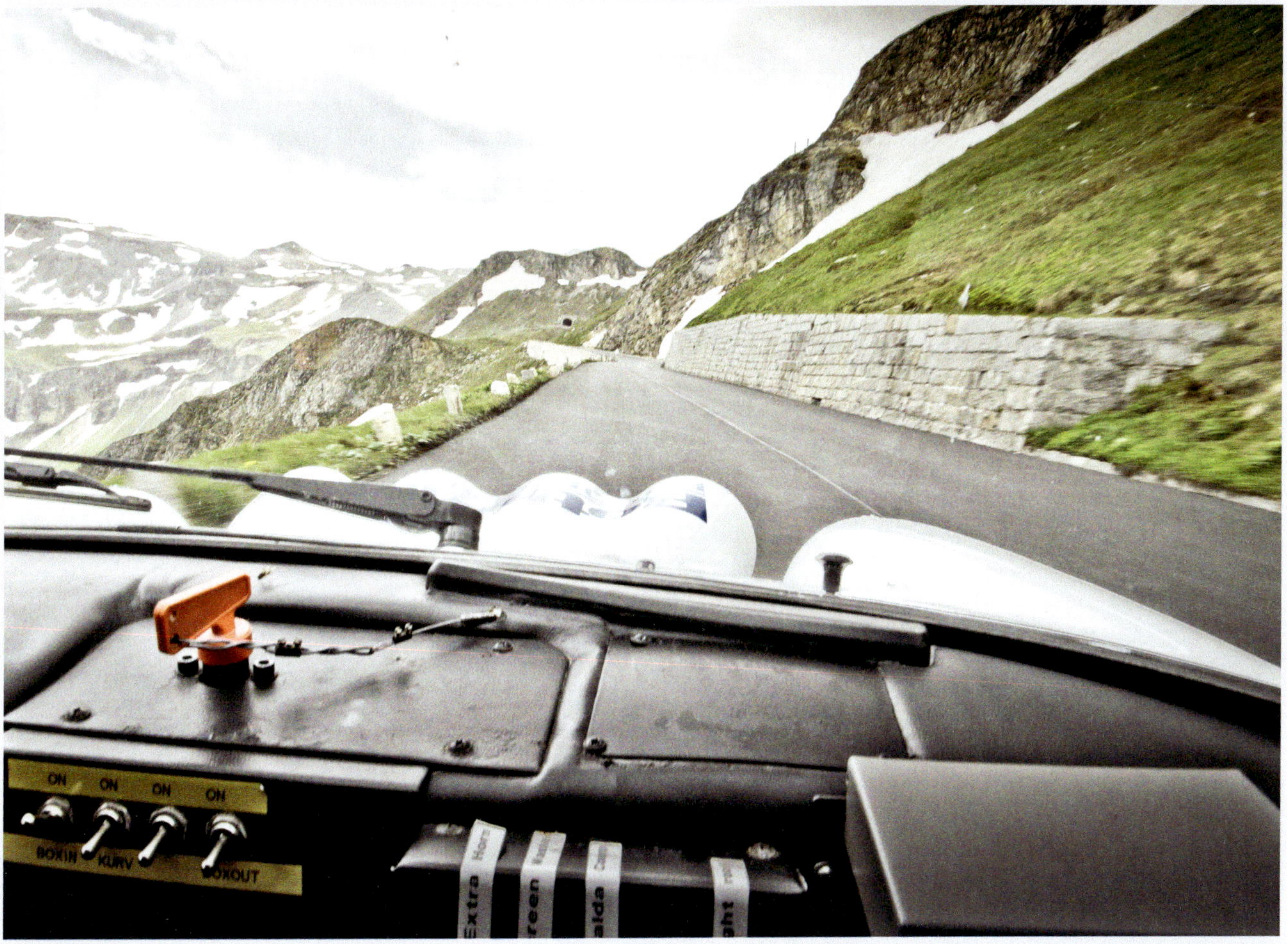
ON
ON
ON
ON
BOXIN
KURV
BOXOUT

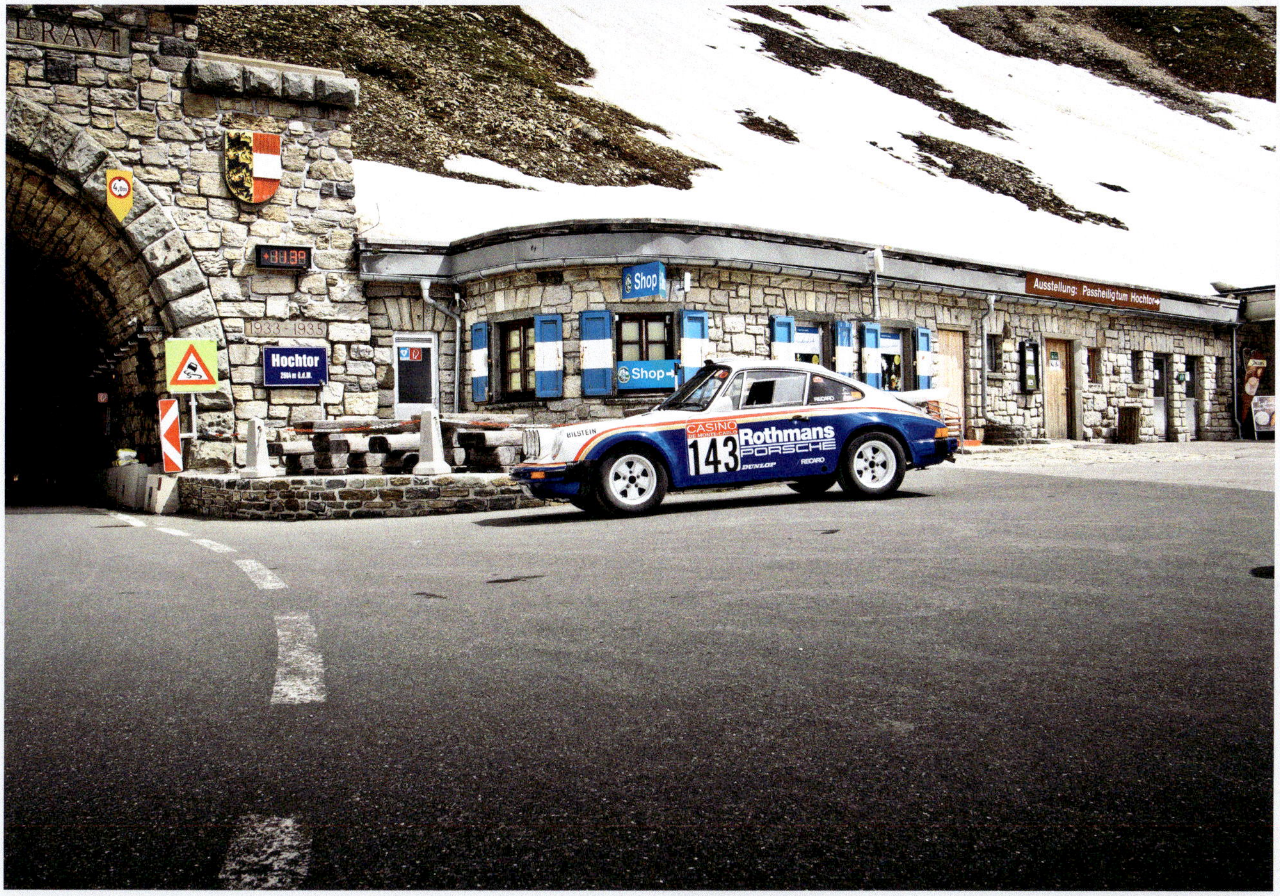
1933-1935
Hochtor
Shop
Ausstellung: Passheiligtum Hochtor
CASINO
143
Rothmans
PORSCHE
DUNLOP

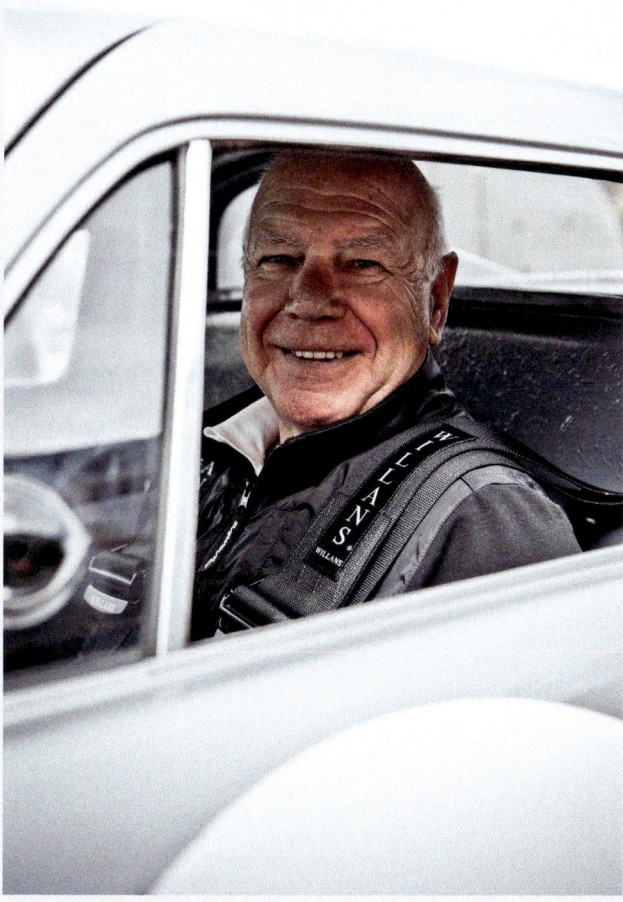

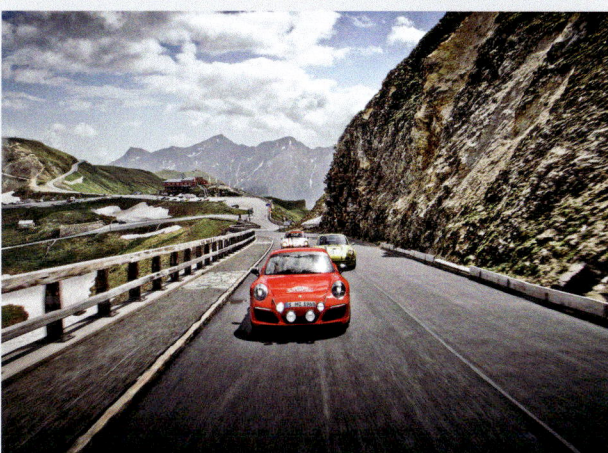

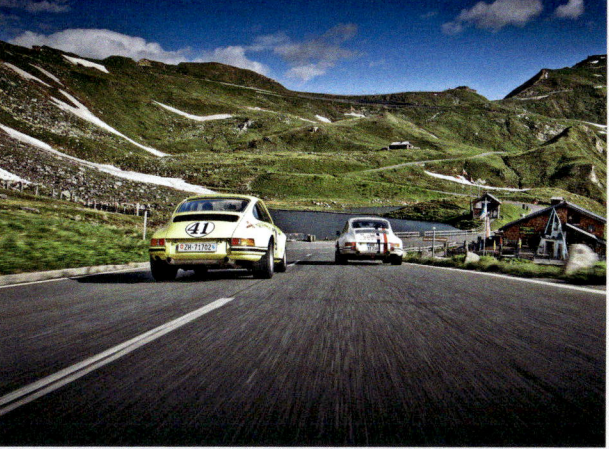

GROSSGLOCKNER HOCHALPENSTRASSE · PORSCHE DRIVE

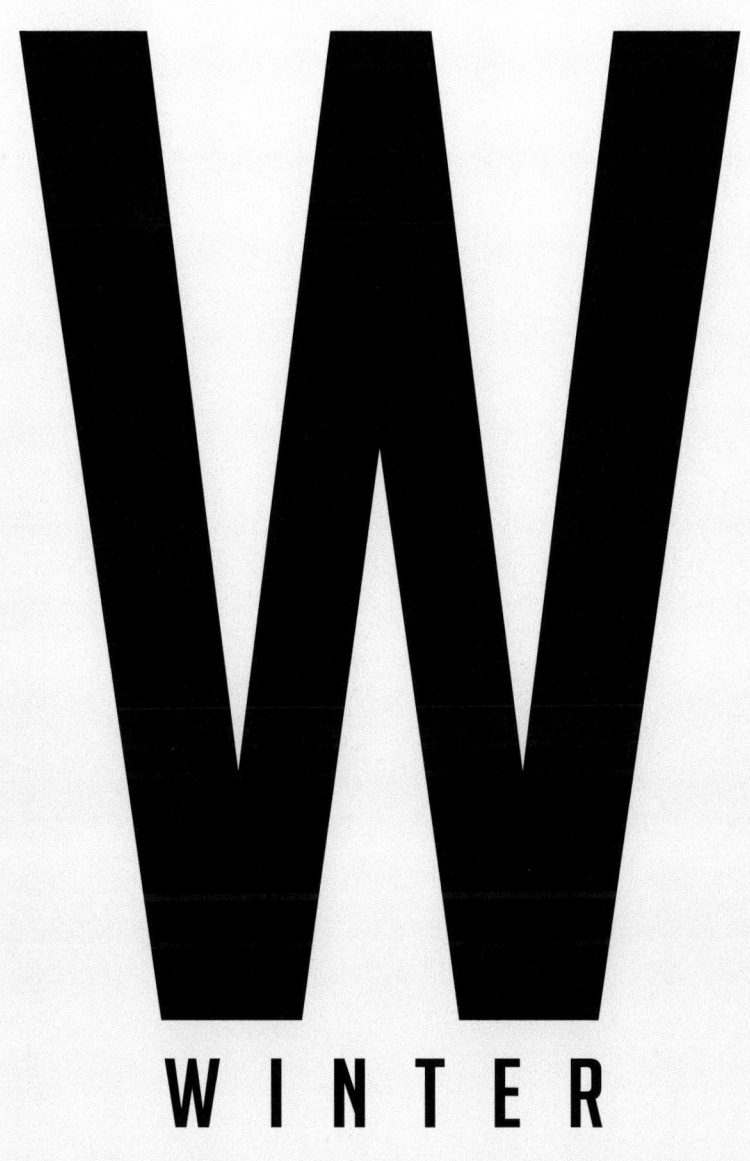

W
WINTER

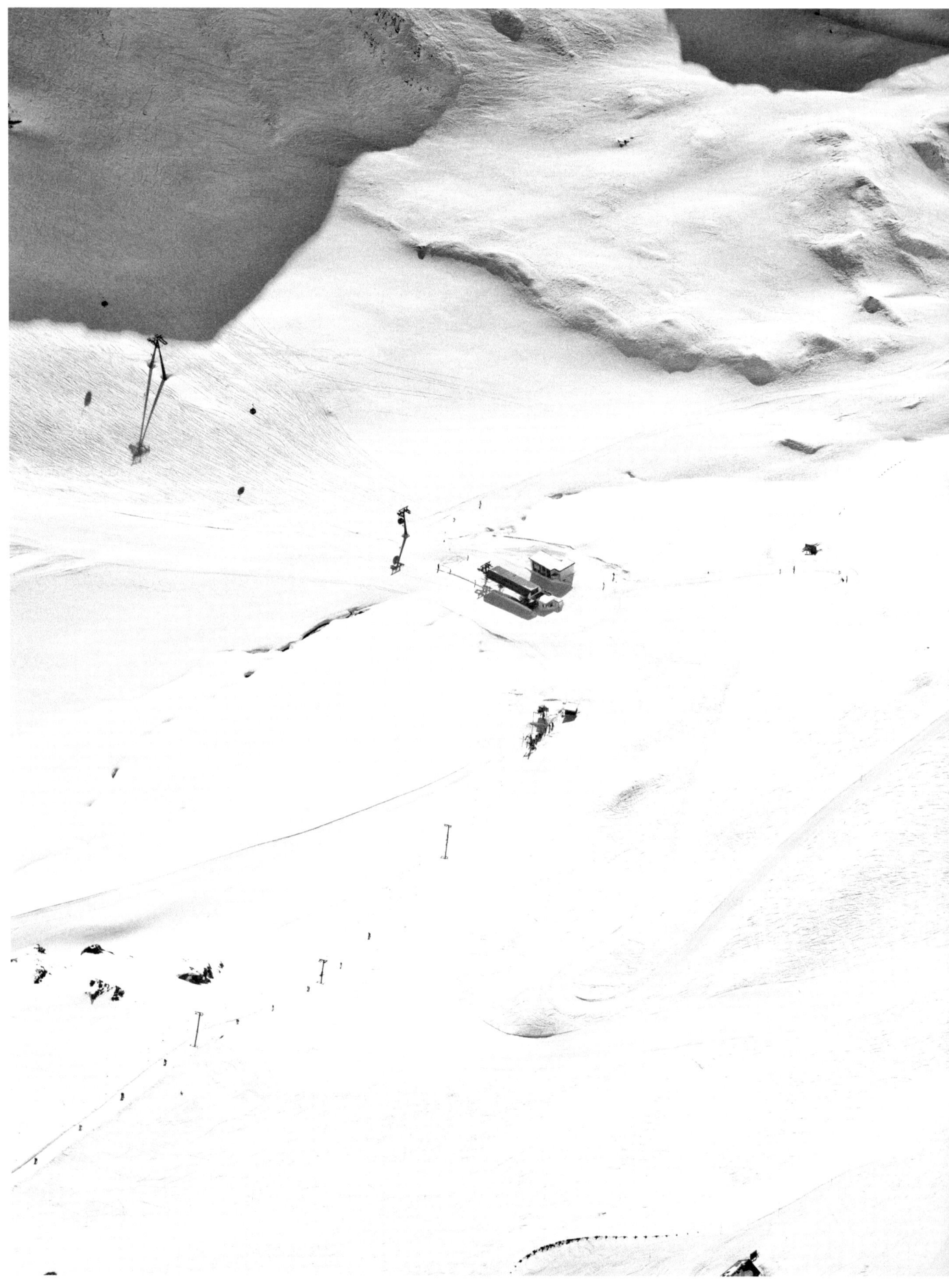

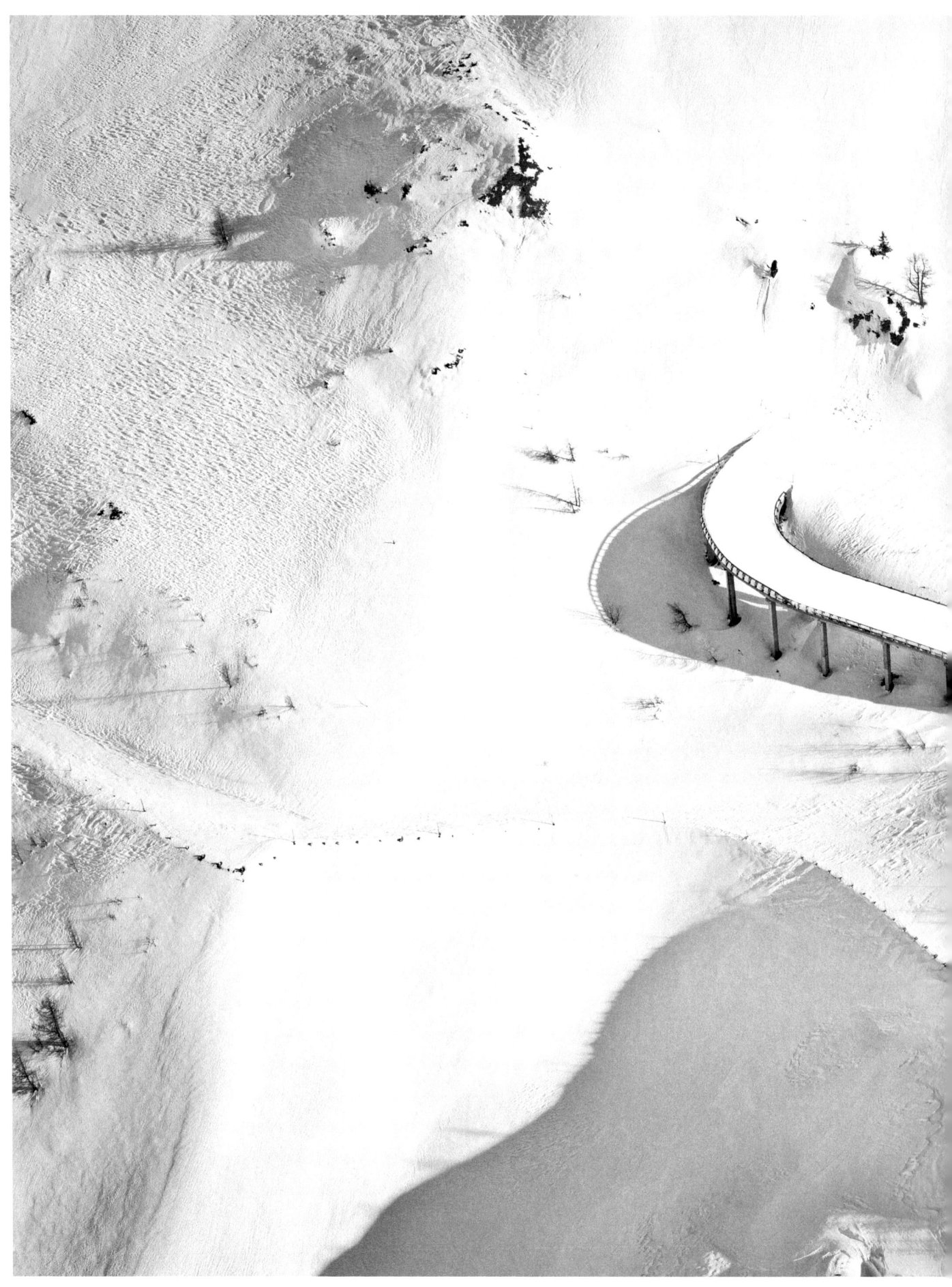

REISETIPPS
TRAVEL TIPS

— DIE STRASSE

Die Großglockner Hochalpenstraße ist in der Regel von Anfang Mai bis Anfang November geöffnet – wobei die Einschränkung schon darauf hinweist, dass der Faktor Natur hier ausschlaggebend ist. Die Öffnungszeiten ändern sich je nach Saison. Dabei sollte man nicht vergessen, dass die Straße durch hochalpine Berglandschaft führt und sich das Wetter auch im Sommer schnell ändern kann. Deshalb ist es ratsam, sich vor der Fahrt auf der Website der Großglockner Hochalpenstraßen AG zu informieren, in wieweit und zu welchen Zeiten die Straße befahrbar ist. Auch ein Blick auf den lokalen Wetterbericht und die aktuellen Temperaturen am Berg ist ratsam. Die letzte Einfahrt wird 45 Minuten vor der Nachtsperre gewährt.

Die Großglockner Hochalpenstraße ist eine Mautstraße. Die Mautstation auf Salzburger Seite befindet sich in Ferleiten, in Kärnten liegt das Mauthaus oberhalb von Heiligenblut. Das Tagesticket für ein Automobil kostet derzeit rund 36 Euro, Motorradfahrer bezahlen etwa 26 Euro. Für Elektromobile werden ermäßigte Preise und Ladestationen angeboten. Radfahrer müssen keine Mautgebühren zahlen.

Weitere Informationen finden sich unter **www.grossglockner.at**

— THE ROAD

The Grossglockner High Alpine Road is generally open from early May until the beginning of November – this limitation already suggests that nature is what really counts here. The opening times vary depending on the season. It is important to remember that the road leads through high alpine mountain landscape where weather conditions can change suddenly even during the summer months. That's why you should check the Grossglockner Hochalpenstraße AG website before embarking on your journey to find out the extent and times at which the road is navigable. It's also worth taking a look at the local weather forecast and the current temperatures on the mountain. The last entry is permitted 45 minutes prior to the night closure.

The Grossglockner High Alpine Road is a toll road. The toll road on the Salzburg side is located in Ferleiten; in Carinthia the toll road is situated above Heiligenblut. The day ticket for a car currently costs approx. 36 euros and motorcyclists pay around 26 euros. Discounted prices and charging stations are available for electric vehicles. Cyclists do not have to pay any toll charges.

You can find additional information at **www.grossglockner.at**

— STATIONEN ENTLANG DER STRECKE

Wer die Großglockner Hochalpenstraße wirklich erleben möchte, sollte Zeit mitbringen. Denn entlang der 48 Kilometer langen Panoramastrecke gibt es nicht nur atemberaubende Aussichten zu bewundern und elegante Kurven und Kehren zu durchfahren, sondern auch zahlreiche interessante Themenausstellungen zur alpinen Natur und Geschichte der Straße, die wir allen Besuchern ans Herz legen möchten.

Von der Mautstation in Ferleiten kommend, zweigt vom **Piffkar (1.620 m)** ein Naturlehrpfad ab, der in etwa 30 Minuten zu erkunden ist. Im alten Straßenwärterhaus findet sich auch eine erste Sonderschau zur Faszination Berg. Im Hochmais (1.850 m) kann man sich als nächstes über den Gletscher und die verschiedenen Vegetationsstufen informieren, die man entlang der Glocknerstraße durchfährt. Einsichten in die Ökologie des Hochgebirges eröffnet das Haus Alpine Naturschau (2.260 m).

Kurz bevor man das **Fuscher Törl (2.428 m)** mit seiner Gedenkstätte für die verunglückten Straßenarbeiter und der Aussichtsterrasse erreicht, zweigt die Straße nach links ab und führt über abenteuerlich-historische Pflastersteinkehren hinauf zum höchsten Punkt der Glocknerstraße, zur **Edelweiß-Spitze (2.571 m)**. Von hier kann man bei klarer Sicht einen herrlichen Panoramablick auf mehr als 30 Dreitausender genießen.

Zurück auf der Durchgangsstraße geht es zunächst wieder ein Stück hinab zur **Fuscher Lacke (2.262 m)**. Im alten Straßenwärterhäuschen neben dem See kann man sich über den Bau der Straße informieren und sogar einigen betagten Glocknerbarabern beim Feierabendbier zusehen. Nachdem man den Tunnel durchs **Hochtor (2.504 m)** passiert hat, kann man sich in der Ausstellung neben dem Südportal über das alte Passheiligtum informieren. Von beiden Seiten des Tunnels erreicht man zudem einen alten Pfad, auf dem schon die Kelten, Römer und Saumhändler die Passhöhe des Hochtors überquerten. Er lässt sich in etwa 30 Minuten begehen. Auf Kärntner

— STATIONS ALONG THE ROUTE

You will need plenty of time if you want to take full advantage of the Grossglockner High Alpine Road. This is because the 48-kilometer-long panoramic stretch not only offers breathtaking vistas and the prospect of driving around elegant curves and bends, but also numerous interesting thematic exhibitions on Alpine nature and the history of the road – which we urge all visitors to visit.

Coming from the toll station in Ferleiten, the **Piffkar (1,620 m)** branches off from the nature trail, which you can explore in around 30 minutes. The first special exhibition on the Faszination Berg [Fascination Mountain] can be found in the old Straßenwärterhaus [Roadman's House]. During the next stage, Hochmais (1,850 m) will provide you with information about the glacier and the different levels of vegetation that you drive through along the Glocknerstraße. The Haus Alpine Naturschau (2,260 m) [Alpine Nature House] provides insights into the ecology of the high mountain region.

Shortly before you reach the **Fuscher Toerl (2,428 m)** with its memorial to road workers who lost their lives there and the panoramic terrace, the road branches off to the left and leads over an adventurous, historic cobblestone bend to the highest point of the Glocknerstraße: the **Edelweiss-Spitze (2,571 m)**. From here, on a clear day, you can savor the superb panoramic view spanning more than 30 three-thousand-meter summits.

Once you are back on the through road, at first you dip down a bit towards **Fuscher Lacke (2,262 m)**. In the old Straßenwärterhäuschen next to the lake, you will find out about how the road was constructed and may even see some elderly Glockner laborers enjoying their after-work beer. After having passed the tunnel through **Hochtor (2,504 m)**, you can learn about the old Passheiligtum [Pass Sanctuary] at the exhibition next to the south portal. From both sides of the tunnel you can reach an old trail where the Celts, Romans and mule traders once crossed the pass summit of the Hochtor. It takes around 30

Seite weiter der Straße ins Tal folgend, kann man beim **Schöneck (1.935 m)** zudem einem rund 10 Minuten langen botanischen Rundwanderweg durch die Glocknerwiesen folgen.

Kurz darauf zweigt die Gletscherstraße in Richtung der **Kaiser-Franz-Josefs-Höhe (2.369 m)** ab. Der Ausblick auf den Großglockner, den Johannisberg und den Pasterze-Gletscher ist eindrücklich – und es lohnt sich, hier etwas länger zu verweilen, denn es gibt viel zu entdecken. Eine **historische Gletscherbahn** führt 144 Meter hinunter in Richtung Pasterze; ab der Talstation (die dem Gletscherstand im Jahr 1960 entspricht) erreicht man den Gletscher nach einer halbstündigen Wanderung. Empfehlenswert ist auch der **Gamsgrubenweg**, der in einem etwa einstündigen Fußmarsch mit eindrucksvollen Gletscherblicken von der Kaiser-Franz-Josefs-Höhe zum Wasserfallwinkel führt.

Wer das Sonderschutzgebiet nicht zu Fuß erkunden will, findet im Besucherzentrum an der **Kaiser-Franz-Josefs-Höhe** neben der Info-Stelle des Nationalparks eine ebenso lehrreiche wie unterhaltsame Ausstellungen zum Lebensraum Gletscher, die einem viele Fragen, die sich angesichts der schmelzenden Pasterze stellen, beantworten kann. Im selben Gebäude findet sich auch eine Sonderschau zur Erfolgsgeschichte des Automobils mit Schwerpunkt auf der Mobilitätsgeschichte der Großglockner Hochalpenstraße. Aus der einem Bergkristall nachempfundenen Wilhelm-Swarowski-Beobachtungswarte kann man zudem mit Ferngläsern die Steinböcke, Murmeltiere und Alpinisten beobachten, die sich bei schönem Wetter zwischen den Felsen tummeln.

Bei der Informationsstelle **Kasereck (1.911 m)** erhält man schließlich letzte Informationen zur Natur- und Kulturlandschaft des oberen Mölltals, bevor man schließlich den Endpunkt der Großglockner Hochalpenstraße in **Heiligenblut (1.288 m)** erreicht. Der spitze gotische Kirchturm des Bergsteigerdorfes mit der Pyramide des Großglockner im Hintergrund gehört zu den beliebtesten Fotomotiven Österreichs, doch auch ein Besuch der Pfarrkirche und des Friedhofs, auf dem auch zahlreiche anonyme Bergtote begraben liegen, ist lohnenswert. Wer es selbst wagen und die Pasterze erwandern oder sogar den Großglockner besteigen möchte, findet beim Bergführerverein in Heiligenblut immer einen kompetenten Alpinisten.

— RESTAURANTS UND HOTELS

Auch wenn Franz Wallack, der Erbauer der Großglockner Hochalpenstraße, einst von anspruchsvollen Hotels und Restaurants entlang der Strecke geträumt hatte,

minutes on foot. At **Schöneck (1,935 m)**, on the Carinthian side continuing along the road into the valley, you can also follow an approx. 10 minute-long botanical hiking circuit through the Glocknerwiesen [Glockner meadows].

Shortly afterwards, the glacier road branches off towards the **Kaiser-Franz-Josefs-Höhe (2,369 m)**. The view of the Grossglockner, the Johannisberg and the Pasterze-Gletscher [Pasterze Glacier] is an impressive one – it is worth lingering a while as there is so much to discover! A **historic Glacier Cableway** leads down 144 m in the direction of Pasterze. From the valley station (which corresponds to the position of the glacier in 1960), you can reach the glacier after a half-hour hike. It is also worth visiting the **Gamsgrubenweg**: this approx. one-hour walk that showcases spectacular views over the glacier runs from the Kaiser-Franz-Josefs-Höhe to the Wasserfallwinkel [Waterfall Corner].

Those who don't wish to discover the area of special conservation on foot will stumble upon exhibitions about the glacial habitat in the visitor's center at the **Kaiser-Franz-Josef-Höhe** next to the national park info point. These exhibitions, which are both educational and engaging, provide answers to a range of questions concerning the melting Pasterze. The same building also hosts a special exhibition on the success story of the automobile with a focus on the history of mobility on the Grossglockner High Alpine Road. Why not visit a Wilhelm-Swarowski observational tower modeled on a rock crystal where you can also use binoculars to observe the ibexes, marmots and mountaineers that cavort between the rocks during good weather conditions.

The Kasereck (1,911 m) information point will enlighten you about the latest information on the natural and cultural landscape of the upper Moelltal valley before finally reaching the end point of the Grossglockner High Alpine Road in **Heiligenblut (1,288 m)**. The marvelous Gothic church tower of the mountaineering village with the pyramid of the Grossglockner rising up in the background ranks among one of the most popular photo scenes in Austria. It is also well worth visiting the parish church and the cemetery in which a number of anonymous people killed in the mountains lay buried. Those who want to risk it themselves and hike the Pasterze, or even climb the Grossglockner, will always find a competent mountaineer at the mountain guide association in Heiligenblut.

— RESTAURANTS AND HOTELS

Even though Franz Wallack, the constructor of the Grossglockner High Alpine Road, had once dreamt of upmarket hotels and restaurants along the route, the road is

finden sich entlang der Straße doch vor allem klassische touristische Gastronomiebetriebe, in denen man sich mit einem Kaffee, einer Mehlspeise oder einem Schnitzel stärken und teilweise auch übernachten kann. Empfehlenswert sind etwa das **Restaurant Fuschertörl**, der **Berggasthof Edelweißhütte**, das **Gasthaus Fuscherlacke »Beim Mankeiwirt«**, das **Glocknerhaus**, das **Gasthaus Schöneck** und das **Kaiser-Franz-Josef-Haus**.

Wer im Tal nächtigen und morgens in aller Frühe hinauf zum Hochtor und zur Edelweiß-Spitze fahren möchte, dem sei neben dem eleganten Zell am See – wo man im Garten des historischen **Grand Hotel Zell am See** den Panoramablick auf die Hohen Tauern und das Steinerne Meer genießen kann, als sei die Belle Époque nie zu Ende gegangen – auch das gemütlich-bodenständige **Bruck an der Großglocknerstraße** oder **Fusch** als Basislager empfohlen. Im **Gasthaus Lukashansl** (gleich beim Kilometer Null der Straße) bekommt man abends alternativ zum Schnitzel auch ein zünftiges Blutwurstgröstl vorgesetzt. Und in der alten holzgetäfelten Stube des **Gasthof Zacherlbräu** kann man sich zum traditionellen Hausbier eine exzellente Pinzgauer Käsknödelsuppe im Zwiebel-Lorbeersud und einen frischen Saibling aus der Fuscherache servieren lassen. Tipps für Hotels in Fusch: Das **Lampenhäusl** oder **Hotel Wasserfall**.

– TAGESAUSFLÜGE

Die Großglockner Hochalpenstraße bietet freilich nur einen kleinen Einblick in den **Nationalpark Hohe Tauern**, der mit 1.856 km² Fläche zu den größten Nationalparks Europas zählt. Weitere Informationen zu Wanderungen durch die faszinierende Alpenlandschaft erhält man in den Besucherzentren in Mittersill, Matrei und Mallnitz sowie auf der Website www.hohetauern.at.

Selbst eine Zeitreise in die Geschichte des kaiserlichen Bädertourismus kann man von der Glocknerstraße aus unternehmen: Im einst beliebten **Bad Fusch**, zum Beginn des Straßenbauprojektes als Startpunkt geplant, zeugen derzeit nur Ruinen mit morbiden Charme vom einstigen Glanz, während das mondäne, etwa 45 Fahrminuten von Zell am See entfernte **Badgastein** gerade seine Auferstehung als neuer Sehnsuchtsort der Instagram-Bohème feiert.

Wer auf den Spuren der Automobilgeschichte wandeln will, dem seien zudem ein Ausflug ins kleine **Vötter's Oldtimer Museum** in Kaprun oder – bei etwas großzügigerem Zeitbudget – die **Ferdinand-Porsche-Erlebniswelten »Fahr(t)raum«** am Mattsee im Norden von Salzburg sowie das **Porsche Automuseum Helmut Pfeifhofer** in Gmünd empfohlen. Die letzten beiden Museen befinden sich etwa 90 Autominuten von Zell am See entfernt.

mostly lined with classic tourist restaurants where you can regain your strength with a coffee, pastry or a schnitzel and some also offer accommodation. We can recommend **Restaurant Fuschertoerl, Berggasthof Edelweisshütte, Gasthaus Fuscherlacke "Beim Mankeiwirt"** [The Marmot Host], **Glocknerhaus, Gasthaus Schöneck** and **Kaiser-Franz-Josef-Haus**.

For those of you who would like to spend a night in the valley and drive bright and early to the Hochtor and the Edelweiss-Spitze, besides the elegant Zell am See – where you can relish the panoramic view over the Hohe Tauern [High Tauern] and Steinerne Meer as if the Belle Époque was still in its heyday from the garden of the historical **Grand Hotel Zell am See** – we can also recommend the cozy down-to-earth base camp of **Bruck an der Grossglocknerstraße** or **Fusch**. At **Gasthaus Lukashansl** (right at kilometer zero of the road) you can get a hearty Blutwurstgröstl [blood sausage] as an alternative to Schnitzel. You can enjoy an excellent Pinzgauer Käsknödelsuppe im Zwiebel-Lorbeersud [bread dumplings with cheese served in a clear broth] and a fresh char from the Fuscherache river to complement a glass of traditional house beer in the old wood-paneled dining room of the **Gasthof Zacherlbräu**. We recommend the following Hotels in Fusch: **Hotel Lampenhäusl** or the **Hotel Wasserfall**.

– DAY TRIPS

Naturally, the Grossglockner High Alpine Road only offers a small insight into the **Nationalpark Hohe Tauern** [Hohe Tauern National Park], which is one of Europe's largest national parks with an area covering 1,856 km². You can get more information about hikes through the fascinating Alpine landscape at the visitor centers in Mittersill, Matrei and Mallnitz as well as on the www.hohetauern.at website.

Even a journey back in time to imperial spa tourism can be undertaken from the Glocknerstraße: in the once popular **Bad Fusch**, originally planned as a starting point when the construction of the road began, it is now only the ruins with their morbid charm that bear testimony to its former glory. Whereas the sophisticated **Badgastein**, a 45-minute drive from Zell am See, is celebrating its resurrection as the new magical place of Instagram bohemians.

For those of you wanting to retrace the history of the automobile, we recommend a trip to the small **Vötter's Vintage Car Museum** in Kaprun or – if you have a bit more time on your hands – **the Ferdinand-Porsche-Erlebniswelten Fahr(t)raum** [Ferdinand Porsche Driving Dream Experience World] at Mattsee in the North of Salzburg as well as the **Porsche Automuseum Helmut Pfeifhofer** in Gmünd. The last two museums are located approx. 90 minutes by car from Zell am See.

VIELEN DANK/THANK YOU:

Patricia Lutz, Daniela Laimer und Dr. Johannes Hörl von der Großglockner Hochalpenstraßen AG.
Peter Embacher, dem technischen Betriebsleiter der Straße. Erika und Robert Sallaberger sowie Hartmut Henkel vom Restaurant Fuschertörl.
Herbert Haslinger, dem »Mankeiwirt« vom Gasthof Fuscherlacke. Nadja Kneissler, Birgit Radebold und Ed Baaske vom Delius Klasing Verlag.

Danke den Kurvenverstehern bei Porsche, die uns unter die Arme greifen. Dr. Wolfgang Porsche, Dr. Josef Arweck von der Porsche AG.
Michael Mauer und Walter Röhrl.

Martin Brandenburg, Ferdinand Wolf, Roland Richter, Florian »Fred« Singer, Yehonatan Richter, Annemarie Falk, Vincent Haldy (Skynamic) von DJI
David zu Elfe – what a film! Philipp Hohenthanner for beeing the »Insta«. Michael Dorn für den letzten Schliff.

For bringing the cars: Michael Barbach, Egon Zweimüller, Jürgen Boden, Thomas Beckmann, Max Braunmühl, Florian Geissler, Stevie Fahr-Becker, Matthias Laimer, Niki Knoll, Marco Halter, Franz Schwarz, Mike Gnani, P&P Patt, Daniel Maier, Mark Porsche, Hermann Köpf, Jonas Bierschneider und Michael Behr.

Wucher Helikopter für die grandiosen Flüge!

–

Jan Karl Baedeker: Für Laura und Anton – gemeinsam über alle Berge.
Stefan Bogner: Für Micha, Maxi & Dominik, die die Kurven im Alltag driften und Michi »The Driver«.

Bibliografische Information der Deutschen Nationalbibliothek
Die Deutsche Nationalbibliothek verzeichnet diese Publikation in der Deutschen Nationalbibliografie; detaillierte bibliografische Daten sind im Internet über http://dnb.dnb.de abrufbar.

Bibliographic information published by the Deutsche Nationalbibliothek. The Deutsche Nationalbibliothek lists this publication in the Deutsche Nationalbibliografie; detailed bibliographic data are available in the Internet at http://dnb.dnb.de.

1. Auflage / 1st edition
ISBN 978-3-667-11394-8
© Delius Klasing & Co. KG, Bielefeld

Konzept/Concept: Stefan Bogner
Einbandgestaltung und Layout/Cover Design and Layout: Stefan Bogner
Text: Jan Karl Baedeker
Übersetzung ins Englische/Translation: Kaye Mueller
Fotos/Photos: Stefan Bogner
Motivausarbeitung/Artwork: Michael Dorn

Karten mit freundlicher Genehmigung von/
Maps with courtesy of: Arthur Gfrei,
Touriseum Meran & Centro studi storici Alta Valtellina

Projektmanagement und Lektorat/
Projectmanagement and Editor: Birgit Radebold
Produktion/Production: Jörn Heese
Druck/Printing: Firmengruppe APPL, aprinta-druck, Wemding.
Printed in Germany 2018

Alle Rechte vorbehalten! Ohne ausdrückliche Erlaubnis des Verlages darf das Werk weder komplett noch teilweise reproduziert, übertragen oder kopiert werden, wie z. B. manuell oder mithilfe elektronischer und mechanischer Systeme inklusive Fotokopieren, Bandaufzeichnung und Datenspeicherung.

All rights reserved. The work may neither be entirely nor partially reproduced, transmitted or copied – such as manually or by means of electronic and mechanical systems, including photo-copying, tape recording and data storage – without explicit permission of the publisher.

Delius Klasing Verlag, Siekerwall 21,
D - 33602 Bielefeld, Germany
Telefon/Phone +49 (0)521 559-0,
Telefax/Fax +49 (0)521 559-115
E-Mail: info@delius-klasing.de
www.delius-klasing.de

»STELVIO«
STILFSERJOCH
ITALIEN
IM HANDEL ERHÄLTLICH

PORSCHE DRIVE
15 PÄSSE IN 4 TAGEN
IM HANDEL ERHÄLTLICH

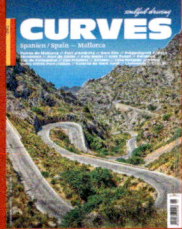

MALLORCA
MALLORCA
Ab Dezember 2018/Available Dec. 2018

PYRENÄEN
PYRENEES
Im Handel erhältlich/Available in stores

ÖSTERREICH
AUSTRIA
Im Handel erhältlich/Available in stores

SCHWEIZ
SWITZERLAND
Im Handel erhältlich/Available in stores

SCHOTTLAND
SCOTLAND
Im Handel erhältlich/Available in stores

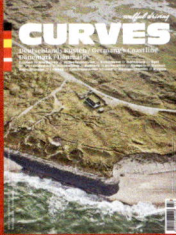

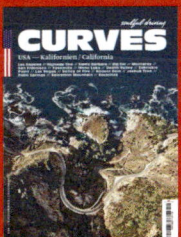
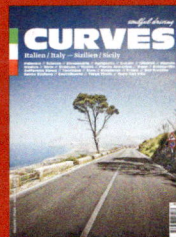
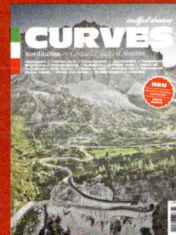

DEUTSCHL./DÄNEMARK
GERMANY/DENMARK
Im Handel erhältlich/Available in stores

FRANKREICH
FRANCE
Im Handel erhältlich/Available in stores

USA · KALIFORNIEN
USA · CALIFORNIA
Im Handel erhältlich/Available in stores

SIZILIEN
SICILY
Im Handel erhältlich/Available in stores

NORDITALIEN
NORTHERN ITALY
Im Handel erhältlich/Available in stores

ESCAPES WINTER
TRAUMSTRASSEN IM SCHNEE
IM HANDEL ERHÄLTLICH

ESCAPES
TRAUMROUTEN DER ALPEN
IM HANDEL ERHÄLTLICH

TRACKS
NÜRBURGRING NORDSCHLEIFE
IM HANDEL ERHÄLTLICH

Map

Labels visible on the map:

- Lengfeldkäsl
- Schäflermahdl
- Sauloch
- Gisenmahdl
- Wiednasfl
- Kalbertradl
- Ochsenreichwald
- Wiesbach
- Vogeralm
- Finsterwald
- Fießwald
- Tränke
- Lebermoos
- Piffgrundalm
- Stangenhagriedl
- Baleitboden
- Brunnlöcher
- Baleitrain
- 1571
- Br
- Tau- oder Tauernbach
- Taubachalm
- Ahornboden
- löcherboden
- Wiesach
- Foißen
- 1265
- Welzenboden
- 1624
- Schap
- Königsstuhl
- 1260
- Tauernwald
- 1265
- Pfal
- Piff...oos
- Kalber...
- 1270
- 1269
- 1275
- ...der Maiß